Coastlines of
BRAZIL

This volume is part of a series of volumes on Coastlines of the World. The papers included in the volume are to be presented at Coastal Zone '89.

Volume edited by Claudio Neves
Series edited by Orville T. Magoon

ASCE
1852
®

Published by the
American Society of Civil Engineers
345 East 47th Street
New York, New York 10017-2398

D0071498

ABSTRACT

These papers were presented at Coastal Zone '89 the Sixth Symposium on Coastal and Ocean Management held in Charleston, South Carolina, July 11-14, 1989. This volume is a part of a series of volumes on Coastlines of the World. Some of the topics covered include environmental economics, marine bioindicators, coastline programs, fisheries, heavy metals pollution, and ovaluation of coastal areas. This volume provides the civil engineer with a broad understanding of coastal and ocean management issues related to the coastlines of Brazil.

Library of Congress Cataloging-in-Publication Data

Coastlines of Brazil.

(Coastlines of the world)
Includes index.
1. Coasts—Brazil—Congresses. 2. Shore protection—Brazil—Congresses. I. American Society of Civil Engineers. II. Series.
GB459.15.C63   1989   333.91'7'0981   89-14943
ISBN 0-87262-707-1

FOREWORD

Coastal Zone '89, a major American Society of Civil Engineers (ASCE) Specialty Conference, was the sixth in a series of multidisciplinary meetings on comprehensive coastal and ocean management. Professionals, citizens and decision makers met for four days in Charleston, South Carolina to exchange information and views on matters ranging from regional to international in scope and interest. This year's theme was entitled "Spotlight on Solutions", emphasizing a recurrent focus on practical problem solving.

Other sponsors and affiliates besides ASCE included the National Oceanic and Atmospheric Space Administration, the American Shore and Beach Preservation Association, Department of Commerce, the Coastal Zone Foundation and many other organizations (see title page). The range of sponsorship hints at the diversity of those attending. The presence of viewpoints will surely stimulate improved coastal and ocean management through the best of current knowledge and cooperation.

This volume is part of the "Coastlines of the World" series produced in conjunction with the Coastal Zone '89 Conference. The purpose of this special regional volume is to focus on one geographical area in depth.

Each volume of the "Coastlines of the World" series will have a guest series editor representing the particular geographical area of interest discussed in that volume.

All papers have been accepted for publication by the Proceedings Editors. All papers are eligible for discussion in the Journal of Waterway, Port, Coastal and Ocean Engineering and all papers are eligible for ASCE Awards.

A seventh conference is now being planned to maintain this dialogue and information exchange. Information is available through the Coastal Zone Foundation, P.O. Box 26062, San Francisco, CA 94126, USA.

Orville T. Magoon
Series Editor

CONTENTS

vi

THE COASTAL MANAGEMENT PROGRAM IN BRAZIL

Enio R. Frischeisen [1]   Mauro Sergio F. Argento [2]   Renato Herz [3]

Ronaldo Paschoalette Carneiro [1]

1 INTRODUCTION

The coastal zone is an area where the marine, the atmospheric and the terrestrial environments interact. Thus, it constitutes a unique geographical system of special relevance, not only because of these environmental factors, but also due to the appeal that it exerts. As concerns the Brazilian coastal zone, some important aspects should be considered: the littoral is 7,408 km long, it concentrates most of the country's population, it is where the largest oil resources are located, and the coast has a high touristic potential. Consequently, anthropic pressure on the environment is very strong and the occupation is not always done in a planned way.

Therefore, the coastal zone requires attention from different points of view such as physical, chemical, biological and geographical as well as economical, political and social.

The complexity of coordinated action in such a vast area requires a careful integration of actions in order to guarantee the effectiveness and feasibility of any project.

As a proposal to guide the rational utilization of coastal resources, the Brazilian government established the National Coastal Zone Management Plan (PNGC), according to the Federal Law no. 7,661, promulgated by President José Sarney on May 16, 1988. The PNGC comprises the National Policy for the Environment (PNMA) and the National Policy for Sea Resources (PNRM).

SECIRM (Secretaria da Comissão Interministerial para os Recursos do Mar) is responsible for conducting the coastal zone management, and for directing a Coordination Group in the federal level. Other government agencies belong to this group which has legal authority on all coastal matters. The "Subsecretaria para o Gerenciamento Costeiro" is in charge of coordinating the activities with the States where the Plan is in progress. The basic approach is to provide the technical and financial support to the coastal states in a systematic and harmonic way, encouraging

---

[1] Comissão Interministerial para os Recursos do Mar, Min. Marinha, 4. andar, Brasília, DF 70055, Brazil.

[2] Departamento de Geografia, Universidade Federal do Rio de Janeiro, Rio de Janeiro, RJ 21945, Brazil.

[3] Instituto Oceanográfico, Universidade de São Paulo.

the creation of their own management plans according to a common methodology. Consequently, the PNGC has a fundamentally decentralized character, each State being responsible to elaborate and develop its own Coastal Management Plan, without violating general aspects of a common methodology established by the general coordination of PNGC.

So, the "Comissão Interministerial para os Recursos do Mar" (CIRM) — the governmental agency for sea resources which includes representatives of eleven federal ministries — promotes through its Secretary for Coastal Zone Management technical and financial support to state and municipal agencies, in order to make the plan viable.

2 AN INTEGRATED VIEW OF THE COASTAL MANAGEMENT

The coastal zone is a transition environment presenting various characteristics according to the functional categories of each space. For this reason, but mostly because of the decentralized character of the PNGC, each State must establish its line of action for managing the coastline.

For systematic purposes, information concerning each state must be organized by geographical sectors measuring 30′ in latitude and 30′ in longitude, adjusted to Marsden's sub-squares of 1° × 1°. The whole set of these sets, established for each State, corresponds to the total area to be covered by the PNGC.

Figure 1 shows the planned subdivision of the entire littoral zone, corresponding to approximately 1,000 sectors. Figure 2 shows the areas being covered in the first six states involved in the Plan (from south to north, Rio Grande do Sul, Santa Catarina, São Paulo, Rio de Janeiro, Bahia, and Rio Grande do Norte).

The need for an integrated view of the coastal systems resides on the fact that, until the 70's, most of the research programs in Brazil resulted on particularized and disperse information. There was no normalization to integrate the knowledge obtained, adjusted to the space-time scales suitable for regional planning as the PNGC does.

The tasks of the Program include the systematical gathering of existing data and previous works. This should be accomplished on an integrating form and following a systemic perspective which takes into account the resulting forms, the mechanisms which generate these forms, the constitution of the terrain, and the soil occupation by man.

Figure 3 presents an schematic view of the environmental inter-relationships which serve as basis for the survey of information for the Project.

The systematic survey of such information, for each sector, is transformed into thematic maps, by means of traditional cartographic methods, in different levels of representation: in 1:100,000 for macro-scale data, in 1:50,000 for meso-scale, and in better than 1:25,000 for micro-scale. These scales were directly related to different levels of zoning. The first level (1:100,000) which was adopted is appropriate for the macro-zoning of the coast, currently in progress in six states.

The **Macro-zoning of the Coast** is being done with the help of a consensual methodology approved after several presentations in conferences, seminars and meetings. The methodology was adjusted according to the effective participation of the involved states. At this point, the essence of the philosophy of GERCO Project

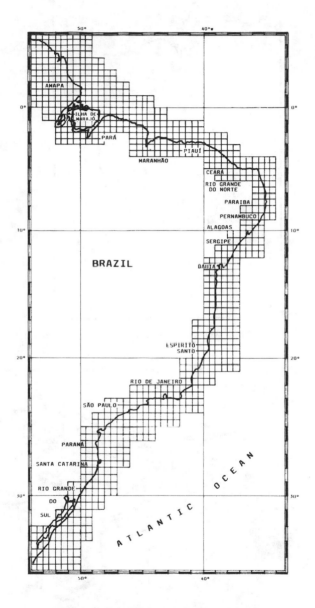

Figure 1: Subdivision of the littoral zone.

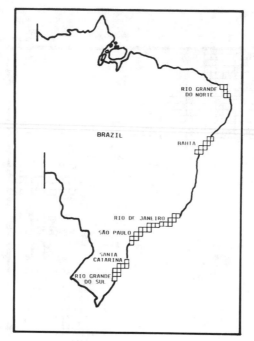

Figure 2: Areas where the coastal zoning is in progress.

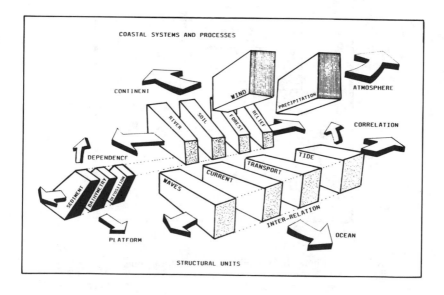

Figure 3: Schematic view of the coastal environment.

is revealed, as an integrating action of the participants is required as well as the strengthening of decentralized points of view.

The criteria for sampling data, mapping information in conventional cartographic base (in 1:100,000 scale), and titles should be initially chosen and normalized, before surveying information for the macro-zoning, so that the internal structure of the coastal systems could be properly represented. Twelve themes serve as guidelines to the application and to the development of techniques of static cartographic representation, containing the survey of coastal resources in their current state of use or preservation. Basically, these twelve themes include the main parameters needed for the diagnosis and management of the coastal environment.

The thematic maps contain: topography and bathymetry; geology/faciology; agricultural vocation; aquatic and terrestrial ecosystems; oceanographical parameters; climatic information; socio-economical information; soil cover; land use; geomorphology; declivity; water quality; and planned and current zoning. These constitute the foundations of the diagnosis stage of the Project.

This cadastral survey of information is restricted to sectors measuring 30' of latitude and 30' of longitude, the information is geocoded in a matrix format, which serves as input for the data bank of the Geographical System of Information of the Coastal Management (GEOSYS). (See Argento, elsewhere in this conference.)

This information, when inserted into the system, will form the initial stored data which will serve as basis to prepare different environmental scenarios. A "Regional Collegiate" will then be able to establish a thematic map called *Projected Use*, which reflects the dialectical result between technical data and the definition of political and social needs.

Figure 4 illustrates the symmetric superposition of the information, by a matrix view corresponding to sectors of 30' by 30'.

Consequently, the results of this zoning will be linked to the preparation of geocodes and will be stored in the Data Bank of GEOSYS, using a cellular and/or polygonal basis. GEOSYS follows the same criteria of decentralization, and both numerical and alphabetical data are distributed in a cartographic grid superposed to the 30' sectors adopted in the macro-zoning.

Figure 5 shows the methodology used by the GEOSYS for the Coastal Management Program.

It is possible to obtain thematic information about groups of same identification from the thematic matrices, already in geocode format, as well as to search for relationships through cross-references. Output is furnished in video display or dot-matrix printers for use in diagnosis or synthesis reports.

Automation was introduced in the methodology of coastal management with the purpose of obtaining faster and more effective control about the information traditionally produced. The actualization of the data which generates the thematic maps is also done automatically, by using the Digital Treatment of Satellite Imagery, which makes easier to determine the dynamics of geo-environments studying their variations as time passes.

Integrated handling of this information permits to obtain a final product to plan the use of the coast. By means of some definitions relative to its organization, its dynamics, the vocations for the use of soil, and the environmental reaction, it is possible to obtain a wide perspective of the coastal zone, without losing the basic proposal which is to preserve the environmental quality of that area in Brazil.

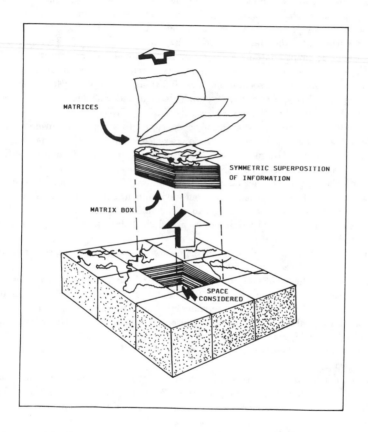

Figure 4: Conceptual view of the information matrix.

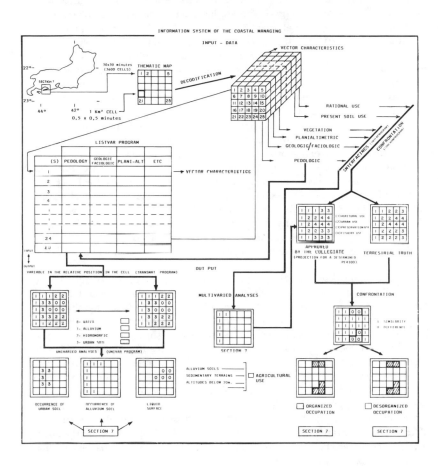

Figure 5: The Geographical System of Information (GEOSYS).

Some of these definitions are related to the establishment of areas for: ecological preservation; exploitation of natural biological resources; localization of ports and terminals; prospective of urban expansion; localization of potentially polluting industries; cultural, political and recreational activities; national security sites; exploitation of mineral or energy resources; historical, artistic, archaeological and landscape sites; development of scientific and technological activities; aquaculture, agriculture and forestry activities. The agents of the administration, defined by the Regional Collegiates representative of the community and of institutions (federal, state or municipal) responsible for or existing in the area, become the ultimate step of the process which results on the thematic map of projected use. This map, which encompasses all of the parameters mentioned above, constitutes the operational basis for the Coastal Zone Management.

As administrations and the environment change with time, a continuous feedback of the process is expected. This activity is foreseen by the GERCO Project as the **Coastal Monitoring** program. This program accounts, not only for the renewal of information, but also for the dynamization of the GEOSYS data bank.

One of the tasks belonging to the monitoring program is to follow the functional dynamics of the region and the resulting changes in the coastal environment. Other examples are the use or transformation of the structure of independent ecosystems, and the verification whether the environmental quality indexes are within the established criteria for purity or contamination. The coastal monitoring requires the actualization of information and continuous follow up of the interactions with the environment.

It must be emphasized that the process of monitoring always uses advanced technologies, like airplanes and satellites equipped with sensors able to furnish low cost information in a short period of time. To observe an area 7,408 km long, it is not possible to overlook improved research techniques. As it is concerned, the GERCO Project counts on technical and scientific assistance from the remote sensors laboratory ("Laboratório de Sensoreamento Remoto") of the Instituto Oceanográfico da Universidade de São Paulo (IOUSP) as well as on the formation of human resources capable of conducting the coastal zone management programs. The Project also counts on support from the Universidade Federal do Rio de Janeiro (through its Department of Geography) and from the Instituto de Pesquisas Espaciais (INPE) for the development of software for GEOSYS. These institutions, together with SECIRM and the State coordinating agencies, have been operating jointly in order to guarantee the effectiveness of the National Coastal Zone Management Plan (PNGC) in Brazil.

3 CONCLUSION

PNGC has legal support from the Federal Law 7,661 of May 16, 1988. The plan brings within its philosophy, a conservationist view of the coastal zone proposing an orderly utilization of this region, and at the same time, transferring the responsibility of carrying it out to State level.

The Project also presents in its context, the commitment to create and enhance human resources. This should be accomplished by encouraging courses and interaction with research institutions which are responsible for developing methods and new technologies.

The Brazilian Coastal Management Project is directed towards a rational use of the coastal zone, following two principles:

1. a decentralized coordination, with decisions issued from Regional Collegiates;

2. that the involved communities are always consulted.

REFERENCES

[1] Almeida, E.G. (1985). Gerenciamento Costeiro: Uma proposta para preservar o ambiente na zona costeira. *Manchete*, special edition: "O Mar Brasileiro".

[2] Argento, M.S.F. (1985). O Sistema de Informações do Gerenciamento Costeiro. Proc. Simp. Bras. Gerenciamento Costeiro.

[3] Argento, M.S.F. (1989). The Geographical Information System of the Brazilian Coastal Management Program. *in:* Proc. Sixth Symp. Coastal and Ocean Management, Charleston.

[4] Diegues, A.C. *et alli.* (1985). Subsistemas "Conservação dos Recursos Vivos do Mar". Rel. COPPETEC, Rio de Janeiro.

[5] Herz, R. (1987). Organização do Espaço Informativo. CIRM, Sep./87. *in:* Propriedades e Critérios Normativos para o Desenvolvimento da Cartografia Temática para o Gerenciamento Costeiro.

[6] Oliveira, L.L. (1988). O Plano Nacional de Gerenciamento Costeiro. *in:* Informativo – Atividades da Comissão Interministerial para Recursos do Mar.

ENVIRONMENTAL ECONOMICS OF THE SOUTHERN BRAZILIAN COAST

Antônio Libório Philomena *

Abstract

The goal of this study is a large-scale synthesis of the ecological and economic characteristics of the Southern Brazilian Coast. The coastal area is formed by a watershed, a lagoon, and a continental shelf, covering 202,978 km^2.

Energy Systems Analysis played a central part in the methodology used to synthesize interactions between ecologic and economic activities.

Concepts like Emergy and Transformity was used to evaluate contributions of resources and services to the coastal area studied.The analysis showed the importance of the renewable resources(i.e., nonmarket resources such as sun, rain,and wind)in comparison to the nonrenewables(market resources like fuel, fertilizer,services and labour). The methodology has proven to be useful as a mesure of value for evaluating environment, resources, and public policy alternatives.

Introduction

Environmental Economics a few years ago was just a fuzzy concept in classical economic and ecologic literature. Today it is a necessity and increasingly will be the answer to most of the problems involving man and nature.

----

*Departamento de Oceanografia. Fundação Universidade do Rio Grande. Caixa Postal 474. Rio Grande, RS 96200. Brasil.

This interface between ecology and economy through the application of the priciples of systems approach and energy analysis will demonstrate that economic and environmental problems have the same roots and as such, should be treated as one subject.

In this paper I used the Energy Language , or Energese developed by Odum (Odum,1983), and two new measures: EMERGY, as the "energy memory", since it is all energy transformed to generate that of another type; and TRANSFORMITY, which is the equivalent solar energy required to generate a unit of an object(of more concentrated energy) (Odum, 1986, 1988). To consider all interactions that nature and man participated, Solar Emergy (in solar emjoules) and Solar Transformities (in em joules per joule) are used. In that way different sources, flows, storages, feedbacks, and losses can be compared. (See Odum, 1986 for methods, and Philomena, 1988 for calculations).

Study Area

The Southern Brazilian Coast considered here comprises the Lagoa dos Patos (Lagoon of the Ducks in English), its watershed, and the continental shelf (considering the isobath of 100 m)that borders them. These systems are located in the southernmost state of Brazil, around latitudes 30 and 32 South, and longitudes 52 and 51 West (See Figure 1). It covers $2/3$ of the Rio Grande do Sul State, i.e., 202,978 km^2, and the watershed, the lagoon, and the continental shelf represent in areal proportion 67%, 5%, and 28% respectively.

Most of the area covers low flat land. Sixteen percent of the watershed area is less than 100 m. high where agricultural activities are concemtrated on rice plantations. This flat land is bordered by higher land rising more than 1,000 m. where soybean plantations and pasture-stock are the principal economic functions.

Since the Lagoa dos Patos is shallow and unprotected, winds are a very important forcing function. Kjerfve(Kjerfve, 1986)cited Lagoa dos Patos as a typical example of a choked system, characterized by a single entrance, a small ratio of cross-sectional entrance channel area, riverine dominated,low tidal range (mean variation of 30 cm.), and medium wave energy.

The air temperature ranges from -2ºC to 42ºC, with a
mean temperature of 19ºC over the entire area. The cycles of
cold fronts arriving every seven to ten days set up homogeneous
spatial and temporal weather conditions with a mean precipitation of 1,552 millimeters a year (equal to 61 inches/year).

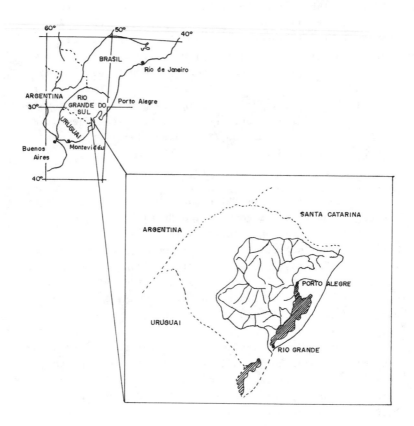

Figure 1. Map of the Southern Brazilian Coast.

Maximum precipitation occurs in July, August, and September
while the minimum occurs in November, December, and March.

Environmental Economics

The emergence of Environmental Economics was possible
only when a common denominator to scale economic and ecologic
values could be assessed. Emergy is the common denominator
used in this paper.

Figure 2 is an aggregate model, retaining all important flows, resources, and compartments of the Southern Brazilian Coast. This figure shows the main components of the economy of man and nature in Rio Grande do Sul, Brazil.

Tables 1, 2, and 3, which generated Figure 2, have all
flow depicted to show large scale compartments and the interactions among them.(See Philomena, 1988, for details).

Based on Table 1 (especially the data in emdollar,which
is the dollar contribution that item makes directly or indirectly to the gross economic product), the largest inflow of
renewable resources (renewable here means one year or less of
turnover)are solar energy (with 12 billions of emdollar/y)and
rain (chemical and potential energy, with one billion of em-
dollar/y). Together they create 93% of the natural energy inputs. The wind, with less energy input (875 millions of em-
dollar/y) than solar energy and rain, neverthless is very
important in the hydrologic cycle(especially to the agriculture systems) and at the soil-water interactions in the lagoon and continental shelf(directly related to fisheries).

In relation to nonrenewable resources, fertilizer(with
8 billions of emdollar per year) is the largest input, responsible for 55% of the total. The second largest, petroleum (with
3,5 billions of emdollar per year) is about 23% of the input
of nonrenewable resources. Firewood, coal, and hydropower,
make 22% of the total, while alcohol and other biomass sources
were negligible in 1983.

Of the economic activities on the Lagoa dos Patos Com-
plex(the Southern Brazilian Coast), market activities brought
2,4 billions of emdollar per year while investments were in the
order of 800 millions of dollars, i.e. equivalent to 36% of the
market budget. Tourism injected 6,7 millions of dollars or,

compared to market activities, only 3%.

Goods and services, considered as imports to the area, cost 990 millions of dollars.

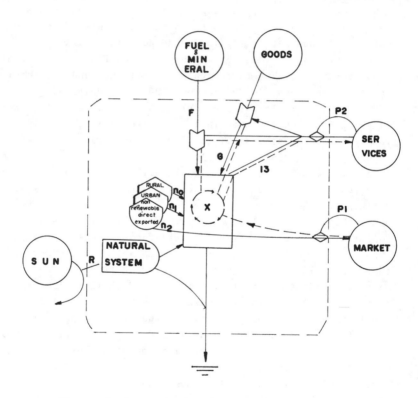

Figure 2. Aggregated Model of the Southern
Brazilian Coast(1983)

TABLE 1

Evaluation of the Resource Basis of the
Southern Brazilian Coast in 1983

item	transformity (SEJ/J)	emergy (E20SEJ/y)	emdollar
RENEWABLE RESOURCES			
solar (land)	1	183.0	7.63E09
(shelf)	1	88.7	3.70E09
(lagoon)	1	17.8	7.42E08
wind (winter)	6.23E2	20.6	8.58E08
(summer)	6.23E2	0.28	1.17E07
wave (shelf)	2.59E4	0.07	2.92E06
(lagoon)	2.59E4	0.00	0.00
rain over the land			
(potential)	8.89E3	64.8	2.70E09
(chemical)	1.54E4	160.0	6.67E09
over the shelf			
(chemical)	3.54E4	15.2	6.33E08
tide (shelf)	2.35E4	1.03	4.29E07
(estuary)	2.35E4	0.08	3.33E06
geocycle	2.90E4	11.5	4.79E08
firewood	3.49E4	244.0	10.2E09
river (chemical)	4.8E4	0.0	0.00
hydroelectricity	1.59E5	36.9	1.54E09
IMPORTS AND OUSIDE SOURCES			
coal	3.98E4	22.0	9.17E08
petroleum	5.30E4	44.6	1.86E09
fertilizer (N)	1.69E6	30.6	1.28E09
(P)	1.41E10	35.3	1.47E09
goods and services	2.4E12	23.9	9.96E08
market	2.4E12	59.5	2.48E09
tourism	2.4E12	4.4	1.83E08
investment	2.4E12	21.5	8.96E08
EXPORTS			
soil loss	6.30E4	0.2	8.33E06
waste(liquid)	4.10E4	0.2	8.33E06
general production	2.4E12	59.5	2.48E09

TABLE 2

Summary Flow for the Southern Brazilian Coast in 1983

Symbol	Item	Magnitude (dollar/y)	(SEJ/y)
R	Renewable Resources		2.90E22
N	Flow from indigenous nonrenewable Resources (total)		2.82E20
	No dispersed rural source		4.28E20
	N1 concentrated use		2.82E24
	N2 exported without use	2.67E7	4.84E19
F	Imported Fuels and Mineral		1.32E22
G	Imported goods	1.68E10	
I	Dollars paid for Imports	1.68E10	
P2I	Emergy Value of Goods and Services		4.03E22
I3	Dollars paid for Imports minus services in goods, fuels, and minerals	6.20E9	
P2I3	Imported services minus F & G	4.23E6	7.70E18
E	Dollars paid for Exports	13.5E8	
P1E	Emergy value of goods and services exported		9.32E21
B	Exported products transformed within the Southern Brazilian Coast	6.75E8	4.66E21
E3	Dollars paid for exports minus goods	6.48E8	
P1E3	Exported services		4.47E21
X	Rio Grande do Sul Gross Internal Product	112E8	
X1	Southern Brazilian Coast Gross Internal Product	53.8E8	
P2	Brazil Emergy to dollar of imports	1.82E12 SEJ/$	
P1	Brazil Emergy to Gross Internal Product	6.9E12 SEJ/$	
P1LPC	Southern Brazilian Coast to Gross Internal Product	5.35E14 SEJ/$	

Debt in 1983 for Rio Grande do Sul = 1.79E9$
Ratio cruzeiro/dollar in 1983 = 980

TABLE 3

Indices using emergy for overview of
the Southern Brazilian Coast in 1983

name of Index	Expression	Magnitude
Renewable emergy flow	R	2.90E22SEJ/y
Flow from indigenous nonrenewable resources	N	2.82E24SEJ/y
Flow of imported emergy	F+G+P2I3	4.03E22SEJ/y
Total emergy inflows	R+N+G+ P2I3+F	2.89E24SEJ/y
Total emergy used	No+N1+R+ F+G+P2I	2.92E24SEJ/y
Total emergy exported	B+P1+E+N2	9.13E21SEJ/y
Fraction of emergy used derived from indigenous sources	(No+N1+R)/U	0.98
Imports minus exports	(F+G+P2I)- (N2+B+P1E)	3.11E22SEJ/y
Ratio of exports to imports	$\frac{(N2+B+P1E)}{(F+G+P2I)}$	0.23
Fraction used locally renewable	R/U	0.01
Fraction of used-purchased	(F+G+P2I)	0.01
Fraction used that is imported	P2I/U	0.01
Fraction used that is free	(R+No)/U	0.01
Ratio of concentrated to rural	$\frac{(F+G+P2I+N1)}{(R \cdot No)}$	173
Use per unit area(energy density) U/(area)		2.12E13SEJ/m^2
Use per capita	U/(population)	3.14E17SEJ
Renewable carrying capacity at present living standard	$\frac{(R/U)}{population}$	4.30E4 p.
Developed carrying capacity at the same living standard	$\frac{8(R/U)}{population}$	3.44E5 p.
Ratio of used to GIP	U/GIP	2.59E14SEJ/$
Fraction electric	$\frac{(total\ elec)}{U}$	0.01
Fuel per person (only oil)	(fuel)/(pop)	1.08E16SEJ/p.

Figure 3 portrays emergy value of all economic and
environmental resources involved at the Southern Brazilian
Coast. They are already transformed to comparable values and
in the same unit(E20 solar emjoules per year or billions of
emdollar). Although society controls and rely only on the nonrenewable resources(through the market mechanisms)it is the
sun and the rain that have the largest value in this area.
This confirms the agricultural and aquatic nature of the Rio
Grande do Sul State.

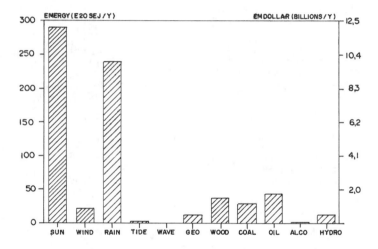

Figure 3.   Emergy and dollar values of nonmarket and
            market resources in the Southern Brazilian
            Coast , in 1983.

        The role that environmental resources play in a state's
economy is likely to be considered only after a holistic theory of value is exrcised by economists and ecologists. The
fundamental concept here is equity. In the future , as fuel
costs change, wood and oil will decrease in importance. Coal
and alcohol can increase while hydroelectricity will increase
just a small fraction in the next years(Eletrosul,1985). As

can also be seen in Figure 3, the partition of nonrenewable
energy will have to be carefully done among agriculture,
industry, and commerce to benefit of the whole state,these
activities should not interfere with the life supporting
systems and, the best way to accomplish this is to adopt
the Input Management Approach(See in same Symposium :
"Input Management: A Proposal for the Largest Coastal Lagoon
in Brazil") .

REFERENCES

ELETROSUL. 1985. Boletim Estatístico, 1969-1984. Eletrosul.
        Porto Alegre,RS . 120pp.
Kjerfve, B.J. 1986. Comparative Oceanography of Coastal Lago-
        ons. In "Estuarine Variability", edited by D.A.Wolfe.
        Academic Press. New York.:63-81.
Odum, H.T. 1983. Systems Ecology. John Wiley and Sons. New
        York. 644pp.
Odum, H.T. 1986. Energy in ecosystems. In "Ecosystem Theory
        and Application", edited by N.Polunin. John Wiley
        and Sons. New York.:337-369.
Odum, H.T. 1988. Self-Organization, Transformity, and Infor-
        mation. Science, vol.242.:1132-1139.
Philomena, A.L. 1988. Preliminary study toward an Integrative
        Management of a Coastal Lagoon. Ph.D.Dissertation.
        University of Georgia. The Institute of Ecology.
        Athens, GA. 155pp.

INPUT MANAGEMENT: A PROPOSAL FOR THE LARGEST COASTAL LAGOON IN BRAZIL.

Antônio Libório Philomena*

Abstract

Principles of General System Theory and Energy Analysis are used to study the best management technique al Lagoa dos Patos (in southern Brazil), including its watershed and contiguous continental shelf. This synthesis will provide a framework to solve specific problems raised by the development and exploitation of these systems. Due to the large scale involved(around 202,978 km^2) and to their characteristics of cascading systems, the Lagoa dos Patos Complex shows that most of the energy involved are controled by the inputs. Consequently, management efforts should be concentrated in the inputs, too.

Introduction

The rise of ecology to include the understanding of large systems as functional wholes has promoted the development of solutions to a variety of long-range problems of society. An important characteristic of hierarchical levels of organization is that new properties emerge at different integrative level(Odum, 1977).
From the first thoughs presented by Ludwig von Bertalanffy(1968 , 1975)until the management of large systems centered on computer technology, considerable developments in General System Theory have taken place.

----

* Departamento de Oceanografia, Fundação Universidade do Rio Grande, Caixa Postal 474, Rio Grande, RS -96200. Brazil.

In this paper I have studied a large system. Using
a classification proposed by Chorley and Kennedy (Chorley
and Kennedy, 1971) the studied subject composed of a watershed, a lagoon, and a continental shelf could be viewed as
a cascading system characterized by tresholds and a chain
of subsystems dynamically linked by a cascade of mass or
energy. In this cascade the mass or energy output from
one subsystem becomes the input for the next one.
       To achieve these goals, a methodology known as
Energy Systems Analysis (Odum, 1986)was used. Calculations
involving "Emergy" and "Transformity" were performed in a
preceeding paper (Philomena, 1989).

Study Area

       "Lagoa dos Patos Complex" comprises the area of the
Lagoa dos Patos (Lagoon of the Ducks, in English), its
watershed, and the continental shelf that borders them.
These area are located in the southernmost state of Brazil,
around latitudes 30 and 32 South, and longitudes 52 and 51
West (Figure 1). It coyers $2/3$ of the Rio Grande do Sul
State, i.e., 202,972 km^2 . This area contains the following
natural components: forests(Araucaria,Atlantic,Subtropical,
Corridors, and Capão or Forest Islands), grasslands,rivers,
marshes, coastal lakes and lagoons, islands, and continental
shelf.
       The Lagoa dos Patos Complex can be characterized by
at least five very important environmental settings:
(1) The lagoon is a large shallow water body, with only one
    opening to the ocean, and with a strong riverine in-
    fuence from the watershed;
(2) The Lagoa dos Patos Complex is under the influence of
    two air masses which give intermediate characteristics
    of subtropical and temperate climates;
(3) Three masses of water : the Brazil, Falkland, and Coast-
    al currents influence the eastern border of the lago-
    onal area;
(4) The Lagoa dos Patos'watershed has densely branched
    streams. It has the second largest area of streams (5%
    of the sate area, i.e., 14,656 km2)of the Brazilian
    watersheds, second only to the state of Pará;
(5) The coastal plain of the Lagoa dos Patos has the large-
    st areal percentage of water bodies in Brazil.
       One of these characteristics, the air masses influ-
enced by oceanic and continental masses and different land
altitudes form the weather patterns over the Lagoa dos Patos Complex, especially the arrival of cold fronts every
seven to ten days, with subsequent changes in wind direction.
These cycles set up homogeneous spatial and temporal weather
conditions over the entire area with a mean precipitation of
1,552 millimeters a year(equal to 61 inches/year).
       The air temperature ranges from -2ºC to 42ºC, with
a mean temperature of 19ºC over the entire area.
       Another important factor is the diurnal tide with
a mean of 0.47 m(characterized as a microtidal system)
and variation in amplitude positively related to wind
direction and force (Herz, 1977).

Input Management

At Table 1, all resources of the Lagoa dos Patos
Complex, during the year of 1983, are listed. We can divided
the energy inputs to the lagoon in three types: the renewable and natural sources(such as sun,wind,rain,tide,and
waves), the nonrenewable but man-controlled sources (like
geocycle, firewood, coal, petroleum, hydroelectricity, and
fertilizer), and the man-controlled economic resources (
goods and services, tourism, investment, and market).

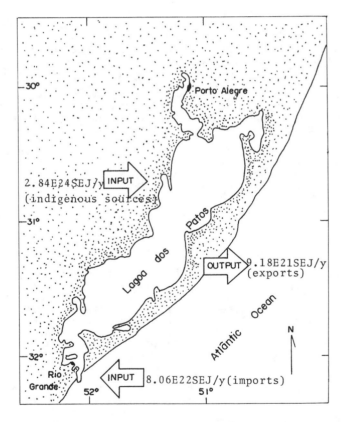

Figure 1. Map and synthesis of Lagoa dos Patos Complex.
(units are in solar emjoules per year).

Inputs of every source flows through the system's boundaries(watershed and continental shelf at the isobath of 100 m)causing interactions among and feedbacks between the compartments. This network of components and processes shows the area as a typical agricultural system with primary and secundary industries parallel to it as power generation, petrochemicals, machinery, transport, and advertising.

In energy terms, input of solar radiation is the main forcing function that makes the natural systems work. Although all other natural forcing functions are derived from solar radiation(except the geologic cycles), in this study they are considered separate for the sake of clarity and management.

Most of the agriculture activities are centered on a few monocultures.. On a large scale, rice and soybeans are very importants flows within and out of the Lagoa dos Patos Complex.

The pasture-stock subsystem had been a very noticeable economic and energetic development at the state level. Basically the state developed as a cattle trade center.Now, due to low efficiency rate and change in governmental goals, its growth is much lower than agriculture. The state exports beef(frozen and cooked), shoes, and wool(95% of Brazil's wool production is from Rio Grande do Sul). Economically the pasture-stock subsystem generates 30% of the state production.

Of the man-controlled inputs, petroleum is the one most used(3,495.3E3 tons of oil equivalent in 1983 for the state), although electricity was growing at 10% per year from 1969 until 1984.

Tourism is still to be developed in spite of the presence of mountains, pampas, and large beaches. In 1985 tourism was listed as 31st on the export products list of the Rio Grande do Sul state.

Another input to the lagoon, especially Lagoa dos Patos with so large watershed, is the soil loss resulting from many activities(especially agriculture). Lewgoy cited to Lagoa dos Patos area(personal communication)1.50E8 tons per year of soil loss from the watershed, and on the northwest of Lagoa dos Patos, erosion is equivalent to the loss of 330,000 hectares per year of land no longer able to produce crops(Porto et al., 1980).

The domestic wate, input directly related to the human population growth and runoff was calculated as input to the lagoon as 1.29 l of waste per cubic meter of runoff. Figure 1 summarized the importance of inputs to the Lagoa dos Patos. All the values are already transformed to comparable values and in the same units(solar emjoule/year). Although the economists like to consider only outputs and the nonrenewable resources(through the market mechanisms) it is the sun and rain that have the largest value at Lagoa dos Patos Complex. This confirms the agricultural and aquatic nature of the State of Rio Grande do Sul. It is the environmental sectors that transform environmental sources whose products are used by the economy.

Eugene P.Odum proposed the Input Management Approach (Odum, 1987) where all the decisions relating to resource utilization are taken depending on quantity and quality of

TABLE 1

Evaluation of the Resource Basis of the
Lagoa dos Patos Complex in 1983

	transformity (SEJ/J)	solar emergy (E20 SEJ/y)
RENEWABLE RESOURCES		
solar (land)	1	183.0
(shelf)	1	88.7
(lagoon)	1	17.8
wind (winter)	6.23E2	20.6
(summer)	6.23E2	0.28
wave (shelf)	2.59E4	0.07
(lagoon)	2.59E4	0.00
rain over the land		
(potential)	8.89E3	64.8
(chemical)	1.54E4	160.0
over the shelf)		
(chemical)	3.54E4	15.2
tide (shelf)	2.35E4	1.03
(estuary)	2.35E4	0.08
geocycle	2.90E4	11.5
firewood	3.49E4	244.0
river (chemical)	4.8E4	0.0
hydroelectricity	1.59E5	36.9
IMPORTS AND OUTSIDE SOURCES		
coal	3.98E4	22.0
petroleum	5.30E4	44.6
fertilizer (N)	1.69E6	30.6
(P)	1.41E10	35.3
goods and services	2.4E12	23.9
market	2.4E12	59.5
tourism	2.4E12	4.4
investment	2.4E12	21.5
EXPORTS		
soil loss	6.30E4	0.2
waste(liquid)	4.10E4	0.2
general production	2.4E12	59.5

the inputs.
The application of the Input Management Approach to Rio Grande do Sul would result in full utilization of untapped renewable sources, steady state utilization of non-renewable sources, decrease of externalized economy, less waste production and soil losses, and decrease of population growth.

REFERENCES

Bertalanffy, L.von. 1968. General System Theory.Geroge Braziller. New York. 295p.
Bertalanffy, L.von. 1975. Perspectives on General System Theory. George Braziller.New York. 183p.
Chorley,R.J. and Kennedy,B.A. 1971. Physical Geography: a system approach. Prentice-Hall.London.370p.
Herz,R. 1977. Circulação das águas de superfície da Lagoa dos Patos. Dissertação.Universidade de São Paulo. São Paulo. 318p.
Odum, E.P. 1977. The emergence of Ecology as a New Integrative Discipline. Science 195:1289-1293.
Odum, E.P. 1987. Reduced-input agriculture reduces non-point pollution. Journal of Water Conservation. Vol.42: 412-414.
Odum, H.T. 1986. Energy in ecosystems. In "Ecosystem Theory and Application," edited by N.Polunin. John Wiley and Sons. New York:337-369.
Philomena, A.L. 1989. Environmental Economics of the Southern Brazilian Coast. Coastal Zone 89. Charleston.

LOW COST WAVE MEASUREMENT PROGRAM

Carlos Eduardo Parente Ribeiro [1]

1 INTRODUCTION

One of the dreams of a coastal engineer is to have at his hands decades of continuous and reliable wave observations at the coast. Then he can better understand the coastal processes, estimate extreme wave values for coastal structures design, validate models of wave generation and propagation and discover general features and trends of the wave climate. This is something that everyone involved with oceanographical measurements in general should have in mind: the importance of long term series of ocean data. They can be correlated with different events, show global trends and provide valuable information for a more rational occupation of the coast. However, to have such long series of data it requires political decision and good planning, and the main obstacles are: costs, environmental hazards and thecnological problems. In this paper we address some problems related to a wave measurement program in the coast emphasizing these last three points.

2 COASTAL WAVE MEASUREMENTS

Many countries in the world have now a network of wave sensors along their coasts, as is the case of USA, Japan, Korea, Norway, and Spain, just to mention a few. In the computer age it is possible to handle, to store and to fast analyze such huge amount of data and a centralized network allows for: cost optimization, standardization of calibration and general procedures and, last but not least, it is a warranty that someone is always "waiting and looking for the data", one basic requirement for a long term series to exist. In Brazil wave measurements are still scarce and limited to special places of the coast and did not include, up to now, directional measurements. Deep water measurements are increasing in the offshore oil areas. Extreme wave values for the coastal and offshore areas still depend strongly on hindcasting on meteorological events. We are looking for low cost and reliable systems in order to improve this situation.

[1] Programa de Engenharia Oceânica, COPPE, Universidade Federal do Rio de Janeiro, Caixa Postal 68508, Rio de Janeiro, RJ 21945, Brazil.

3 WAVE MEASUREMENT SYSTEMS

We make here a brief survey of the general characteristics of wave measurement systems used in the coast pointing out some possible low cost alternatives.

3.1 Wave staffs

A wave staff can be attached to a fixed structure or platform at sea and pierce the sea surface and this is the most accurate way to measure waves provided that the structure itself is not disturbing the wave field. Not including the platform cost it is also the least expensive way. Direct resistive and magnetically coupled discrete resistive staffs are low cost sensors that are used in our platforms. Experience shows that the best way is to hang them from the platforms avoiding diver's work. Capacitive wavestaffs are known to have not much endurance; they are extremely cheap (just a piece of thin wire and a simple conditioner) and can be used for quick measurements. A long term directional spectrum measurement program is being started now from an offshore platform in the Campos basin, using an 8 sensor array of this type. Wave staffs can also be attached to spar buoys (Ford, Timme and Trampus, 1968). They tend to lose low frequency information as the buoy has some response to swell.

3.2 Subsurface pressure sensor

This is a low cost alternative for coastal measurements when there are no fixed structures available. A pressure sensor measures the changing wave induced pressure beneath the waves. Higher frequency components are more attenuated with depth so a practical limit for pressure sensors used in the bottom is 20 meters. The high frequency part of the spectrum is less important when the low frequency swell prevails but in local sea conditions or with mixed sea and swell this lost of high frequency information can alter some wave parameters calculated from the spectrum and make difficult to correlate with wave models of the JONSWAP type and the meteorological situation, the high frequency part being directly related with the local wind. With no directional spectrum measurements, a systematic comparison of some parameters like α, γ, peak frequency and energy with wind and fetch can give a better understanding of the wave climate (Parente and Souza, 1988).

It would be interesting to associate this low cost pressure system with another one with a good high frequency response. A pressure transducer suspended from a surface float with a small diameter wire, as shown by Gaul and Brown (1966) will lose low frequency information and preserve the high one. A wave staff suspended from a surface buoy and measuring the relative movement between the buoy and a subsurface body will also have the same characteristics. A combination of a pressure sensor in the bottom with one of these mentioned systems could provide a system with acceptable transfer function and cost.

3.3 Accelerometer buoys

The Datawell waverider buoy is very famous and worldwide used in deep and shallow waters. An accelerometer buoy (Earle and Bishop, 1984) moves with the waves and measures vertical acceleration wich is time integrated twice to provide a record of wave elevations. Vertical accelerations should not be contaminated by horizontal accelerations, a problem often treated by use of a specially gimballed accelerometer, supplemental use of a gyroscope to maintain a vertical reference, or use of mechanical devices, such as pendulums. These buoys and the new ones that give directional information measuring also surface slope in two directions, are very expensive but in most cases they are the only possible alternative (and, closing the cycle, they can solve the problem because they are the product of scientific talent, ingenuity and high technology and so they are expensive). A small accelerometer buoy, like the wavestaff previously mentioned can also be coupled to a moored spar buoy type of structure working decoupled from this structure having practically only vertical movements. The vertical reference is provided by a vertical suspended wire guiding the buoy. This system has been successfully tested only in a semisubmersible platform (Parente and Moreira Lima, 1989).

3.4 Inverted fathometer

Waves can be measured by the travel time of an acoustic pulse transmitted from the bottom to the surface. Data are sent to shore via electric cable. This system is used in the coastal network of Japan. The cost will depend heavily on the distance to shore and the protection near shore.

3.5 Data storage and transmission

Three options for data handling are common: self contained systems, where the data is stored in analog form (graphical or magnetic) or digital (solid state memory); data transmission via radio and via electric cable. Data transmission to shore is always the best option because the data is immediately available and in the case of cable transmission the maintenance costs are much lower. Data can be stored in a coastal station and/or transmited by telephone to a central station. Wave information can be passed to the coastal community in real time. In some coastal areas data can be sent by cable to coastal island and from there to the coastal station by radio.

3.6 Environmental hazards

Wave measurement systems are exposed to several hostile conditions, referred here as environmental hazards. Vandalism, accidents produced by surface vessels and bottom trawlers, lightning discharges and extreme wave conditions (this is included here as an hazard because usually a system is not built to stand the most severe condition expected in a large period of time).

4 WAVE MEASUREMENT PROGRAM

UFRJ-Federal University of Rio de Janeiro is committed with other institutions in Brazil in a wave measurement program for our coast, briefly resumed below.

- systems development: different types of wave sensors are being developed like pressure sensor with radio link to shore, pressure sensor associated with buoy suspended wavestaff, inverted fathometer with cable link to shore, buoy accelerometer for semisubersible platforms, resistive and capacitive wavestaffs arrays for directional spectra measurements from platforms.

• data analysis package: standardized computer programs for point and directional measurements.

• wave observation manual: to serve as a guide for the community.

• wave data bank: a section in the national oceanographic data bank related to wave parameters is being implemented.

REFERENCES

[1] Earle, M. and J. Bishop (1984). A practical guide to ocean wave measurement and analysis, published by Endeco Inc., Marion, MA, USA.

[2] Ford, J.; R.C. Timme and A. Trampus (1968). A new method for obtaining directional spectrum of Ocean Surface gravity waves. *IEEE Trans. on Geoscience Electronics*, Vol.GE-6 (4).

[3] Gaul, R.D. and N.L. Brown (1966). A free-floating wavemeter. Proc. Conf. on Electronic Eng. in Oceanography, London, 1966.

[4] Parente, C.E. and M.H. Souza (1988). Wave climate off Rio de Janeiro coast. Proc. XVII Intern. Conf. Coastal Engineering, Malaga, Spain (in press).

[5] Parente, C.E. and J.A. Moreira Lima (1989). MOPS-A wave sensor for semisubmersible platforms - to be presented at Brazil Offshore 89 Conference in Rio de Janeiro, Aug. 1989.

THE COASTLINE OF RIO DE JANEIRO
FROM A COASTAL ENGINEERING POINT OF VIEW

Enise Valentini [1]   Claudio F. Neves [1]

1 INTRODUCTION

As a result of the growth of the urban population in Brazil, there has been a significant increase of the occupation of coastal areas. In the State of Rio de Janeiro, resort towns have been established in place of fishing villages, harbors were planned to support the economical activities like offshore oil exploitation and fishing, and towns, located on the coast, had their urbanized area expanded. These examples quite often require the construction of works — seawalls, breakwaters, jetties — which affect the shoreline. Therefore, coastal engineering can give an important contribution to the coastal zone management by characterizing the shoreline (before its occupation), by providing technical guidelines on how to build the necessary works, as well as by predicting the effects of these works on neighboring beaches.

Coastal engineering is a young specialty, which requires knowledge about the sea, the shoreline, and their interaction. In developed countries, the loss of high valued beach properties often justfied the need for coastal studies and research. Those studies turned out to be expensive and to require long periods of observation. Such experience should serve as an alert for Brazil, where vast areas along the coast have not yet been occupied, and where little information on the coastal environment is available.

Having this in mind, the Ocean Engineering Department of COPPE/UFRJ started in early 1988 a project called "Littoral Rio", in order to make an assessment of coastal engineering problems along the coastline of Rio de Janeiro. Consequently, those research needs, which might contribute towards the solution of existing problems and the prevention of new ones, could be better established.

This is a two-year long project whose general description is presented in section 2. The following sections discuss the problems found in different points of the coast, possible remedial measures, and studies which have been suggested to municipalities, State agencies, or are currently in progress as academic research.

[1]Programa de Engenharia Oceânica – COPPE, Universidade Federal do Rio de Janeiro, Caixa Postal 68508, Rio de Janeiro, RJ 21945, Brazil.

2 LITTORAL RIO PROJECT

2.1 General Purposes

This project was conceived with two purposes. First, to serve as a guideline for the academic work and basic research on coastal engineering to be developed at the Federal University of Rio de Janeiro (UFRJ), mainly at its Ocean Engineering Department. Second, to spread the information about coastal engineering and concepts on shoreline preservation, especially among local communities.

The coastline of the State of Rio de Janeiro, approximately 800 km long including the contour of bays, was divided in four segments (Fig. 1).

The northern coast runs from the mouth of Itabapoana River to Cape São Tomé, is roughly aligned in the N-S direction, and its main feature is the delta of Paraíba do Sul River. Section 3.1 describes the main problems found in this area.

Following south from Cape S. Tomé, the coastline has its orientation changed to NE-SW. In this 180 km stretch, which ends in Búzios, the coastline is sparsely populated, except in Macaé where the harbor for the offshore industry is located. This part is presented in section 3.2.

Armação dos Búzios is a rocky formation, with a sequence of pocket beaches and capes, where another sharp deflection of the coastline takes place. From Cape Frio, whose name is due to the cold water which usually upwells near it, the coastline runs E-W for 200 km. The city of Rio is located roughly in the middle of this stretch, which ends on Marambaia Island. Most of the coastal works has been executed in this area, and they are discussed in section 3.3.

The final portion of the coastline is formed by Sepetiba, Ilha Grande and Paraty Bays. It is a sequence of pocket beaches formed by the nearby mountain range. It is a highly valued touristic zone as well as harbors important industries like shipyards, oil and ore terminals, and power plants.

The first phase of the project consisted of a bibliographic survey which was conducted at several institutions in Rio de Janeiro in order to obtain existing information regarding shoreline evolution, previous field measurements, and design of coastal works. Trips along the coastline were then scheduled once in the summer and once in the winter. During these trips, the authors obtained films and slides of the natural features of the coastline as well as of the coastal engineering works. Comparison of slides obtained in the summer and in the winter are very illustrative of change in wave climate and shoreline response to coastal structures. Sand samples were also collected, both on the beach face and at the top of the berm, just for a qualitative picture of the distribution of sediment diameter along the coast.

Finally, mayors, other county commissioners and local residents were interviewed during those trips. To serve as a guideline for the interview, the authors elaborated a questionnaire including questions on the following subjects: description of coastal engineering problems in the county, existence in local libraries of historical information about the shoreline and coastal areas, existence of topographical surveys and localization of monuments near the coast, interest on environmental education programs supported by the county.

This is a long term project with educational purposes which should be started by the university. It aims to disseminate coastal engineering: what can be done in terms of a rational occupation of the shoreline (and to benefit from it). For

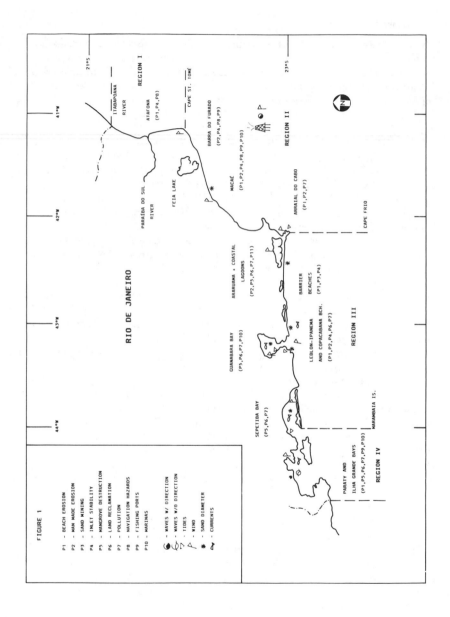

FIGURE 1

P1 - BEACH EROSION
P2 - MAN MADE EROSION
P3 - SAND MINING
P4 - INLET STABILITY
P5 - MANGROVE DESTRUCTION
P6 - LAND RECLAMATION
P7 - POLLUTION
P8 - NAVIGATION HAZARDS
P9 - FISHING PORTS
P10 - MARINAS

 - WAVES W/ DIRECTION
 - WAVES W/O DIRECTION
 - TIDES
 - WIND
 - SAND DIAMETER
 - CURRENTS

RIO DE JANEIRO

REGION I

ITABAPOANA RIVER
ATAFONA (P1,P4,P8)
CAPE ST. TOME

BARRA DO FURADO (P2,P4,P8,P9,P10)

REGION II

PARAÍBA DO SUL RIVER
FEIA LAKE
MACAÉ (P1,P2,P4,P8,P9,P10)
ARRAIAL DO CABO (P1,P2,P7)
CAPE FRIO

ARARUAMA + COASTAL LAGOONS (P2,P5,P6,P7,P11)

BARRIER BEACHES (P1,P3,P4)

GUANABARA BAY (P5,P6,P7,P10)

LEBLON-IPANEMA AND COPACABANA BCH. (P1,P2,P4,P6,P7)

REGION III

SEPETIBA BAY (P5,P6,P7)

MARAMBAIA IS.

PARATY AND ILHA GRANDE BAYS (P1,P5,P6,P7,P9,P10)

REGION IV

instance, building a seawall on the beach and a longshore avenue has a large appeal to any municipality, and the cost is usually within its budget. However, any erosional process which may follow and the correctional measures are often beyond the financial capability — or the jurisdiction — of the county.

2.2 Existing Data

Figure 1 schematically summarizes the information collected during the first phase of the project regarding previous field studies. The main sources of information were the Instituto de Pesquisas Hidroviárias (INPH) – the national hydraulic laboratory – and the Diretoria de Hidrografia e Navegação (DHN) – the Navy department for hydrography and navigation. The authors restricted the search to data which would be relevant to coastal engineering, what is next described.

Waves were usually measured without direction. In the most favorable cases, just visual observations were carried out, which may be misleading for instance when swell and seas occur simultaneously.

Regarding tide data, the most significant measurements regarding time span and reliability were conducted in Guanabara Bay (Ilha Fiscal, from 1963 to 1987; Ponta da Armação, since 1984) and in Sepetiba Bay (Ilha Guaíba, from 1970 to 1982). Other stations, in several points of the coast, were active for only one to three months, which is too short for studying meteorological effects or long term sea level variation. Unfortunately there is no tidal station along the coast of the State with reliable, long period time series.

There is a good amount of wind data beacause of networks maintained by the Brazilian Navy, Air Force, and Ministry of Agriculture. The stations are usually equiped with anemographs. Although such data should not be used for wave hindcast, they can be useful in studies of wind set-up on the coast.

On a regular basis, the Navy carries out current measurements on the inner shelf (for instance, GEOCOSTA Operations); other studies which required observation of currents were related to circulation in bays, inlet stabilization, and submarine outfalls.

Regarding bathymetric surveys, there are either nautical charts or those conducted for specific coastal works. DHN has a data bank of all surveys (in the country), indicating period of execution, executor, and surveyed region.

Drillings for sedimentological purposes have been carried out mostly in bays; grain size analysis have been performed either for coastal works or for the study of the evolution of barrier beaches between Rio de Janeiro and Cape Frio, and for evaluation of sediment transport.

Aerophotogrametric surveys, although available, do not cover the entire coastline and are available for a very short period of time. Since 1976 satellite images have been available every two weeks, but their potential use has not been fully realized.

The authors verified that the data has been collected and treated without a systematic approach. As a result, both the access to the information and its optimized use become difficult. This is a too important matter to be overlooked by a coastal management plan, and so far it has not been satisfactorily dealt with by the proposed methodologies within the National Coastal Management Plan.

3 GENERAL DESCRIPTION OF THE COASTLINE

3.1 The coastline of São João da Barra County

The northern stretch of the coastline of Rio, running from the mouth of the Itabapoana River to S. Tomé Cape, is under jurisdiction of S. João da Barra County. It is divided in half by the mouth of Paraíba do Sul River and has a deltaic formation. Argento (1987) made a very extensive overview of the geological features of that region.

In the past ten years, Atafona Beach, located on the southern margin of the mouth of Paraíba do Sul, has been severely eroded. A segment of the coast 400 m wide has disappeared: elsewhere in this conference, Argento presents a possible explanation for this process, which still deserves further study. River discharges vary seasonally from 500 m³/s to 2,000 m³/s, and wave climate also changes from northeastern local generated seas during the summer months, to southeastern storm seas and swell in the winter.

Besides Navy nautical charts in a 1:130,000 scale, there is no detailed bathymetric surveys of the coast in this region. In both trips the authors made to the county, the waves were about 1 m high or less at breaking, and the surf zone was about 200 m wide, indicating a flat beach slope. Clearly, the Paraíba do Sul River represents a dominant feature for the coastal processes in the area, either as a source of sediment or by affecting the wave direction at the shoreline due to current-wave interaction.

The road which runs along the coast south of the river was built at about 50 m from the beach, and the natural vegetation is still preserved. Near Gruçaí, 20 km south of Atafona, though, where houses and restaurants were built along the road, the vegetation which covers the foredunes was removed. After winter, mounds of sand 1 m high had accumulated in the porches of those buildings.

North of Paraíba do Sul, the mouth of Itabapoana River marks the northern border of the State of Rio de Janeiro. The nearby town of Bom Jesus do Itabapoana, located in the estuary, depends economically on fishing. The inlet migrates periodically, and at present a spit is growing towards south. According to some residents, the spit is occasionally broken.

For an extension of 10 km south of this river, the shoreline shows a sequence of clayey bluffs. The cliffs are being eroded: a house originally built on top of one cliff and now destroyed is the only indication of the erosional process. There is no aerophotography of this area, and the authors are trying to obtain satellite images in order to get, at least, a qualitative indication of shoreline retreat.

In other locations, closer to the Paraíba do Sul River, the municipality has built sidewalks along the beach: at some points, though, they seem to be too close to the beach and may be affected by waves during winter storms.

For this area, two studies seem to be necessary. First, the determination of the relative sea level variation near the mouth of Paraíba do Sul River, preferably using the devices developed by Murayama (Mehta et al., 1987), which would allow to determine land subsidence. Although a definite conclusion about the eustatic sea level could only be obtained twenty years from now, in the meantime relevant information would be generated. Second, the development of computer programs to study wave refraction and diffraction caused by bottom topography and/or currents would be an important tool for studying the coastal processes in this area.

3.2 From Cape S. Tomé to Cape Frio

Geological evidence shows that the mouth of the Paraíba do Sul River has migrated from south to north, and Cape S. Tomé would be a remnant feature of the deltaic formation. This stretch of the coastline runs in the general NE-SW direction. The sediment transport has not been quantified so far, mostly due to lack of information on waves, but it certainly has a net component from S to N.

About 30 km south of the cape, two jetties were built in 1976 to stabilize the mouth of Furado inlet, which serves as spillway to Lagoa Feia, the largest lake in the State. The channel is about 10 km long and, before reaching the sea, it crosses mangrove and shallow flooded areas. Also, the jetties would allow for the use by the local fishing community of a small harbor in the lagoon side. The project originally required the construction of a sand by-pass system which has not been built. Since then, the beach downdrift from the northern jetty has experienced an accelerated process of erosion, the road which ran along the shore was destroyed, and there are signs of overwashing. Updrift of the southern jetty, though, the beach has accreted approximately 150 m.

On the other hand, the fishermen do not use the harbor inside the lagoon because of navigation hazards at the inlet: they complain it is not safe to enter the canal during storms from the South quadrant, and claim a couple of boats have been thrown towards the jetties. Therefore, they use tractors to tow the boats onshore or to launch them, and use the beach as a parking lot.

Following south, there is a dozen small coastal lagoons. On their margins, there are sugar cane plantations and/or cattle ranches; also, the local community obtains food supply from the lagoon. A prospect use of these lagoons, according to Annibal (elsewhere in this conference), would be to develop fish farms. Of course this becomes an area of conflict which should be addressed by the coastal zone management program. The water level inside the lagoon depends both on the amount of rainfall and on the opening of the inlet. Occasionally, the local community dredges a channel when the water level is too high, or during some storm the inlet opens naturally. In any case, it stays open no longer than two weeks.

Macaé represents the first discontinuity on the shoreline. The spit at the mouth of Macaé river, growing from N to S, has been eroding in the past 10 years or so. Houses and a nautical club built on the spit have been affected by the erosion, and in August 1988, after a southeastern storm, the remnant of the spit which protected the inlet and the town from wave action was severely destroyed.

Also in Macaé, Petrobras, the Brazilian oil company, built a terminal at Imbetiba beach, where the operational basis for the offshore industry would be installed. The beach is approximately 1 km long, located between two headlands; a breakwater connected to one of the headlands would give shelter for the harbor. Several problems followed the construction of the terminal: the beach started being eroded, sediments were deposited in the harbor, and the remedial measures which were adopted at least compromised the recreational value of the beach.

Along the final segment of this stretch of coastline, there are three natural stable inlets: Ostras river, São João river, and Itajuru, this last one being the inlet for Araruama Lagoon. From the engineering point of view, there are no coastal problems, only sanitary pollution caused by expanding urbanization and lack of appropriate waste treatment.

3.3 From Cape Frio to Marambaia Island

This third portion is oriented in a E-W direction, Cape Frio being at its eastern end and Marambaia Island at the western end. The metropolitan area of Rio de Janeiro is located approximately at the middle of this segment, where are concentrated most of the population, the commercial and industrial activities of the State.

Guanabara Bay represents the main discontinuity of the coast, with a sequence of pocket beaches formed by headlands at both sides of the bay mouth. Dieter (elsewhere in this conference) presents an extensive description of the littoral east of the bay. Its main features are barrier beaches and coastal lagoons whose inlets are occasionally opened. The beaches are exposed to waves from SE (summer regime) and S to SW (winter regime), and the sand diameter varies from medium to coarse. Local winds come from E or NE (good weather) or from SW, during storms associated with cold fronts.

The sea water temperature is cold, ranging from 10 to 18 °C during the summer months due to the upwelling of South Atlantic Intermediate Water close to Cape Frio. Fisheries resources are abundant in this area, causing both sport and commercial fishing to become important activities.

From the coastal engineering point of view, the following problems have been identified: inlet stabilization, water circulation in coastal lagoons, man-related beach erosion, and domestic or industrial sewage disposal in coastal waters. Guanabara Bay constitutes an important case study as it presents all of these problems; it certainly deserves the joint effort of a multidisciplinary team conducting simultaneous studies about its physical, chemical, and biological aspects.

Uncontrolled action of man, in terms of urbanization and exploitation of coastal regions, has aggravated the problems in this area, as well as created new ones due to land reclamations, destruction of mangrove areas, removal of vegetation from dunes, and unplanned urban expansion. For instance, along the barrier beaches between Cape Frio and Guanabara Bay, there are several spots where sand — from dunes and beach — is mined for house construction, landfills or other industrial use. Although this activity is forbidden, it becomes very difficult to enforce the law in such large area without appropriate personnel or equipment.

The only zone still preserved is the barrier island of Marambaia. The beach connecting the proper Marambaia Is. to the continent is 50 km long, and encloses the Sepetiba Bay. The total area is approximately 40 km², and has been used as a training area for the armed forces. The sand diameter on the beach decreases from W to E, similar to what happens in other beaches along this segment of the coast.

3.4 Bays

The last portion of the State littoral is characterized by a sequence of bays, with a large number of pocket beaches and islands. The three largest bays are Sepetiba, Ilha Grande and Paraty (Fig. 1). The mountain range known as "Serra do Mar" runs very close to the sea, the precipitation rate is of the order of 2,000 mm/year, and the vegetation is typically tropical forest, covering the hills, and mangroves at the inner reaches of the bays.

Originally, the population was dispersed in small villages, whose economy depended mostly on fishing and banana plantations. For more than twenty years, a shipyard has been installed near Angra dos Reis (Ilha Grande Bay) and an ore terminal at the entrance of Sepetiba Bay. Nearly ten years ago, after the opening of the road connecting Rio de Janeiro to Santos (the largest port in Brazil, located in the State of São Paulo), urbanization has increased in this area; also, the Port Authority of Rio de Janeiro built a terminal for coal and ore in Sepetiba Bay; an oil terminal belonging to Petrobras and a nuclear power plant were also installed in Ilha Grande Bay.

Real estate and tourism are causing a significant impact on the region, which is ecologically very fragile. Land reclamation projects are being built without proper fiscalization, changing the contour of coves and small bays and thus affecting tidal circulation. On the hills, deforestation and high rates of rainfall are causing serious landslides, as well as accelerating the siltation of bays. The number of marinas is also increasing. Water quality, especially near the terminals and plants, become very poor; besides, serious effects of pollution due to inadequate disposal of heavy metals on Sepetiba Bay are in progress. Therefore, this is a region where an enforced coastal zone management program is urgently needed, including the execution of a series of environmental studies especially on wind and tide driven circulation. Another area of interest would be related to cohesive sediment transport, present in Sepetiba Bay, which is closely associated to the problem of heavy metal pollution described by Malm et al. in this conference.

4 SOME COASTAL ENGINEERING WORKS AND PROBLEMS

This inventory of the littoral of Rio de Janeiro made possible to identify the coastal engineering problems which systematically occur at several points. In the next paragraphs, these problems are addressed separately as well as some of the most important works.

4.1 Beach erosion

This is the most common problem along the coastline of the State, occurring either on exposed or in pocket beaches. Generally, the engineering works are designed without knowledge of coastal zone dynamics, resulting on loss of beach front property. Very often, urbanization is done too close to the top of the berm, or within the reach of exceptionally severe storm waves. Many longshore avenues and sea walls have been destroyed due to this fact.

Three history cases dealing with the evolution of beach profiles have been selected, each on a different scale of importance and with different physiographic characteristics. They are: Cabiúnas beach, located on the northern coast of the State, Leblon beach, in the city of Rio de Janeiro, and Mambucaba beach, inside Ilha Grande bay (see Fig. 1).

Cabiúnas beach, in Macaé County, is located on Region II (according to the scheme previously shown), and subject to waves from NE to S, resulting on a littoral drift with seasonal change of direction, e.g. towards south during summer months, and towards north during winter. Also, during storms, there is strong onshore-offshore action. Two pipelines linking the offshore oil fields to the refineries were planned to land on the Cabiúnas beach, and the construction started in February 1988. Unfortunately, there were neither long term study of the wave climate in the region, nor information about the local beach processes. The first storm, on April 3, piled sand on top of the berm, burying the pipes. The second storm on April 15, 1988, destroyed a total length of 35 meters of sheetpiles, and almost caused the drilling equipment to fall into the water.

Another example of erosion happened at Leblon beach, a highly valued area in the city of Rio de Janeiro. Together with Ipanema beach, Leblon constitutes a physiographic unit, bounded by two headlands, and having the inlet of a small lagoon at one third of the beach arc (Rosman and Valentini describes this problem in more detail). Since the inlet tends to be closed, the county periodically dredges the channel to keep the renewal of the lagoon water. For the past 30 years this procedure has been done without returning the sand to the beach. The total volume of sand dredged in this period was estimated in 100,000 m^3, a significant volume for a 4 km long beach.

The last example happened at Mambucaba beach, in the inner reaches of Ilha Grande bay. It is a pocket beach, about 4 km long, with an arc shape, facing directly the entrance of the bay. At the E and W ends of the beach there are tombolos formed by nearby islands. The mouth of Mambucaba river, in the past 50 years, has migrated from the E end of the beach, next to the rocky headland, to its present situation at the east tombolo.

Wave crests usually arrive parallel to the beach, although wave heights are higher at the middle of the beach arc due to refraction and diffraction effects. The distribution of sand diameter shows a decrease in D_{50} from the center (0.6 mm) to both ends of the beach (0.2 mm). Onshore-offshore processes are dominant, mainly due to storm waves coming from South.

Housing for workers of a nearby plant was established at Mambucaba. The urbanization project included a longshore avenue with wide sidewalks and parking areas, which was located at the edge of the (then) existing vegetation. Since there was no long period record of waves, and the area had not been previously occupied, the establishment of the avenue apparently followed a reasonable criterion. The avenue grade was 2 m above sea level, and the front row of houses was at least 25 m from the high water line. Five years after the village had been built, a strong storm brought waves which destroyed 350 m of the avenue at the center of the beach arc, the berm receded 20 m, and water invaded the nearby houses. As remedial measures, the owners were advised to cut part of the parking area at the most affected site, and replace the rubblemound (used to protect the beach) by sand.

4.2   Beach erosion due to coastal structures

In this section, emphasys is given on erosion directly caused by structures built on the coastline and surf zone, like breakwaters, groins, and jetties. Two examples are given, one at Anjos Cove, near Cape Frio, and the other at Furado Inlet, near St. Tomé Cape.

Anjos beach is located inside a cove, traditionally used by fishermen because of good shelter conditions. It is a long, relatively narrow bay, limited by headlands which are part of the Cape Frio formation. A harbor was established inside the bay, and a 260 m long breakwater was built in order to shelter the ships. The beach response was to erode at the exposed side with loss of beach front property, and sand was transported towards the more sheltered area and into the harbor.

Furado inlet, connecting Feia Lake to the ocean, is located about 30 km south of St. Tomé Cape. There is a 300 fishermen community which needed harbor facilities; at the time of the project, the boats were towed by tractors up the beach or towards the water. The project included the construction of: two jetties to fix Furado Inlet, harbor facilities inside the lagoon, and a sand by-pass system to prevent beach erosion. The sand by-pass was never built; north of the jetties, the beach has severely eroded and the north jetty is already isolated from shore; since 1976, coastline offset between the south and north side of the jetties has reached about 150 m. The fishermen claim the channel is not safe for navigation, and so they keep towing their boats to shore.

4.3 Beach nourishment projects

The most successful and only beach nourishment project in the State was done at Copacabana beach, in the city of Rio de Janeiro. This 4.5 km long beach is limited by two rocky headlands and represents one of the tourist attractions of the city. Winter storms caused waves to pile sand on the longshore avenue and threatened the stability of the seawall; in the early 60's, during a severe storm, waves flooded the underground garages of the buildings along the avenue. The City, in face of this periodical problem, and also intending to build a 6-lane road to improve the traffic circulation in Copacabana, then approved the beach nourishment.

The project was developed by the Laboratório Nacional de Engenharia Civil (LNEC) in Portugal, which carried out field measurements in 1965-67 and executed the physical models for the beach (LNEC, 1968). Apparently this was the first long period observation of waves in Rio. According to the studies, if the beach were widened up to 120 m there would be no loss of sand around the headlands.

The final choice was for a widening of 80 m. The total volume of nourishment was 2,500,000 m^3 at a cost of US\$ 0.80 /m^3 (Nicoletti, 1970). The borrow material came mostly from a source inside Guanabara Bay, transported through 5,200 m of pipelines, and pumped out at 6 outlets along the beach. Out of the total volume, about 400,000 m^3 was transported by a hopper dredge and dumped right offshore of the breaking zone.

Unfortunately, there has been no follow up of the beach evolution after the nourishment. No other episode of water reaching the avenue had happened until August/88 when, during the same storm which destroyed the sewer pipelines in Leblon, the waves reached the seawall near Posto 6 — the southern end of the beach.

4.4 Stability of tidal inlets

Most of the coastal lagoons along the coastline of Rio have unstable inlets which stay open for short periods. The potential for building marinas and developments along the margins of these lagoons is very high, and may happen in the future. One of these cases is Itaipu lagoon, near the city of Rio de Janeiro, where jetties were built; however, the planned marina has never been built.

When the inlet is closed, water is not renewed, water level inside the lagoon increases, and flooding of marginal areas occurs. These are typical problems of the coastal lagoons (Jaconé, Maricá, Guarapina, Saquarema) between Rio de Janeiro and Cape Frio. Also, uncontrolled land reclamation along the margins of the lagoons causes a change of the tidal prism, and the consequent variation of the stable cross section area of the channel.

In the northern part of the littoral, where a significant net longshore sediment transport is present, the opening of stable inlets may bring damages to the coastline, as it is happening at Furado Inlet, or because the lagoons may work as sediment traps.

In the city of Rio de Janeiro there are three stabilized inlets, all with jetties. The one which separates Ipanema and Leblon beaches is periodically dredged; the other two are located at both ends of Barra da Tijuca beach, next to headlands, with depths ranging from 1 to 2 m.

4.5 Pollution

Coastal and/or sea pollution has increased to alarming degrees in the past years as result of growing industrialization, urbanization, and different uses of the coastal zone. Due to a lack of normalization to control these uses, the works are not always preceeded by a careful plan, causing, in a medium or long time span, damages to the environment.

Most often, problems are related to the disposal of domestic sewerage. In Rio de Janeiro and in Niterói counties, submarine outfall were built, disposing the sewer without any form of treatment at an average distance of 3 km from shore. Usually, the sea water would be able to degrade the sewer. However, during storms, the direction of currents is changed, causing the polluting plume to return towards the beach, eventually reaching the surf zone. Because no treatment is done, the disposed material has high grease content, low density, thus with tendency for buoyancy. Reaching the surface, it can be carried by upper ocean circulation, instead of being dispersed near the bottom.

Designing the future capacity of the disposal system is another problem that has recently proved to be important. The system was designed based on a projected growth of population. However, because of changes in the zoning codes of the city, the occupation density has increased beyond the projected level. Since the sewage system was neither designed nor enlarged for the present discharge, occasionaly the sewer system overspills to the pluvial water system. There are even cases when the domestic sewer lines are illegally connected to pluvial system, which drains directly to rivers, lagoons, or beaches. This form of pollution becomes very difficult to control.

This sort of problem is not exclusive to large cities, though. In small towns, with high tourist value, uncontrolled real state demand is causing serious damages to the environment. For instance, along the coastal lagoons, covering 8 counties, where fishing and tourism were the main activities, water supply was inaugurated without construction of sewer lines.

Another form of pollution is due to industrial sewer, occurring mainly in Guanabara and Sepetiba bays. In spite of federal legislation prohibiting disposal of untreated sewer into waters, the penalties are often lower than the cost of treatment plants. Rivers, estuaries and lagoons are affected by residues of sugar and alcohol industry (northern part of the state), mercury used in gold purification (Paraíba do Sul river and its tributaries), oil spills near terminals, cadmium and heavy metals (Sepetiba bay, see Malm et al. in this conference), and a potential for thermal water pollution after the nuclear power plant starts operation.

5 COASTAL MANAGEMENT

The issue of *coastal management* started being addressed in Brazil in 1983, being regulated by federal law in 1988. It is not the purpose of this article to discuss the political aspects or the methodology of the Program, subject of other papers in this conference (Frischeisen et al., Argento, and Azevedo). Here, emphasys is rather given to the issues directly related to coastal engineering, since a management program should not avoid taking into consideration engineering aspects. As in other types of studies, there is always a strong interface between legal and technical criteria.

As exposed in Section 2, the "Littoral Rio" Project has two purposes: one is strictly of academic nature, the other is to disseminate among the coastal communities the ideas of coastal protection. The reason for this is the fact that coastal engineering is a still unknown specialty in Brazil. Consequently, there are no technical norms and codes regulating or giving directions for engineering works on the coastline.

During the execution of the inventory, the authors also noted the lack of data relevant to coastal engineering, like wave climate, tidal data, current measurements, topographic surveys. Whenever the information was available, though, the data was dispersed among several institutions, often there was no record on the methodology employed for measurement and data reduction, or the data was not in a format for easy analysis. Hopefully, after the consolidation of the National Coastal Zone Management Program these problems should be minimized.

From the questionnaires submitted to the local communities, the answers indicated very often a lack of sense about the sea-coast interaction or the consequences from an improper intervention. For instance, municipal laws omit aspects related to the occupation of coastal areas, and many works are built without adequate technical analysis (by state or federal agencies). Some of the problems detected could have been avoided if the municipality exerted a more strict control of coastal works. Certainly it would represent a significant economy for the counties, which can afford to build a longshore sea wall, but certainly can not afford the costs for repairing the coastline. Other examples are land reclamation projects inside lagoons or along inlets, construction of groins, boardwalks and coastal avenues. Of course, one could seldom expect to find within each municipal government, engineers able to design coastal engineering works. Therefore, it would be extremely useful the establishment of minimum criteria to govern the use of the coastline, according to engineering principles and scientific basis.

The present legislation prescribe a long series of steps to be satisfied before the authorization of any coastal work. First, all areas subject to tidal fluctuations are of public access. For this purpose, a strip along the coast 33 m inland from a specific high water line in 1831 belongs to the Union, which receives taxes for private use of the land. This line (hereafter named SPU line) however has not been entirely demarcated along the coast of Brazil, and within the State, only in some urban segments in the county of Rio de Janeiro, parts of Guanabara Bay, along Itajuru Inlet, and short segments of the coast near Macaé. If the area belongs to the Union (for instance, historical sites, or preservation areas), the "Serviço de Patrimônio da União" (SPU), should be first contacted. This agency will give permission to the work after hearing the Navy — regarding navigation or strategical aspects — and the "Serviço de Patrimônio Histórico e Artístico Nacional" (SPHAN), which manages sites and monuments of historical or artistical value. Next, it is necessary to obtain approval from the environmental agency, usually within the State, which forward an opinion after the evaluation by some institution especialized in coastal engineering. Depending on the magnitude of the project, a report on environmental impact may also be required. After all of these agencies have provided their opinion, the project is forwarded to the county government, which is supposed to give the final evaluation, approving or not the work.

6 RECOMMENDATIONS AND CONCLUSIONS

The most urgent coastal engineering problems have been briefly described. As the coastline becomes increasingly more populated, either new problems may appear or the current ones may bring more serious consequences. The solutions require studies which take at least one year of preliminary field work, because few measurements have already been conducted, and very seldom there is enough historical data for determining the evolution of the coast.

The inventory conducted by the authors showed that a very small amount of information — useful for coastal engineering purposes — has been accumulated. As described in section 2.2, information is too much spread, scarce, and not easily retrieved. It becomes evident the need for a systematic approach for collecting, treating and storing data. Besides that, more scientifically oriented field works should be done with the purpose of increasing the general knowledge about Rio de Janeiro coastline.

Collecting data takes a long time; in addition, the cost of equipment and operation is usually high and often the local authorities have other problems to face with higher priority. Having this in mind, a "preventive program" is suggested, and also that funds be allocated for research on monitoring programs employing low cost, but reliable, equipment. Further, taking into account the many difficulties faced by a developing country, the most effective way to carry out such program would be through a joint effort among universities, research institutes, and governmental agencies.

Among the data which needs to be collected on a regular basis, the most urgent are:

- waves:
  At least one permanent wave station should be installed offshore Regions III and IV. The offshore oil platforms, located in Regions I and II, should also be used to obtain information on deep water waves. Besides period and height, wave direction must be measured, otherwise all coastal processes cannot be properly evaluated.

• tide:

The present array of tide gauges should be extended and maintained in a proper way, so that precise information about sea level fluctuations along the coast of Rio may be obtained in the future. Three new stations should be installed (especially on open coast): one near the mouth of Paraíba do Sul river, another near Macaé, and one in the southern part of the littoral.

• topographic surveys:

In order to follow the evolution of the shoreline and plan new works on the coast, a surveyed line should be installed. The SPU line could be a first option, although this issue should be addressed by the national coastal management program (PNGC).

• water circulation:

As more outfalls of industrial and domestic sewer are planned in coastal waters, detailed measurements of inner shelf circulation become necessary, as well as related studies about winds, water quality, biology, and physical oceanography.

Although not directly connected to coastal engineering, another important issue for a coastal management program deals with environmental education. One of the items in the questionnaire addressed exactly this point, and for all counties, it became evident that: they did not have any educational program with emphasis on environmental control; and the counties would be willing to establish such programs. This verification allows one to reason that such a program would be very well received by the local community. Long term results would be felt as much as the population would be aware of environmental issues, would seek an occupation of the coast in a more harmonious way, and would contribute to the solution of environmental problems.

In conclusion, some action must be taken now in order to enable engineers to find solutions in the future, like the establishment of: 1) a systematic data bank for oceanographycal information according to international standards; 2) follow up programs for coastal works; 3) the demarcation of a surveyed line along the coast which may be used to control shoreline evolution, for instance following the SPU line; 4) norms and criteria for construction along the littoral, with rigid enforcement by municipalities; 5) educational programs about environmental (coastal) protection addressed to different levels of the population.

REFERENCES

[1] Argento, M.S.F. (1977). A planície deltaica do Paraíba do Sul – um sistema ambiental. M.Sc. Thesis, Inst. Geociências, Universidade Federal do Rio de Janeiro, 120 pp.

[2] Argento, M.S.F. (1987). A contribuição dos Sistemas Cristalino e Barreira na formação da planície deltaica do Paraíba do Sul. D.Sc. Dissertaion, UNESP.

[3] Argento, M.S.F. (1989). The Geographical Information System of the Brazilian Coastal Management Program. Proc. VI Symp. Coastal Ocean Management, Charleston, July 10–15, 1989, ASCE.

[4] Azevedo, L.H.A.; D.M.W. Zee; D.R. Tenenbaum (1989). Coastal Zone Planning. Proc. VI Symp. Coastal Ocean Management, Charleston, July 10–15, 1989, ASCE.

[5] Frischeisen, E.R.; M.S.F. Argento; R. Herz; R.P. Carneiro (1989). The Brazilian Coastal Management Plan. Proc. VI Symp. Coastal Ocean Management, Charleston, July, 10–15, 1989, ASCE.

[6] LNEC – Laboratório Nacional de Engenharia Civil (1968). Praia de Copacabana – Estudo de alargamento em modelo reduzido. Lisboa.

[7] Malm, O; W.C. Pfeiffer; L.D. Lacerda; M. Fiszman; and N.R.W. Lima (1989). Heavy metals pollution monitoring through the critical pathways analysis: the Sepetiba Bay case. Proc. VI Symp. Coastal Ocean Management, Charleston, July, 10–15, 1989, ASCE.

[8] Mehta, A.J; R.G. Dean; W.R. Dally; and C.L. Montague (1987). Some considerations on coastal processes relevant to sea level rise", University of Florida, Coastal and Oceanographical Engineering Report no. 87/012.

[9] Nicoletti, M.V. (1970). The Copacabana Beach reclamation project. Proc. World Dredging Conference, Singapore: 65–105.

[10] Rosman, P.C.C. and E. Valentini (1989). Recent erosion in the "stable" Ipanema-Leblon beach in Rio de Janeiro. Proc. VI Symp. Coastal Ocean Management, Charleston, July, 10–15, 1989, ASCE.

[11] Valentini, E. and G.O.M. Fialho (1986). Estudo de erosão na praia de Mambucaba, Angra dos Reis. Relatório COPPETEC ET-17121, 164 pp.

SELECTION OF MARINE BIOINDICATORS FOR MONITORING RADIOACTIVE WASTES RELEASED FROM NUCLEAR POWER PLANTS

Letícia M. Mayr [1]   Rosane B.C. Moraes [1]   Jane B.N. Mauro [1]

Aura C.L.F. Ferreira [1]

1 INTRODUCTION

Aiming for the solution of the problem of energy deficit in the most industrialized and most populated area of Brazil, the region comprising three big cities (São Paulo, 16.2 million inhabitants; Rio de Janeiro, 10.7 million, and Belo Horizonte, 3.3 million) — (Fig. 1), the federal government has decided to build three nuclear power plants in the region between São Paulo and Rio de Janeiro.

The Brazilian Nuclear Program comprehends: the Angra I Nuclear Power Plant, in operational tests; the Angra II Nuclear Power Plant, under construction, expected to be completed in 1992; and Angra III Nuclear Power Plant, still in its project stage.

Those plants are located on the coast, in the inner reaches of Ilha Grande Bay, Angra dos Reis (RJ), which is characterized by a humid tropical climate (2240.6 mm of rainfall/annum) and also by important tourism activities and fisheries.

Following the decision of their construction, a broad research program on radionuclides became necessary, particulary environmental impact studies. These three nuclear power plants have a pressurized water refrigeration system. The liquid effluent released in Ribeira Bay makes radiological studies a priority in this area. These studies will determine the radionuclides pathways, its concentrations and dispersion in the environment and in the biota, taking into account the possible effects on the local population.

As part of this program, the Institute of Biology/UFRJ began, in 1978, a research project to estimate the radiation doses which the population of the region might be exposed to and to determine the suitable biological indicators to radioactive contamination.

The information obtained in the present work will contribute greatly to the monitoring program, helping in the making of decisions in the Brazilian Coastal Management Program related to this area.

[1]Departamento de Biologia Marinha, Instituto de Biologia, Universidade Federal do Rio de Janeiro, Rio de Janeiro, RJ 21941, Brazil.

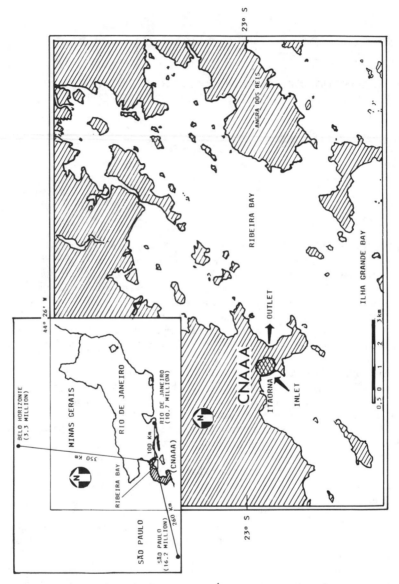

Figure 1: Localization of the Admiral Álvaro Alberto Nuclear Power Plant (CNAAA) and its distance from three country's big cities (with their population). –▷ Refrigeration water.

Among the radionuclides released by the power plants, the radioisotopes of cobalt (Co), strontium (Sr), iodine (I) and cesium (Cs) were selected for the present work because they are potentially harmful to man, mainly when introduced in the food chain.

Up to the present moment, the bioaccumulation factors (BF) of ^{60}Co, ^{131}I and ^{137}Cs by the "clam" *Anomalocardia brasiliana* and the biological half-life of cobalt and cesium in this animal were determined, as well as the BF of ^{131}I by the "barnacle" *Megabalanus tintinnabulum* and the incorporation of ^{85}Sr by the "snail" *Strombus pugilis*. These studies were made using the standard methodology for bioaccumulation and elimination in closed water systems.

The microbial activity was also studied because of its importance related to the remobilization of the radioactive elements released by the power plant. Thus ^{60}Co, when released in its ionic form, is strongly retained by the bottom sediment, and it is liberated by the interference of the microorganisms, becoming thus available in the water and then being incorporated by other animals of the food chain.

2 MATERIAL AND METHODS

2.1 Selected Biological Material

With the objective of evaluating environmental pollution by using either living animals or plants and also because there is the possibility of human contamination, the biological indicators of pollution should have basic characteristics, which are:

• minimum mobility;

• abundance in the area;

• all year availability;

• ease of collection,

and they should preferably be edible organisms.

The following organisms were selected because they have all if not most of the required characteristics so as to be a biological indicator.

They are:

• *Anomalocardia brasiliana* (Gmelin, 1971)
  Edible bivalve ("vôngole"). Occurring in the sand-muddy bottom of the medium-littoral (Narchi, 1972), being abundant at the Ribeira Bay (RJ), where the Angra I Nuclear Power Plant is situated. It feeds by filtration on the suspended material at the sediment-water interface (Fig. 2).

• *Megabalanus tintinnabulum* (Linnaeus, 1758)
  Sessile arthropod crustacean, occurring mainly on rocks, shells or any hard substratum. It is a suspension feeder (Oliveira, 1941) (Fig. 3). Industries that use sea water for refrigeration create ideal conditions for the development of these organisms in the circulation tubes, making it necessary to use biocides and/or antiincrustants. It is not an edible animal, but as part of the ecological food web, it can reach men.

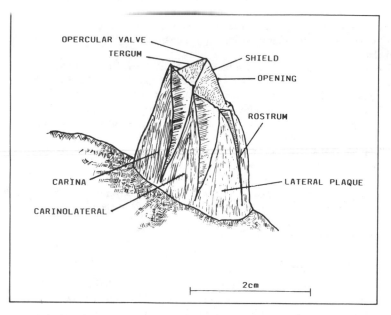

Figure 2: *A. brasiliana* in its habitat showing its external left side. The arrows indicate the direction of the inhaling and exhaling currents.

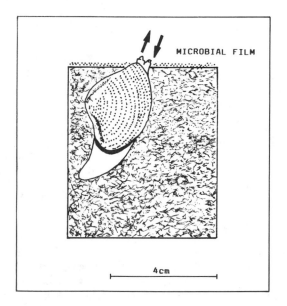

Figure 3: External aspect of *M. tintinnabulum*.

- *Strombus pugilis* (Linnaeus, 1758)
  Edible snail ("preguari"). It occurs on the sand-muddy bottom of the infra littoral (Matthews, 1980), being abundant at the Ribeira Bay. It is a grazing feeder, eating mainly microalgae and detritus (Fig. 4 and 5).

2.2 Selected Radionuclides

Among the critical radionuclides released by the Angra I Nuclear Power Plant ^{60}Co, ^{85}Sr, ^{131}I and ^{137}Cs were chosen as tracers. They are good emitters of highly energetic gamma radiation and also easily obtained, facilitating the laboratory radiometrical work.

2.3 Methods

The experiments of radionuclide bioaccumulation from the water were made in aquaria with aeration and no biological filter. In the studies of radionuclide transference from the sediment to the biota(^{60}Co in *A. brasiliana*), the animals were put inside bechers containing mud in an aquarium with a biological filter.

The radionuclides were added to the aquaria water in its ionic form. The bioaccumulation dynamics was almost always observed until reaching its equilibrium phase. In each experiment the animals were periodically taken out of the aquarium, washed with uncontaminated sea water and, after the determination of the radiation level, put back in the aquarium.

To measure the concentration of the elements in different parts of the animals in the experiments of ^{60}Co and ^{137}Cs, they were dissected after being killed with liquid nitrogen. This type of killing was used in order to preserve their internal structures. Water samples were measured simultaneously with the organisms.

The measurements of the radionuclides activities were taken in a "Tracerlab" manual cintilometer, Model SC-57 A with a 7.6 × 7.6 cm NaI (Tl) crystal connected to a monochannel gamma spectrometer.

After ^{60}Co and ^{137}Cs incorporation and the equilibrium of the bioaccumulation factors, the animals were transferred to another aquarium with no contaminated water, and the radionuclide elimination was observed so as to determine its biological half-life.

3 RESULTS AND DISCUSSION

The bioaccumulation factor (BF) is given by:

$$BF = \frac{\text{radionuclide concentration/g of organism}}{\text{radionuclide concentration/ml of water}}$$

The ^{60}Co, ^{137}I and ^{131}I BF for *M. tintinnabulum* and *A. brasiliana* are shown on Table I.

The ^{131}I BF for *M. tintinnabulum* was the highest value found among the studied organisms (average of 13 animals after 13 days). As 100 is a good BF (Portmmann, 1976), *M. tintinnabulum* can be considered a reasonable but not ideal biological accumulator.

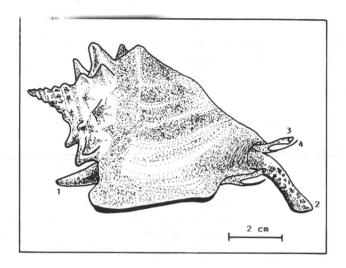

Figure 4: External aspect of *S. pugilis* showing its foot[1], proboscid[2], omatophores[3] with eyes at its ends, and antennae[4].

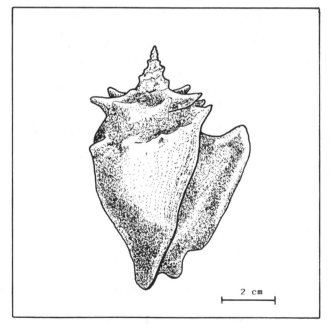

Figure 5: Ventral aspect of the shell of *S. pugilis*.

Table I: Values of bioaccumulation factor of ^{60}Co , ^{137}Cs and ^{131}I from water by
M. tintinnabulum (wet weight) and *A. brasiliana* (dry and wet weights). WW - wet
weight; DW - dry weight.

Animal	Radionuclide					
	^{60}Co		^{137}Cs		^{131}I	
	WW	DW	WW	DW	WW	DW
M. tintinnabulum	–	–	–	–	43.0	–
A. brasiliana						
- Whole animal	5.3	7.8	1.5	2.2	3.9	5.8
- Shells	4.3	4.5	0.1	0.1	4.7	4.9
- Soft Tissues	6.5	64.0	6.1	60.0	4.9	33.0

For *A. brasiliana*, ^{60}Co showed a higher BF (7.8) and, although of low value,
the found BF of the soft tissue (64.0) was significant. *A. brasiliana* showed higher
BF for ^{60}Co than for the other studied radionuclides. This can be explained by
the fact that this organism feeds on the bottom sediment by filtration. ^{60}Co, put
in the aquarium in its ionic form, was "organified" by the microorganisms present
in the bottom sediment, becoming the nucleus of cobalamins, molecules of great
biological importance. The obtained ^{60}Co and ^{137}Cs BF for *A. brasiliana* cannot be
considered of high values (Lowman, Rice and Richards, 1971; Lowman and Ting,
1973; Harrison, 1973; Amiard-Triquet, 1975; and Cranmore and Harrison, 1975).

In the soft tissue subdivisions obtained by dissection, the ^{60}Co BF corresponded
to the following activity distribution: Viscera - 85.2%; Gills - 5.9%; Muscles - 3.3%;
Mantle - 2.5%; Foot - 2.4% and Siphons - 0.8%. For ^{137}Cs, the BF corresponded to
the following activity distribution: Viscera - 27.5%; Gills - 25.8%; Siphons - 13%;
Mantle - 13%; Foot - 12.3% and Abductor Muscles - 8.4% (See Table II).

The results of ^{60}Co and ^{137}Cs elimination experiments are shown on Table III.
The highest biological half-life found was of ^{60}Co (460 days). After a few days of
elimination, we could observe that the percentages of ^{60}Co and ^{137}Cs concentration
in the subdivisions of the soft tissue suffered alterations, indicating different biological half-lives for each compartment. Cobalt maintained the highest percentage
in the viscera, which can indicate the incorporation of cobalamins containing ^{60}Co
by the digestive gland. For cesium, the highest biological half-lives found were for
the abductor muscles and the foot. The recycling of cesium was relatively fast in
the soft tissue. This observation agrees with the metabolic behavior of potassium
in animal cells (Amiard-Triquet, 1975), confirming analogous chemical behavior of
the two elements.

The ^{85}Sr bioaccumulation experiments with *S. pugilis* showed an increasing incorporation of this radionuclide (Fig. 6). Its BF, however, was not determined,
since we are still studying the better counting geometry for this organism.

Table II: Values of bioaccumulation factor of ^{60}Co and ^{137}Cs by the soft tissues of *A. brasiliana* obtained by its dissection (dry weight) (approximate values).

Parts of Organism	Radionuclide	
	^{60}Co	^{137}Cs
- Viscera	21.0	113.0
- Gills	1.0	106.0
- Abductor Muscles	1.0	34.0
- Mantle	1.0	53.0
- Foot	1.0	50.0
- Siphons	0.2	53.0

Table III: ^{60}Co and ^{137}Cs biological half-life (days) in *A. brasiliana*.

Parts of Organism	Radionuclide	
	^{60}Co	^{137}Cs
- Whole animal	460	39
- Shells	–	18
- Soft tissues	81	20

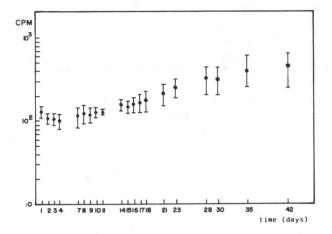

Figure 6: ^{85}Sr bioaccumulation by *S. pugilis*.

4 CONCLUSIONS

The determined BF values do not classify the studied organisms as good biological indicators for the tested radionuclides. Considering, however, that the highest concentrations of the radionuclides were found in the soft tissue, and since *A. brasiliana* and *S. pugilis* are eaten and commercialized by the local population, we recommend their monitoring in relation to radioactive material contamination.

It is advisable to restate the importance of the microbial population in the distribution of radionuclides in the marine environment:

1. By its great total biomass;

2. By its significant role in the change of the physico-chemical state of the radioactive material, and

3. In the remobilization of radioactive ions retained in the bottom sediment.

Nowadays we are studying the incorporation of ^{60}Co by *S. pugilis*. The research project will continue testing other radionuclides and other organisms.

Acknowledgements: The authors would like to thank to the "Comissão Nacional de Energia Nuclear" (CNEN), the "Conselho Nacional de Desenvolvimento Científico e Tecnológico" (CNPq) and the "Universidade Federal do Rio de Janeiro" (UFRJ) for the financial support.

REFERENCES

[1] Amiard-Triquet, C. (1975). Étude du Transfert des Radionucleides entre le Milieu Sedimentaire Marin et les Invertebrés qui y Vivent. Doctorate Thesis. Centre d'Études Nucléaires de Fontenay-aux-Roses, France.

[?] Cronmarci, G. and F. L. Harrison (1975). Loss of ^{137}Cs and ^{60}Co from the oyster *Crassostrea gigas*. Health Physics Pergamon Press, **28**: 319–333.

[3] Harrison, F.L. (1973). Accumulation and loss of cobalt and cesium by the marine clam *Mya arenaria* under laboratory and field conditions. *in:* "Radioactive Contamination of the Marine Environment", Proceedings of a Symposium, 10–14 July 1972, AEA, Vienna.

[4] Lowman, F. G.; T. R. Rice and F. A. Richards (1971). Accumulation and redistribution of radionuclides by marine organisms. *in:* "Radioactivity in the Marine Environment". Committee on Oceanography, National Research Council. National Academy of Sciences, Washington. Chapter 7, pp. 161–199.

[5] Lowman, F. G. and R. Y. Ting (1973). The state of cobalt in sea water and its uptake by marine organisms and sediments. *in:* "Radioactive Contamination of the Marine Environment". Proceedings of a Symposium, Seattle. IAEA, Vienna, 369–384.

[6] Mathews, H. R. (1980). Moluscos Brasileiros da Família Strombidae (Gastropoda, Prosobranchia). M.Sc. Thesis. Coleção Mossoroense **CXXIX**.

[7] Narchi, W. (1972). Comparative study of the functional morphology of *Anomalocardia brasiliana* (Gmelin, 1971) and *Tivela mactroides* (Boen, 1778) (Bivalvia, Veneridae). *Bulletin of Marine Sciences*, **22**: 643–670.

[8] Oliveira, L. P. H. (1941). Contribuição ao Conhecimento dos Crustáceos do Rio de Janeiro, Sub-ordem Balanomorpha (Cirripedia, Thoracica). Memórias do Instituto Oswaldo Cruz, Tomo **36** (1).

[9] Portman, J. E. (1976) The role of biological accumulation in monitoring programs. *in:* "Manual of Methods in Aquatic Environment Research, Part 2. Guidelines for the Use of Biological Accumulators in Marine Pollution Monitoring". J. E. Portman (Ed.), FAO Fisheries Technical Paper **150**, Rome.

STATUS OF THE SPINY LOBSTER (CRUSTACEA : PALINURIDAE) STOCKS
OFF NORTHEAST BRAZIL IN RELATION TO FISHING EFFORT AND
ENVIRONMENTAL CONDITIONS

Antônio Adauto Fonteles-Filho

ABSTRACT

Conditions for the development of relatively abundant
populations of spiny lobsters of genus Panulirus, mainly
P. argus and P. laevicauda, off Northeast Brazil are con
sistent with hydrologically stable waters and associated
fluctuations in productivity that bear out balanced communities
in response to two main features: high-salinity waters owing
to low level of drainage into the continental shelf and
abundance of the sedimentary facies known as calcareous
algae, comprised of a mixture of species of family Coralli
naceae. The lobster stocks have been submitted to heavy
fishing since 1972, 17 years after fishery began, in 1955,
exerted at first by traps and, more recently, also by non-
selective bottom gillnets in nearshore areas, where there
is a predominance of juvenile individuals, what has led to
a diminishing breeding stock and a reduction in recruitment.
This trend for depletion has somewhat been halted by an
expansion of the fishing area and consequent decrease in
fishing intensity, allowing larger and older individuals
to be added up to the overfished stocks. Nevertheless, species
P. laevicauda seems to be losing biomass to the competing
species (P. argus) by having been submitted to heavier
effort over the last 5 years. Spiny lobsters are particu
larly vulnerable to salinity variation, and mass mortality
of larval forms may occur when the threshold value of
$20^{\circ}/oo$ is reached, as a result of the inflow of low-salinity
waters into the coastal nursery areas caused by heavy rainfall that
periodically affect the Northeast region of Brazil in some
years. At present, the lobster fishery, for its economic
importance as a producer of high-price food items, is being
closely monitored for signs of yield decline and identifi
cation of its causes, either from fishing pressure or changes
in environmental conditions.

(1) Senior Professor at the Federal University of Ceará
and bursar-researcher of Brazil's National Research
Council (CNPq). Current address: Laboratório de Cien
cias do Mar, Av. da Abolição 3207. P.O. Box 1072,
60.165 Fortaleza, Brazil.

INTRODUCTION

The fishing for spiny lobsters off Northeast Brazil began 1955 and thenceforth it has reached an outstanding position as a producer for the world trade market on account of the high prices and increasing demand, which have boos ted commercial exploitation causing the stocks to be submitted to very high fishing effort, with a consequent decline of productivity.

The need for enquiring into the status of the spiny lobster stocks stems from the fact that they are not only very important fishery resources, but also outstanding elements of a benthic biocenosis in the tropical zone of southern Atlantic. In Northeast Brazil, the fishery activities have been monitored since 1965 by the National Fisheries Service of Brazil (SUDEPE, 1985) together with data collection by University institutions on length and age structure (Buesa Más et al. 1968; Paiva and Costa 1968; Fonteles-Filho et al. 1988), reproduction (Mesquita and Gesteira 1975; Soares and Cavalcante 1985), growth (Ivo 1975), feeding (Fernandes 1972), migration (Paiva and Fonteles Filho 1968; Fonteles-Filho and Ivo 1980), and population dynamics and fisheries management (Paiva 1967; Paiva and Bezerra 1969; Paiva et al. 1973; Oliveira and Pereira 1980; and Fonteles Filho 1979 and 1986; Fonteles-Filho et al. 1985.

The objetive of this paper is to evaluate the biolo gical status of the stocks under fishing and density-inde pendent environmental factors, e.g. salinity, as shown by two important relationships: stock/recruitment (reproduction curve) and yield/fishing effort (production curve), with the pertinent underlying factors being taken into account, such as stabilization of age structure, regulatory mecha nisms, attainment of maximum sustainable yield and occurrence of growth and/or recruitment overfishing. Besides, the interspecific relationship of P. argus and P. laevicauda will be taken into the picture so as to provide discussion on how their relative abundance has changed and may interfere with the energy transfer between these competing species, leading to a likely, but yet to be confirmed, replacement in favor of P. argus.

THE BIOLOGICAL BACKGROUND

The Caribbean spiny lobster (P. argus) and the smoothtail spiny lobster (P. laevicauda) are decapod crustaceans with distribution in the Western Atlantic from Bermuda and North Carolina to Rio de Janeiro, Brazil (Williams 1986), but the latter has been considered to be a "Brazilian species" for its commercial fishery being confined practically only the Northest region of Brazil (figure 1).

Palinurids, in general, have a short hatching period and a long larval phase (Phillips et al. 1980). In Northeast Brazil their asymptotic length and weight reach values of 43.8 cm and 3,163 g (P. argus) and 38.0 cm and 1.805 g (P. laevicauda), growing at an average rate of 2.9 cm.yr^{-1} and 2.7 cm.yr^{-1}. Growth through molting is seasonal and its higher intensity occurs in January and July-August, in the adult phase, alternating with the main spawning season that

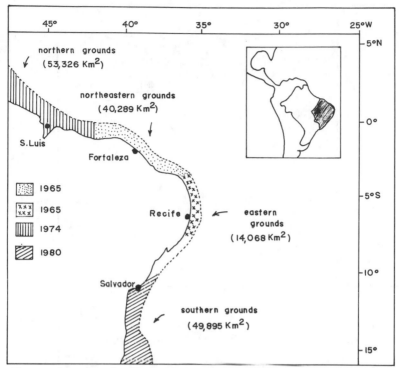

Figure 1 - Chart of fishing grounds (surface area, in brackets) for spiny lobsters, off Northeastern Brazil.

takes place in February-April and September-October (P. argus) and January-March (P. laevicauda), according to Fonteles-Filho (1979) and Soares and Cavalcante (1985).

Absolute fecundity, calculated from equations determined by Ivo and Gesteira (1986) presented mean values of 252,819 eggs and 141,235 eggs per female, corresponding to a relative fecundity of 608.9 eggs per gram and 579.5 eggs per gram of body weight of P. argus and P. laevicauda. Species P. argus is larger in individual size (21.6 cm of mean total length) and weight (404 g) than P. laevicauda (18.2 cm and 247 g), and it has a bigger population both in numbers (71.4 million individuals from age group I) and biomass (13,843 tons), against 44.4 million individuals and 5,435 tons of the other species.

Their spatial distribution is partially overlapping with a seaward trend of size increase in both species, but P. laevicauda concentrates itself in more coastal areas, as it can be shown by the variation of the ratio "CPUE of P. laevicauda/CPUE of P. argus" by depth where an even ratio of 1 is reached at about 40 meters (figure 2). P. argus, being the dominant species, seem to have access to a wider area, but the coexistence of these competing species can only have been achieved by the occupation of breeding and nursery sites at different times of the year so as to

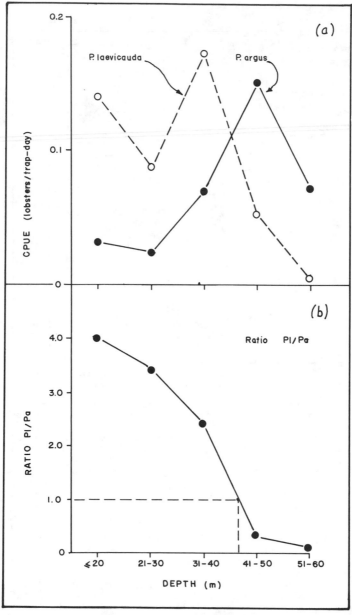

Figure 2 - Variation of CPUE (lobsters per trap-day) of P. argus (Pa) and P. laevicauda (Pl), and ratio "CPUE of Pl/CPUE of Pa" in relation to the depth of fishing grounds off Northeastern Brazil.

avoid maximization of competition for space   in   terms   of
food and shelter.

Fishery operations are carried out by a large number
of motor-boats that use mainly traps   and   by   sail-boats
intended for fishing with gillnets, in shallower   waters.
Lobsters are beheaded at sea soon after being hauled aboard,
so that only the tail is marketed, accounting for one third
of the individual's weight. This system is peculiar to the
Brazilian fisheries and it stems from   the   centralization
of 75% of the landings in the port of Fortaleza (figure 1),
that harbors a fishing fleet that covers an area   as large
as 60,000 sq. mi., in trips that may last as long   as   50
days (Fonteles-Filho et al. 1985).

METHODOLOGY

The basic data used in this paper refer to statistics
of catch and fishing effort by means of log-books,   length
distribution obtained by sampling of the catch   landed   at
Fortaleza and convertion of length to age by means of growth
equations, in centimeters:

P. argus   : $l_t = 43.8 (1 - e^{-0,163 t})$

P. laevicauda : $l_+ = 38.0 (1 - e^{-0,171 t})$

The number and biomass of the total and virtual popu
lations were calculated by Cohort Analysis according to a
method developed by Pope (1972), starting   with   values of
F = 0.8 and M = 0.3 from the oldest age group and working
upwards until age group I. Estimates of   total   mortality
coefficient Z were obtained from the catch   equation,   by
regression of log_e CPUE against age, starting   with   the
biggest CPUE value.

The yield curve was obtained by   the   Fox   method
(Fox, 1970) that assumes a curvilinear relationship between
CPUE (Y/f) and effort (f), so that

$$log_e Y/f = log_e A - bf$$

Using estimates of A and b, values of the maximum sustaina
ble yield (MSY), optimum fishing effort (f_{opt}) and maximum
sustainable CPUE (U_{opt}) will be given by:

MSY = A/be $\therefore$ f_{opt} = 1/b $\therefore$ U_{opt} = A/e

A relationship between recruitment index   (Y)   and
rainfall (X) was established by a parabolic   curve,   fit
through a regression of Y/X against X, tested for   signifi
cance with the correlation coefficient (r) for a 5% level.

RESULTS

In order to understand variations caused by fishing
the stocks shall be analysed in four time periods from 1965
to 1987, in which effort increased from a mean   value   of
4.6 million traps-day, in 1965/68 to 35.7 million traps-day
in 1980/87, in relation to age structure, fecundity, breed
ing stock size and reproductive potential, yield and producti

Table 1   Relative age structure of lobsters P. argus and
P. laevicauda, off northeastern Brazil, by year
periods from 1965 to 1987.

Age groups (year)	Mean length (cm)	Age structure (%)			
		1965/68	1969/73	1974/79	1980/87
Panulirus argus					
I	9.5	-	-	0.04	0.02
II	14.6	1.0	6.4	8.4	4.3
III	19.0	32.7	53.6	49.3	29.0
IV	22.8	45.8	27.8	27.1	34.1
V	25.9	15.6	8.8	10.4	21.1
VI	28.6	3.6	2.7	3.7	8.7
VII	30.9	0.8	0.5	0.8	2.0
VIII	32.8	0.2	0.1	0.2	0.4
IX	34.5	0.1	0.1	0.1	0.2
X	35.9	0.04	0.04	0.04	0.1
XI	37.1	0.02	0.02	0.02	0.05
XII	38.1	-	-	-	0.02
Total	-	100.0	100.0	100.0	100.0
Panulirus laevicauda					
II	13.2	1.2	1.5	5.8	10.6
III	17.1	60.3	60.2	61.3	54.8
IV	20.4	35.6	34.8	28.3	26.2
V	23.2	2.7	3.0	3.6	6.3
VI	25.5	0.2	0.3	0.6	1.2
VII	27.5	0.1	0.1	0.2	0.4
VIII	29.1	0.02	0.1	0.1	0.2
IX	30.5	-	0.04	0.05	0.1
X	31.7	-	0.02	0.03	0.1
XI	32.7	-	-	0.02	0.04
XII	33.5	-	-	0.01	0.02
Total	-	100.0	100.0	100.0	100.0

vity as measured by catch per unit effort (CPUE).
The catchable stocks were comprised of lobsters   from
age groups I to XII years (P. argus) and II to XII years
(P. laevicauda), with corresponding total length   ranges
6.6 - 38.5 cm and 11.0 - 33.9 cm. In years   from   1965   to
1987, the age structure of P. argus undergoes some   changes,
but there is a predominance of early adults (age   groups
III - VIII years) in periods 1965/68 (66.1%) and 1980/87
(´66.3%) and of juveniles (age groups I - III years) in
1969/73 (56.0%) and 1974/79 (57.7%). In respect   to
species P. laevicauda, there has been a regular predominance
of the juvenile age groups in all year periods, with   an

Table 2 - Data on absolute and relative fecundity, and po
pulation's reproductive potential of lobsters
P. argus and P. laevicauda, in northeastern Bra
zil, by year periods from 1965 to 1987.

Year period	Body weight (g)	Absolute fe cundity (num ber of eggs)	Relative fecundity (eggs per gram)	Population's reproductive potential (10^9 eggs)
Panulirus argus				
1965/68	420.8	257,414	611.7	646
1969/73	432.1	266,604	617.0	768
1974/79	372.4	216,057	580.2	674
1980/87	497.7	317,154	637.2	1,600
Mean	418.2	252,819	608.9	969
Panulirus laevicauda				
1965/68	254.8	149,502	586.7	206
1969/73	254.8	149,502	586.7	358
1974/79	225.9	127,456	564.2	335
1980/87	262.3	155,013	591.0	272
Mean	243.7	141,235	579.5	304

average proportion of 63.9%. The age structure also shows
that commercial catch has been maintained by 3 age groups
(III - V years) in P. argus, and 2 age groups (III - IV
years) in P. laevicauda, which account for 88.8% and 90.2%
of total production, respectively (table 1).

Mean body weight, and absolute and relative fecundity
of both species showed an upward trend which is followed
by the reproductive potential of P. argus' population, but
not by that of P. laevicauda (table 2). Since reproductive
potential is a function of both breeding stock size and
mean fecundity, and the ratio between their respective mean
fecundity (1.8) is less than that between reproductive
potential (3.2), it means that the breeding stock of
P. argus must have shown a bigger increasse along the years.
According to Table 3, total length groups 21.1 - 28.0 cm
(P. argus individuals with 4 to 6 years of age) and 18.1 -
23.0 cm (P. laevicauda individuals with 4 and 5 years of
age) make the largest contribution to the breeding stock
and reproductive potential (measured by IPR), P. laevicauda being once again at a disadvantage position in relation
to P. argus inasmuch as the relative proportion of spawning
females is smaller.

The number of eggs per spawning female has been shown
to be linearly related to size (Ivo and Gesteira 1986) ,
which in turn is density determined through growth rate,

Table 3 - Estimates of the breeding stock (S), as per
centage of total number of females, and index
of reproductive potential (IPR) of lobsters
P. argus and P. laevicauda, off northeastern
Brazil, by year periods from 1965 to 1987.

Year period	Panulirus argus					
	≤ 21.0 cm		21.1 - 28.0 cm		> 28.0 cm	
	S (%)	IPR	S (%)	IPR	S (%)	IPR
1965/68	13.8	100	30.9	485	1.6	48
1969/73	21.7	100	14.9	181	0.6	15
1974/79	16.6	100	24.6	355	2.3	91
1980/87	12.3	100	30.8	372	5.4	139

Year period	Panulirus laevicauda					
	≤ 18.0 cm		18.1 - 23.0 cm		> 23.0 cm	
	S (%)	IPR	S (%)	IPR	S (%)	IPR
1965/68	12.7	100	26.0	333	0.5	11
1969/73	12.1	100	27.1	353	0.4	10
1974/79	12.7	100	22.6	334	1.3	34
1980/87	11.6	100	20.7	382	2.8	85

that sets up the mean age of sexual maturity. Since there
has been a decrease in density of the lobster populations,
they seek to maintain their size at first   maturity   and
mean fecundity by lowering their age.
   Population numbers and biomass of lobsters   calculated
by Cohort Analysis, rather than just the   catchable   stock
numbers, attest to the fact that population size of P. argus
(but not necessarily its yield) has been increasing, the
reverse being true of P. laevicauda. Virtual   population
numbers, as a fraction of total population,   provide   an
estimate of the exploitation rate, which   presents average
values of 8.6% in age group II (absolute recruitment) and
63.0% in III + age groups, for P. argus, and 9.0% and 74.7%,
for P. laevicauda (table 4), and this may be the   reason
why P. laevicauda abundance has been decreasing at a faster
rate, with a confirmation by the higher values of the total
mortality coefficient over time (table 6).
   The maximum sustainable yield of both species (6,414
tons and 2,716 tons) was attained in 1972, 17 years after
the onset of exploitation, and thenceforth   both   annual
yield and CPUE have been decreasing, though at small drops
from year to year, but this trend is not   proportionally
matched by the faster rate of fishing   effort   increase
because of the expansion in size of the exploitation area,
whereby additional biomass of virgin stocks has been   made

Table 4 - Estimates of population numbers and biomass of lobsters P. argus and P. laevicauda, off northeas tern Brazil, by year periods from 1965 to 1967.

Age group (year)	Panulirus argus		Panulirus laevicauda	
	population numbers (1,000)	population biomass (ton)	population numbers (1,000)	population biomass (ton)
1965/68				
I	17,696	672 (7.1)	11,550	381 (11.1)
II	13,110	1,730 (18.2)	8,556	890 (26.0)
III-VI	17,148	6,851 (72.3)	8,682	2,150 (62.7)
VII +	174	223 (2,4)	8	6 (0.2)
Total	48,128	9,476	28,796	3,427
1969/73				
I	32,211	1,224 (8.3)	18,402	607 (11.0)
II	23,863	3,150 (21.4)	13,634	1,418 (25.6)
III-VI	26,471	10,024 (68.1)	13,949	3,458 (62.3)
VII +	240	312 (2.1)	63	59 (1.1)
Total	82,886	14,710	46,048	5,542
1974/79				
I	29,178	1,109 (7.9)	24,290	802 (11.0)
II	21,612	2,853 (20.4)	17,995	1,871 (25.6)
III-VI	24,792	9,700 (69.2)	17,841	4,509 (61.6)
VII +	275	352 (2.5)	158	137 (1.9)
Total	75,857	14,014	60,284	7,319
1980/87				
I	28,048	1,066 (6.2)	16,858	556 (10.2)
II	20,776	2,742 (16.0)	12,488	1,299 (23.8)
III-VI	29,429	12,623 (73.5)	12,870	3,413 (62.6)
VII +	574	742 (4.3)	212	184 (3.4)
Total	78,827	17,173	42,428	5,452

Obs.: numbers in brackets are percentage figures.

available, and perhaps because of differential year-class strengths from either species (tables 5 and 6).

Optimum fishing effort (f_{opt}) was reached in 1969/73, at 20.1 million traps-day, equalling the observed annual figure, and in the two following periods annual effort out weighed f_{opt} by 32.8% and 77.8% (P. argus) and 37.6% and 84.2% (P. laevicauda). This has brought about an average

Table 5 - Data on yield, fishing effort and catch per unit
effor (CPUE) of lobsters P. argus and P. laevicauda, off northeastern Brazil,   in   period
1965-1087.

Year	Yield (ton.)		Fishing effort (1,000 traps-day)	CPUE (kg. trap--day^{-1})	
	P. argus	P. laevicauda		P. argus	P. laevicauda
1965	2,564	1,123	2,604	0.985	0.432
1966	2,735	1,364	3,886	0.701	0.350
1967	3,136	925	5,206	0.603	0.178
1968	4,020	1,806	6,566	0.609	0.274
1969	5,624	2,612	14,251	0.396	0.184
1970	6,022	2,798	14,936	0.404	0.188
1971	5,441	2,106	16,957	0.320	0.124
1972	6,650	2,334	24,110	0.276	0.097
1973	6,411	1,901	30,253	0.212	0.063
1974	7,219	2,495	26,991	0.267	0.092
1975	4,762	2,267	22,040	0.216	0.103
1976	3,578	2,739	24,135	0.148	0.114
1977	5,991	2,747	27,949	0.215	0.098
1978	6,553	3,275	29,084	0.225	0.112
1979	6,887	4,232	29,839	0.231	0.142
1980	5,072	3,370	33,012	0.154	0.102
1981	6,401	2,902	35,078	0.182	0.082
1982	6,906	2,340	30,825	0.224	0.076
1983	3,755	1,519	33,400	0.112	0.045
1984	6,528	2,331	36,918	0.177	0.063
1985	5,940	1,614	39,872	0.149	0.045
1986	3,869	1,506	40,524	0.096	0.037
1987	5,356	1,579	35,984	0.149	0.044

reduction in productivity (CPUE) of the two species, of
4.2% and 6.6%, respectively (table 6).

Although the nominal fishing effort has shown, from
1965 through 1987, an upward trend, fishing intensity (num
ber of traps-day.(km^2)$^{-1}$) and density (number of lobsters.
(km^2)$^{-1}$) increased until 1968/73, declining afterwards, as
it can be seen from the figures for both species together:
83.8 , 369.4 , 247.7 and 226.5 (fishing intensity), and
1,415 , 2,372 , 1,264 and 770 (density).

The dome-shaped relationship between the index of
recruitment (R) and rainfall (P), with 2-year time-lag, was
represented by the following equations:

P. argus : R = (0.1052-0.0000408 P) P
P. laevicauda : R = (0.1083-0.0000437 P) P

The parabolic curves show that, for the range of
values used for adjusting this model, there is an optimal
rainfall annual index of 1,300 mm that is supposed to be
related to a higher recruitment index, with decreased values
on both sides of the rainfall range. Thus, above-average

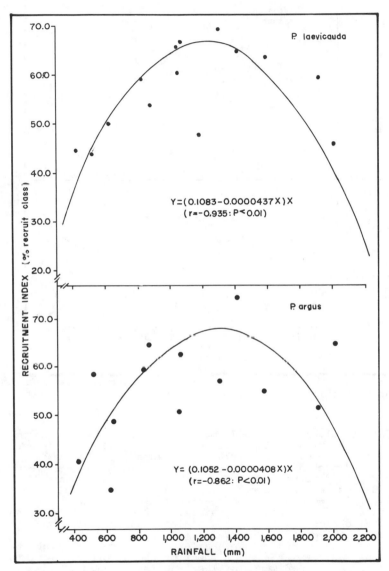

Figure 3 - Parabolic curves of the relationship betw
een recruitment index of lobsters P. argus and P. laevicauda and rainfall, off Northeastern Brazil.

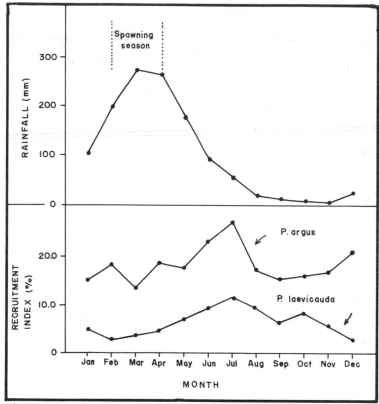

Figure 4 - Monthly variation of recruitment in P.   argus
and P. laevicauda, and comparison with rainfall.

rainfall values of 1,923.7 mm, 2,037.7 mm and 1,420.8 mm
in years 1973/75 could be responsible for the low values
of recruitment in years 1976/78 (figures 3 and 4).
      The mechanisms that explain this variation pattern
are supposed to work towards an increase in larval mortality
via decreasing salinity, at high values of rainfall,   and
via density-dependent pressures operating on the nursery
grounds, via low values of rainfall, at a critical period
of the lobster's life cycle when food supply will be brought
to bear at the time of larval settlement. The lack of water
discharge by rivers of northeastern Brazil during droughts
periods would bring about a lowering of the organic matter
content in the sediments of the inner continental shelf,
necessary to form the substrate of calcareous algae, known
as the most suitable habitat for tropical spiny lobsters.
      Since the decrease in CPUE after the MSY was reached,
in 1972, actually reflects a real loss of biomass,   this
must be caused by a reduction either of the breeding stock
or absolute recruitment, or both. Breeding stock seems to

Table 6 - Annual values of yield, fishing effort and CPUE in relation to optimum values of maximum sustainable yield (MSY), optimum effort(f_{opt}) and optimum CPUE (U_{opt}) of lobster P. argus and P. laevicauda, with estimates of mortality coefficient (Z) and mean body length.

Year period	Yield as percentage of MSY	Effort as percentage of f_{opt}	CPUE as percentage of U_{opt}	Mortality coeffi cient (Z)	Mean length (cm)
Panulirus argus					
1965/68	48.6	22.7	212.5	1.30	22.2
1969/73	94.0	100.0	94.0	1.26	20.6
1974/79	90.9	132.8	86.6	1.23	20.9
1980/87	85.4	177.8	48.0	1.16	22.6
Panulirus laevicauda					
1965/68	48.0	23.6	202.1	0.88	18.4
1969/73	86.5	103.7	83.6	0.96	18.4
1974/79	108.9	137.6	79.3	1.21	18.0
1980/87	79.0	184.2	42.8	1.77	18.2

have remained quite stable over the years and so has repro ductive potential. Therefore, growth overfishing (diminished recruitment because the juveniles are caught in large numbers before they reach maturity) should be thought of as the main cause, evidence for this being found in the smaller numbers of age group II (table 4), and in the higher proportion of juveniles in the catch. In addition, from 1979 through 1984, the Northeast region was affected by severe droughts, which means low pluviosity and probably a higher rate of mortality of postlarvae and early juveniles in the coastal nursery areas.

One important finding to be gathered from the analy sed data is that species P. laevicauda seems to be losing biomass in comparison to that of its principal competitor (species P. argus), since 1980, probably owing to its being submitted to a heavier predation by fishing, repre sented by the action of gillnets, fishing gears far more efficient in shallower water (up to 20-meter deep) where that species is more abundant.

BIBLIOGRAPHY

Buesa Más, R.J., M.P. Paiva and R.S. Costa, 1968. Comporta miento biológico de la langosta "Panulirus argus" (La treille) en el Brasil y en Cuba. Rev. Bras. Biol., 28 (1) : 61 - 70.
Fernandes, L.M.B., 1972. Sobre a alimentação da lagosta Panulirus argus (Latr.). II - Estágios pós-puerulus e adulto. SUDENE, ser. Est. Pesca, (1) : 7 pp.

Fonteles-Filho, A.A., 1979. Biologia pesqueira e dinâmica populacional da lagosta Panulirus laevicauda (Latreille), no Nordeste setentrional do Brasil. Arq. Ciên. Mar, 19: 1 - 43.

Fonteles-Filho, A.A., 1986. Influência do recrutamento e da pluviosidade sobre a abundância das lagostas Panulirus argus (Latreille) e Panulirus laevicauda (Latreille) (Crustacea : Palinuridae). Arq. Ciên. Mar, 25 : 13 - 31.

Fonteles-Filho, A.A. and C.T.C., 1980. Migratory behaviour of the spiny lobster Panulirus argus (Latreille). Arq. Ciên. Mar, 20 : 25 - 32.

Fonteles-Filho, A.A., M.O.C. Ximenes and P.H.M. Monteiro, 1988. Sinopse de informações sobre as lagostas Panulirus argus (Latreille) e Panulirus laevicauda (Latreille). Arq. Ciên. Mar, 27 : (in press).

Fonteles-Filho, A.A. et al, 1985. Parâmetros técnicos e índices de rendimento da frota lagosteira do Estado do Ce ará, Brasil. Arq. Ciên. Mar, 25 : 89 - 100.

Fox, W.W., 1970. As exponential surplus yield model for optimizing exploited fish populations. Trans. Amer. Fish. Soc., 99 : 80 - 88.

Ivo, C.T.C., 1975. Novo estudo sobre o crescimento e idade da lagosta Panulirus laevicauda (Latreille), em águas costeiras do Estado do Ceará (Brasil). Arq. Ciên. Mar, 15 (1) : 29 - 32.

Mesquita, A.L.L. and T.C.V. Gesteira, 1975. Época de repro dução, tamanho e idade na primeira desova da lagosta Panulirus laevicauda (Latreille). Arq. Ciên. Mar, 15 (2) : 93 - 96.

Oliveira, G.M. and H.L. Pereira, 1980. A pesca de lagostas no Nordeste do Brasil. PDP, ser. Doc. Téc. : 26 pp.

Paiva, M.P., 1967. Algunos problemas de la industria langos tera en el Brasil. Arq. Est. Biol. Mar. Univ. Fed. Ceará, 7 (2) : 105 - 112.

Paiva, M.P. and R.C.F. Bezerra, 1969. Algumas tendências recentes da pesca de lagostas no Estado do Ceará. Bol. Soc. Cear. Agron., 10 : 11 - 15.

Paiva, M.P. and R.S. Costa, 1968. Comportamento biológico da lagosta Panulirus laevicauda. Arq. Est. Biol. Mar. Univ. Fed. Ceará, 8 (1) : 1 - 6.

Paiva, M.P. and A.A. Fonteles Filho, 1968. Sobre as migra ções e índices de exploração da lagosta Panulirus argus (Latreille), ao longo da costa do Estado do Ceará. Arq. Est. Biol. Mar. Univ. Fed. Ceará, 8 (1) : 15 - 23.

Paiva, M.P. et al. 1973. Pescarias experimentais de lagos tas com redes de espera, no Estado do Ceará (Brasil). Arq. Ciên. Mar, 13 (2) : 121 - 134.

Phillips, B.F., J.S. Cobb and R.W. George, 1980. General biology, pp. 2 - 82, in J.S. Cobb and B.F. Phillips (eds.). The biology and management of lobsters. Vol. I. Academic Press, XV + 463 pp., New York.

Pope, J.G., 1972. An investigation on the accuracy of vir tual population analysis using cohort analysis. Res. Bull. ICNAF, 9 : 65 - 74.

Soares, C.N.C. and P.P.L. Cavalcante, 1985. Caribbean spiny lobster (Panulirus argus) and smoothtail spiny lobs ter (Panulirus laevicauda) reproductive dynamics on the Brazilian Northeastern coast. _FAO_ _Fish._ _Rep._, (327) : 200 - 217.

Sousa, M.J.B., 1987. Distribuição espacial e relação inter específica das lagostas _Panulirus_ _argus_ (Latreille) e _Panulirus_ _laevicauda_ (Latreille) no Nordeste do Brasil. _Tese_ _de_ _Graduação_ _no_ _Departamento_ _de_ _Engenharia_ _de_ _Pesca_, 33 pp., Fortaleza.

SUDEPE, 1985. Relatório da segunda reunião do Grupo de Tra balho e Treinamento (CTT) sobre avaliação de estoques. PDP, _ser._ _Doc._ _Téc._, (34) : 1 - 439.

Williams, A.B., 1986. Lobsters - identification, world dis tribution, and U.S. trade. _Mar._ _Fish._ _Rev._, 48 (2) : 1 - 36.

COSTAL ZONE PLANNING

Luiz Henrique A. Azevedo[1]   David. M.W. Zee[1]   Denise R. Tenenbaum [1]

1 INTRODUCTION

Coastal zone planning derives its importance from the high economic interest relative to environmental resources and from man's extensive and growing use of these areas. In developing countries there is growing pressure to utilize marginal lands to satisfy the needs of urban expansion and to improve living standards.

The first objective of this methodology is to provide a feasible and practical tool to identify the potentialities of the coastal zone. It has no intention of having the definite and universal solution for all conflicting demands upon the coastal area, but one hopes that the developed methodology will help in selecting better use options for these regions (Archer, 1982).

The coastal environment constitutes a fragile, little known and complex ecosystem that is an important resource for most nations. The protection of these areas through a balanced analysis between conservation, rational use of coastal resources, and living standards, is also an objective of this methodology (Brahtz, 1972).

The second objective is to provide a democratic planning of coastal zone uses. A council composed of representatives from several working fields such as the scientific, political, legal, social, technical, national security, etc., will define the uses of coastal zone. This definition is supported by several information plans which provide a broad view about the potentialities of coastal area (Edmunds and Letey, 1975).

2 RESEARCH TECHNIQUES

A multidisciplinary group constituted by professors, specialists, and students developed a research during the period between 1983 and 1985, with the objective of establishing a methodology of coastal zone planning. This project was coordinated by the Department of Oceanography of the Rio de Janeiro State University. The results of this research form the basic methodology of coastal zone planning in Brazil, coordinated by CIRM.

It was developed an interdisciplinary study to define the environmental information that should be obtained to select coastal areas to be planned.

[1]Dept. Oceanografia, Inst. Geociências, Universidade do Estado do Rio de Janeiro, Rua São Francisco Xavier, 524, Rio de Janeiro, RJ 20550, Brazil.

Specialists from several areas of knowledge were invited to work as consultants in a seminar in order to give a broad view of the problem. Every speech was recorded and the main topics were summarized in a report (Azevedo *et alli.*, 1984). With these guidelines the research team started to develop the methodology of coastal zone planning. The research group was composed by professors and researchers from oceanography (physical, chemical, biological and geological), climatology, cartography, geology and geography.

3 RESULTS

3.1 Proposed Methodology

The developed methodology presents the following stages:

1. *Characterization of the coastal space*
   An integrated analysis of the social-economical characteristics and environmental parameters was done throughout the diagnosis. Conventional techniques and processes as well as remote sensing were used in this stage of the project, to establish a complete physical and spacial inventory.

   The littoral was divided in sectors (Fig. 1, having the same dimension and maintaining a lateral spacing of 30'. In doing so, it was intended: 1) to make the handling of thematic maps easier; 2) to allow the use of geocodification of the information plans; and 3) to have a uniform system for the entire country. This systematization is compatible with the international cartographic system as well as with Marsden's squares. It should be pointed out that such division is only applied to the thematic maps and the basic ones: the coastal sector to be 'zoned' and later 'monitored' should necessarily be enclosed within those spaces.

2. *Definition of vocations and potentialities*
   The confrontation of information plans that characterize the area, allowed the determination of its predominant vocations and potentialities. Digital and analytical processes lead to the detailed definition of these spaces.

3. *Council's analysis and final coastal zone plan*
   The coastal zone plan was established by a council which represents the community and the government basic needs.

For the characterization of the coastal space, one must accomplish a physical space inventory, taking into consideration natural and human resources (Curso de Analises, Planeamiento y Gestion del Medio Litoral, 1973 and 1974). This diagnosis is represented by thematic maps in the scale of 1:100,000 as listed in Table I.

Thematic maps listed above describe the coastal space within its economical potentialities and ecological vocations.

It is important to remind that the data of the above mentioned maps will cover an area larger than the assumed geographical limits of the "Coastal Zone". These limits will be defined considering the integrated analysis of data from information plans.

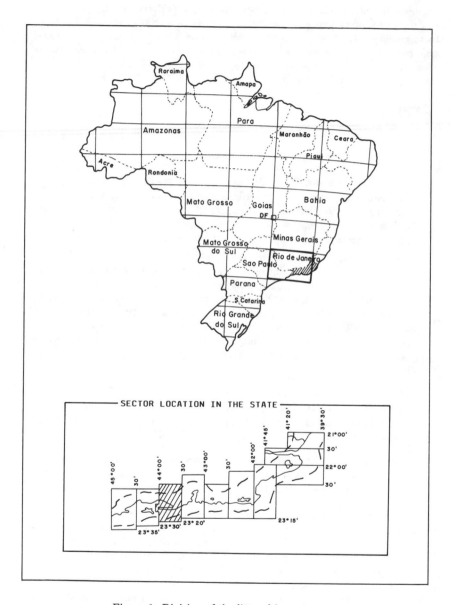

Figure 1: Division of the littoral in sectors.

Table I: List of thematic maps.

1. Cartographic base	7. Water quality map
2. Actual land use and cover map	8. Living resources map
3. Geomorphologic map	9. Oceanographic parameters
4. Declivity map	10. Climatologic and Meteorologic map
5. Geological/Faciological map	11. Existing plans and projects
6. Agricultural potentialities	12. Social-economic information

The thematic maps are part of "information plans" that characterize the coastal space. Those plans represent assemblages of related characteristics of environmental parameters.

The data must be introduced in the Geographical Information System for graphical treatment, which allows fast access, manipulation, and generation of new environmental scenarios.

Integrated analysis of the "plans", achieved manually and digitally, permitted the division of the coastal space in areas that have potentialities for certain projected uses (AIAM, 1965; Azevedo et alli., 1974).

As concerns Coastal Zoning, the foreseen uses or classes are presented in Table II.

Each area selected and projected for a specific use, must possess a number of characteristics that satisfy the required conditions for that class. It is also important to have in mind the minimization of impacts that could occur due to the projected use selection. The implementation of projected use should be done without environmental impacts, otherwise the plan must be revised.

The map which presents the vocations and potentialities, has to be compatible to the real occupation of the space, expressed by the actual land use and cover map.

In this stage, the document which presents the potentialities of the space is submitted to the representative council of the organization that acts directly or indirectly in the area, at Federal, State, Municipal and Community level.

The council, based on the technical documents available, formulates the projected use in a coherent form, thus, establishing the Coastal Zoning.

In this stage, it is already defined the Coastal Zone Limits in the continent and in the sea. In this space, the actions of coastal zone planning and posterior monitoring will be accomplished.

3.2 Information Plans

The design technique for coastal zone planning is based on an adequate pool of information composed of several information plans and accomplished by the respective thematic reports.

Information needs for land-use planning and coastal zone monitoring are environmental, social, economical, legal, oceanographical, actual uses and ecological inventories.

The main characteristics and parameters of proposed information plans (thematic maps) are described in the following:

1. *Cartographic Base*
   The cartographic base is fundamental for coastal zone planning. It is the first map that should be done. The map scale is 1:100,000 and the others maps are based on its drawings .
   The main information of the cartographic base includes: planimetry, bathymetry, altimetry, urban areas, pipelines, drainage network, and transportation routes.

2. *Actual Land Use and Cover Map*
   This information plan should contain the main actual soil uses such as urban occupation, forest cover, swamp area, agricultural/ranching area, water covered surface (lakes, reservoirs, estuaries, etc.), maritime routes, industrial zones, commercial and fisheries activities, tourist and recreation areas, jurisdictional lines, and others.

3. *Geomorphologic Map*
   The geomorphologic map contains the qualitative representation of topographical features such as, land morphology, mountainous and flat areas, physiography, and others (Neves, 1977).

4. *Living Resources Map*
   This map should contain information about biological resources of aquatic and land ecosystem (organisms, communities, vegetation, wild life, etc.). It also defines and characterizes the main ecosystems and their association in a specific region (Magnanini and Nehab, 1978).

5. *Water Quality Map*
   The water quality cartographic representation should contain information about the chemical and sanitary aspects of coastal waters. Data on type of sewage, location of pollution sources, critical points and pollution of drainage network should be pointed out in this map (Pazzaglini and Greco, 1978).

6. *Geological and Faciological Map*
   The geological and faciologic map contains information about earth materials, environmental geology, dredging and mining activities, marine facies, land forms, and geological structures (Keemas, 1980).

7. *Oceanographic Parameters*
   This map contains information about physical and hydrodynamic parameters of coastal region. Data about water temperature, salinity, currents, tidal regime and wave characteristics should be pointed out in this map.

8. *Climatologic and Meteorologic Map*
   This map expresses the variability in space and time of climatological and meteorological phenomena — information on temperature, wind regimes, and pluviometry is represented in the Climatology Information Plan.

9. *Existing Plans and Projects*
This map contains information about important plans or projects previously designed for the region. A search should be done in every private or public agency related to coastal zone planning in order to verify any possible and conflicting superposition of previously planned land use. Maps of existing plans and project, if compared to natural region tendencies, can show evidence of incompatible proposals. This map will be helpful to the council responsible for the final coastal zone use proposal.

10. *Declivity Map*
This information plan contains land morphology information and quantitative data relative to declivity. This information is important for the comprehension of spatial organization and for the evaluation of potentialities and or limitations of available physical space (Neves, 1977).

11. *Social-Economic Information*
The overcrowding and the accelerated development in some areas cause the destruction of valuable resources. Due to this misuse, natural habitats of plant and animal species are threatened. The living standards could decay to critical levels.
The social-economic information map will help formulate all classes of coastal zone uses by giving information about economical activities, population characteristics, urban expansion, public health, energy needs, industrial activities, shipping, commercial, and others.

12. *Agricultural Potentialities*
The agricultural potentialities map contains information that could help locate the better areas for farming activities soil classes, fertility, rockiness, erodibility, and drainage pattern which are important parameters shown in this map (Keemas et alli., 1980).

3.3 General Conditions to define the Classes of Coastal Zone Uses

Classes of coastal zone uses must be defined in order to characterize the required environmental data (Ketchum, 1972). This information will help the selection of coastal zone uses according to coastal area potentialities when a coastal zone planning is made.

The definition of classes of coastal zone uses is based on the main characteristics of Brazilian coastal zone uses at the time and the potential uses of the area.

As previously mentioned, the main conditions required by the classes are pointed out in the thematic maps named here *information plans*.

The basic characteristics of each class, as defined below, permit to define the best site to implement one or more classes.

- *Ecological Conservation Areas*
Any critical site with fragile life support systems, scenic landscapes, and pleasant places of the coastal zone which future generations will benefit from must be classified in ecological conservation class and must be protected from antropic action (Davis, 1980; Magnanini and Nehab, 1978).

Table II. Classes of coastal zone use.

1. Ecological Conservation Areas	7. National Security Areas
2. Renewable Natural Resources Exploitation	8. Mineral and Energetic Resources
	9. Historical, Artistic and Landscape Heritage
3. Ports and Terminals	
4. Urban Expansion	10. Scientific Research Areas
5. Industrial Development	11. Aquacultural Activities
6. Cultural, Tourism and Recreation Activities	12. Farming Activities
	13. Forestry Activities

• *Renewable Natural Resources Exploration*
Sites that present a favorable biological productivity for food, fertilizers, chemicals, and other living resources with economical value should be included in this class.

• *Ports and Terminals*
This class of coastal zone use defines the appropriate regions for commercial ports, fishery terminals, marinas, airports and railways installations.

Some basic conditions should be available in these areas in order to be eligible for this class of use such as the availability of inland and offshore communications, construction materials, energy, fresh water, bathymetry, climate, etc.

• *Urban Expansion*
Sites that have favorable conditions for food, transportation, commerce, moderate climate, jobs, recreation and available area for housing, should be considered as urban expansion class (Neves, 1977).

• *Industrial Development*
Industrial Development class requires areas that present a high volume of water circulation as this kind of activity usually produces waste disposal, oil spills, and the escape of toxic materials into aquatic ecosystems which will affect the coastal environment if there is not enough water available to dilute these undesirable by-products of industry. This class should be placed in areas that cause less impacts on the local environmental quality (Pazzaglini and Greco, 1978).

• *Cultural, Tourism and Recreation Activities*
Public or private areas that present natural qualities for culture, tourism and recreation such as climate, natural and cultural resources, historic sites, infrastructure, access and other aspects should be planned for that class.

• *National Security Areas*
Some areas strategically located due to their particular pattern should be

preserved for national security purposes. Governmental uses of coastal zone include military installations, power plants, immigration or quarantine stations and others.

- *Mineral and Energetic Resources*
Sites that present potentialities of mineral or energetic resources.

- *Historical, Artistic and Landscape Heritage*
Any region that present artistic and historic sites or monuments, unusual landscape whose preservation is important should be considered in this class of coastal use.

- *Scientific Research Areas*
Sites that have favorable conditions and characteristics for scientific research interest.

- *Aquacultural Activities*
Sites where these activities may be introduced or implemented for economical or scientific purpose.

- *Farming Activities*
Inland sites that produce food (vegetal or animal) for human or animal consumption.

- *Forestry Activities*
Appropriate areas to develop reforestation for soil erosion control or economical purposes (Magnanini and Nehab, 1978).

4 APPLICATION TO A PARTICULAR AREA: SEPETIBA BAY

The coastal management program includes coastal zone planning and coastal zone monitoring.

The coastal zone planning main structure is defined here but much more should be done in order to make the methodology complete. Due to the diversity of coastal ecosystems it is almost impossible to have a unique way to represent or to obtain the required data for each information plan. The proposed parameters are not definite. It is possible, in particular situations, to find other important parameters for the coastal zone planning.

One of the complexities of coastal zone planning is the definition of what constitutes the coastal zone. There are several aspects that should be considered in that definition, such as: scientific, legal, geographical, ecological, oceanic and land influences, and social ones. Experience indicates that it is useful to do a first estimate of coastal zone boundaries in order to guide the cartographic base and the information plans data gathering. During the data gathering phase it is possible to analyze the information in order to establish the definite limits of coastal zone.

This methodology was tested on a section of the State of Rio de Janeiro, referred hereafter as Section 7 – Sepetiba Bay. This bay is located 60 km southeast of the city of Rio de Janeiro. It is one of the most important ecosystems in the State due to its multiple uses, and to the benefits to the local community. Recreation (of primary and secondary contact), fishing, navigation, and tourism are examples of the most important activities in the region. Moreover, the biological community finds diversified natural areas as mangroves and beaches (rocky, sand, and muddy), shoals and artificial substrata, which allow the existence of an abundant and varied fauna and flora (Pedrini, 1980). Being a sheltered area with varied micro-regions, Sepetiba Bay is a place of migration and spawning of shrimps, fish and other animals (Oliveira, 1972). Nevertheless, the association of natural and antropic actions has contributed to environmental degradation.

Unplanned urban expansion caused by growing industrial and tourism development, has brought serious problems. Oil and ore terminals, together with industrial effluents, have highly endangered environment quality. Valentini and Neves elsewhere in this conference present several coastal engineering problems in this area, while Malm et alli. describe the problems of pollution caused by the presence of heavy metals in the water regarding contamination of living resources.

As a consequence, Sepetiba Bay proved to be an excellent study area, where emergency measures should be taken aiming the establishment of a monitoring program for environmental and human conditions.

As shown in Figure 2, techniques for interpretation of environmental data based either in conventional or in digital processes were used. The area in study could then be divided according to its economical and ecological suitability.

Twelve classes of Macrozoning were established for Section 7, based on the following criteria:

1. Ecological Conservation Areas:
   Areas covered by forests and all other forms of significant natural vegetation existing on the slopes of the mountain range that crosses this area ("Serra do Mar") were chosen. Part of the *Mata Atlântica* — the tropical rain forest typical of this region — would be preserved, maintaining the local hydric balance. The mangroves were also included in this class, as well as the springs of the most important rivers.

2. Renewable Natural Resources Exploitation:
   As fishing is the traditional activity of the region, the productive areas limited by the islands were selected.

3. Ports and Terminals:
   This class is represented in Section 7 by the Guaíba Island iron ore terminal and the Port of Sepetiba, which belongs to the Rio de Janeiro Port Authority.

4. Urban Expansion:
   Three areas were selected as favorable for urban expansion. All satisfied the necessary conditions (utilities, transportation, adequate geography) for the expansion of industrial, residential and service sectors of nearby towns.

5. Industrial Development:
   Based on ecological conditions, the areas for the establishment of industries — especially polluting ones — were limited by the BR-101 road, the São Francisco Canal and da Guarda River. The terrain in these areas does not have accentuated slope, thus facilitating transportation of equipments and goods, and the orientation of winds and currents are favorable.

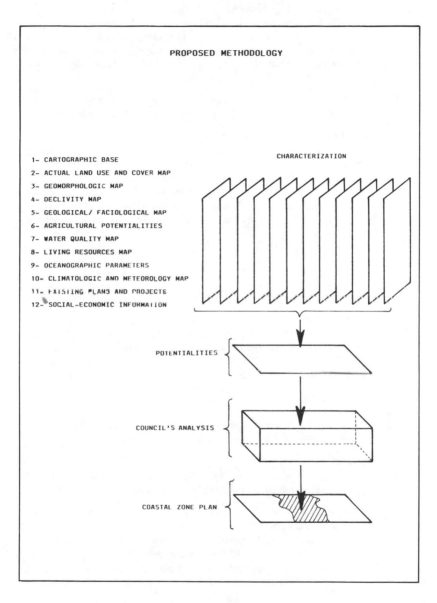

Figure 2: Interpretation of the environmental data.

6. Cultural, Touristic and Recreational Activities:
   The Section 7 - Sepetiba has a very scenic landscape. Marambaia Island, the littoral cut by small coves and bays of "Serra do Mar" mountain range with forests, the islets, and several other natural landscapes were selected as areas that should be used for touristic, recreational and cultural activities.

7. Mineral and Energetic Resources:
   Based on geological information, areas with occurrence of sand, gravel and turf were identified, the latter with potential for economical exploitation.

8. Historical, Artistic and Landscape Heritage:
   Several sites were included in this class, some already preserved by federal or state regulation. The ruins along the old Imperial Road in Mangaratiba, the Jesuits Bridge, some traditional churches, as well as the Fountain in the town of Mangaratiba. Waterfalls on the slopes of "Serra do Mar" and lagoons were selected as landscape heritage. Finally, as an archeological one, it is worth mentioning the burial sites — known as "sambaquis" — remnant from the indian tribes.

9. Scientific Research Areas:
   The chosen sites for scientific research were in three areas: 1) pollution; 2) preservation, and 3) agricultural use. These "research stations" would be responsible for the development of work in appropriate environments.

10. Aquacultural Activities:
    Two areas were selected as adequate for this type of activity. The first near the town of Guaratiba, because it has natural nurseries of several species. The second, in Mangaratiba Bay, because the area is shallow, has no critical pollution, is sheltered, and several species of commercial interest are found there.

11. Farming Activities:
    Plain sites along the basins of important rivers were selected. Topography, soil, and water availability are adequate for these activities.

12. Forestry Activities:
    The selected areas might be used for reforestation projects of economical interest, ecological purposes or areas subject to erosion.

This zoning was conducted by a multidisciplinary staff, which interacted systematically with the SGI (Geographical Information System). Access to environmental information needed for analysis and proposals, could then be made in an easier way.

The proposed zoning (Fig. 3) should then be forwarded to a collegiate, representing different levels of administration (federal, State, and municipal) which act in the area, in order to establish a Projected Use and the zone of the coast to be monitored.

5 CONCLUSION

The application of the referred methodology in Sepetiba indicated that the proposal was feasible and its basic concepts could be extended to a national level. According

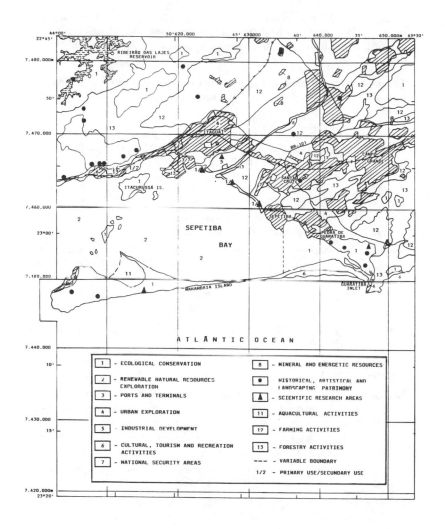

Figure 3: Proposed zoning for Sector 7 – Sepetiba Bay.

to that experience, some recommendations were given:

1. A scale of 1:100,000 for coastal macro-zoning at first stage. If necessary, the system at local level can be detailed following a sequence of scales 1:50,000, 1:25,000, 1:10,000 and 1:5,000, obeying the International Cartographical System.

2. The division of coastal zone in quadrangles equidistant of 30' and compatible with the Mardsen's square which are the units of area for data processing system.

3. Anticipating the coastal zone monitoring, it is suggested that the personnel be prepared for the use of micro-computers compatible with IBM-PC and for Remote Orbital Sensing (LANDSAT, SPOT, CZCS) application.

REFERENCES

[1] Archer, J.H. (1982). "The concept of coastal zone management". U.S. Department of Commerce, NOAA, Washington. 25 pp.

[2] Associação Internacional de Administradores Municipais, ZONEAMENTO. (1965). in: "Planejamento Urbano". Rio de Janeiro, Fundação Getúlio Vargas, p. 306–350.

[3] Azevedo, L.H.A. et alli. (1974). Relatório Preliminar da Metodologia do Zoneamento Costeiro. UERJ/CIRM. Rio de Janeiro. 74 pp.

[4] Azevedo, L.H.A. et alli. (1974). Relatório Final da Metodologia do Zoneamento Costeiro. UERJ/CIRM. Rio de Janeiro. 110 pp.

[5] Brahtz, J.E.P. (1972). "Coastal zone management: Multiple use with conservation". John Willey & Sons. Inc., p. 1–435.

[6] Carpigiani, U.U. (1976). Planejamento e proteção do meio ambiente. in: "Centro de Recursos Hídricos e Ecologia Aplicada". Departamento de Hidráulica e Saneamento da Escola de Engenharia de São Carlos, USP. Ecologia Aplicada e Proteção do Meio Ambiente. São Carlos. Convênio USP/CETESB, p. 1–16.

[7] Castro, D.M.M. (1980) "Diretrizes ambientais para melhor uso de solo na região litoral sul fluminense". FEEMA, 1980.

[8] CENTRE OCEANOLOGIQUE DE BRETAGNE. Departement Environmental Littoral et Gestion de Milieu Marin. "Action du N.E.X.O. dans les études d'environment littoral". 4 pp.

[9] CURSO DE ANALISES, PLANEAMIENTO Y GESTION DEL MEDIO LITORAL. (1973). "Conferencias resúmenes de coloquios y resultados del 1er. Curso de análisis, planeamiento, y gestion del medio litoral". Madrid, Colegio de Ingenieros de Caminos, Canales y Puertos. Centro de Perfeccionamiento Profesional y Empresarial. 530 pp.

[10] CURSO DE ANALISES, PLANEAMIENTO Y GESTION DEL MEDIO LITORAL (1974). 2. "Conferencias y coloquios del 2o. curso de análisis,

planeamiento y gestion del medio litoral". Madrid. Colegio Oficial de Ingenieros Y Caminos, Canales y Puertos. Centro de Perfeccionamiento Profesional y Empresarial. 494 pp.

[11] Davis, G.E. (1980). "Role of underwater parks and sanctuaries in the management of coastal resources in the southeastern United States". 44th. Anual Meeting Nat. Wildlife Ped. Miami Beach, FL (USA). Environ. Conserv. V. 8, no. 1, 1981, p. 67–70.

[12] Edmunds, S. and Letey, J. (1975). "Ordenación y gestión del medio ambiente". Madrid. Inst. de Administración local. 818 pp.

[13] FUNDREM (1979). "Macrozoneamento da região metropolitana do Rio de Janeiro". FUNDREM, Diretoria de Planejamento, 188 pp.

[14] Keemas, V. et alli. (1980). Remote sensing of coastal environment and resources. Proc. Fourteenth Int. Symp. Remote Sensing of Environment. Environm. Res. Inst. Ann Arbor, vol. 1, p. 543–562.

[15] Ketchum, B.H. (editor) (1972). "The Water's Edge. Critical Problems of the Coastal Zone". The MIT Press Design Department.

[16] Magnanini, A. and M. A. F. Nehab (1978). Departamento de Conservação Ambiental – Roteiro para a elaboração do plano diretor: reservas biológicas, áreas estaduais e planejamento de parques estaduais. FEEMA. Rio de Janeiro. 36 pp.

[17] Malm, O.; W.C. Pfeiffer; L.D. Lacerda; M. Fiszman; and N.R.W. Lima (1989). Heavy metals pollution monitoring through the critical pathways analysis: the Sepetiba Bay case. Proc. VI Symp. Coastal and Ocean management, July 1989, Charleston, Paper ref. 367.

[18] Neves, G.R. Geomorfologia aplicada ao planejamento urbano. Notícia Geomorfológica. PUC/Campinas, Instituto de Ciências Humanas, Departamento de Geografia. 17 (34): 95–103.

[19] Oliveira, L.P.H. (1972). Poluição nas Baías de Ilha Grande e Sepetiba. Bol. Clube Naval, Rio de Janeiro, 83 (2): 28–32.

[20] Pazzaglini Fº, M. and M. A. Graco (1978). Zoneamento industrial em áreas críticas de poluição. Comentários à Lei no. 6803/80 de 02/07/80 São Paulo. Conselho Nacional de Desenvolvimento Urbano. Min. do Interior. 178 pp.

[21] Pedrini, A.G. (1982). Algas marinhas bentônicas da Baía de Sepetiba e arredores. Pós-Graduação em Botânica da Universidade Federal do Rio de Janeiro. 397 pp.

[22] Valentini, E. and C.F. Neves (1989). The coastline of Rio de Janeiro from a coastal engineering point of view. Proc. VI Symp. Coastal and Ocean Management, Charleston, July 1989, Paper ref. 356.

THE GEOGRAPHICAL INFORMATION SYSTEM OF THE
BRAZILIAN COASTAL MANAGEMENT PROGRAM

Mauro Sérgio Fernandes Argento [1]

1 GENERAL CONSIDERATIONS

The coastal management program presents, in its content, two modules which are intimately associated and integrated with the system of geoenvironment information: the Zoning and the Monitoring.

The main goal of the SIGECOS concerns the environmental analysis which supports coastal planning as well as its development, and the studies related to the surveys, to the monitoring and, consequently, to the management of the Brazilian coast.

The environmental data, of physical and socio-economic natures, are stored in the system for later processing and information destined for coastal management.

The modules begin with the geocodification of data until arriving at the level of information processing. The "software" which integrates these modules is considered to be the "thinking body" of the coastal management information system. It is composed of submodules that contain approximately 30 programs prepared initially in BASIC and compatible to microcomputers of Apple and PC/XT types. For a better integration with the users of several Brazilian states, this software has been decodified in the following languages: Pascal, Fortran 70 and 87, and C. Thus, there is more probability of compatibility of the mentioned software with the different equipments which might exist near the representative groups of each coastal state and their respective utilization interests.

These packages contain the programs destined to the reading of the environmental data, to the storage of texts, to the following of spatial transformation, to the interfacing of information plans originating multiple environmental sceneries and, also for, programs of statistic analysis: uni-, bi- and multivaried ones. Such programs of integrated action allow for a link between the user and the machine.

The data bank of the SIGECOS presents as INPUT option, *data of descriptive nature* such as: system description, data about the Coastal Management Law, variable contents, data of socio-economic nature such as the ones taken out from the IBGE census, and *data originated from the thematic mapping* in different processing scales (nominal, ordinal, interval and ratio). The Data Bank stores the different

[1]Departamento de Geografia, Instituto de Geociências, Universidade Federal do Rio de Janeiro, Rio de Janeiro, RJ 21945, Brazil.

thematic maps through the geoencoding of the successive information plans. These plans are used to generate automatic information reproductions interfacing and to accompany the data, and also the possibility of evaluating the pattern of the present soil usage and the adaptation of its potentialities.

This information, properly geoencoded, represents the essence of the Geoenviromental Data Bank and makes the Information System operational.

The SIGECOS is an open and interactive system which allows for a close relationship between the user and the machine. It is used not only to create technical reports but, mainly, to support researches developed by different specialists who work in the coastal areas.

The input of the environmental data, the matrix transformations, the interfacing of the information plans, the environmental controls and simulations, besides the detection of critical areas, are some of the programs that can be used by the technical staff involved in the coastal management program. Being an open system, it still foresees the interaction with Compatible Computer Tapes (CCT) and other data banks (oceanographic ones, IBGE, etc.).

Another strong point in the SIGECOS is the possibility of statistically processing data measured in the different scales mentioned above.

Static programs of descriptive variance, correlation and simple and multiple regression, cluster analysis, factorial, and surficial trending besides the "t" and "χ^2" tests, represent some of the options the user has to statistically analyze his data.

Environmental mappings are often begun with the classifying tests, resulting in synthesizing sources of environmental scenarios.

The creation of different new information plans, originated from numerical analysis, permits the choice of the one which best responds to the purpose of the coastal management, and consequently, the one which guarantees consistency of information or, in analysis, less residual value.

The perspective of the use of the information system is ample and varied.

The analysis of declivity classes starting with the planialtimetric basis, the continuity through successive, or expansion of the urban area, spatial confrontations, analysis of which, as the years go by, will automatically furnish the populational dynamics of the studied area, creating a growth coefficient, the capability to diagnose areas covered with varied kinds of soil, following a pedological plan of information. These are some of the examples of the answers which can be obtained from the SIGECOS in a rapid and efficient way.

One of the most important points for the SIGECOS user is the possibility of interaction with several kinds of maps (multivaried analysis).

The shape of a physical space where different environmental characteristics occur simultaneously can be used to solve planning problems in relatively complex areas.

On the other hand, one can still search for the causal characteristics that respond to a determined environmental effect.

This relationship game is one of the most significative way available to make causal analysis of environmental impacts in coastal areas.

In a Geoenvironmental Information System, to simulate means to create new scenarios. The different specialists in environmental analysis will be able to use these devices to discover the best options for planning in the coastal areas merely by counting on the data which are stored in the memory system after the geoencoding.

Here are some examples of what we can accomplish through the Simulation programs, with the interaction of the specialists and the SIGECOS: areas liable to be flooded, better agricultural soil usage, allocation of high voltage power lines and the localization of navigable ports and roads.

Another perspective of the SIGECOS potentiality is related to the analysis of the environmental costs estimation.

The pasture areas which suffered inundation differ significantly from the farming and the urban ones. As the basis of the system is cellular and, in this specific case, the cells measure 1 km^2, it is easy to calculate the whole area involved, as well as the costs (negative and positive) originated from this fact.

The interaction of the Coastal Management Information System with the LASER Laboratory (Laboratório de Sensoreamento Remoto da Universidade de São Paulo) will make a relationship possible between the conventional cartographic basis and the basis obtained by automatic processing, through digital processing. Lastly, this process will be used as basic INPUT to analyze the spatial attendance, a fundamental point for the effective monitoring of the Brazilian coastal space.

2 METHODOLOGY OF THE COASTAL MANAGEMENT INFORMATION SYSTEM (SIGECOS)

A Geoenvironmental Data Bank must be closely associated with an Information System. The fundamental difference between a Data Bank and an Information System consists OF the fact that the former has, as its goal, the storing and the continuous follow up of information while the latter presents the feature of not only storing but of following, mainly, the processing of this information in an adequate scale, in an optimized systematic way.

The Coastal Management Information System is comprised of four modules which are integrated to furnish analysis options to the users. They are: geoencoding, storage, structure programs and data processing.

The Data Bank keeps information in different ways: the descriptive, the numerical, the one originated from thematic maps. This detail makes the INPUT to present specific criteria to each subject.

Information presenting descriptive contents is directly introduced into the memory bank through specific or by the already available test editor. This determines the storage criterion by mere digitation of the descriptive contents.

The data of numeric contents, of the socio-economic information type of municipal basis found in the IBGE's Census, for instance, can be stored in the System by the above mentioned criterion or by specific programs elaborated with matrix logic. These spatial matrices, containing in the rows the spaces (a city, for example), and in the columns the variables (originated from the Census in the mentioned example), consolidated themselves in the basic INPUT to store such information. This storage criterion helps the systematization for the statistic data Processing.

The data originated from the thematic maps is distributed in areas or in points. This information appears in the maps in four basic Processing scales: the nominal, the ordinal, the interval and the ratio one.

Information of the presence of a port or of a historical monument refers to precise information and it is presented in a nominal scale (presence or lack of information). Information concerning hierarchical sequences diagnoses a variable in an ordinal scale. As for the information about temperature, salinity of class distribution, distributed both in points and in areas, represents variables processed in interval scales. When there are no well defined limits of values, or of hierarchical sequences characterization or of interval, the information processing is characterized in a ratio scale.

Figure 1, showing the chart, illustrates the differentiation between the processing scales of a variable completely.

The differentiation of such scales becomes important, not only for adequate definitions of the statistic method, but mainly, for the INPUT procedures in the thematic maps to be stored in the Information System.

The potentiality of the Coastal Management Information System is much related to the processing of the information originated in the thematic maps. A thematic map consists of one or more information plans. These plans are, after being decoded, used as INPUT to the System and constitute the basis for the Geoenvironmental Data Bank. Uni- and multivaried classifying analyses are made, as well as the interfacing, resulting in new environmental scenarios which are reliable support points for coastal space planning (Fig. 2).

The coastal area, limited by latitude and longitude given in degrees, is divided into sections which cover 30 minutes by 30 minutes. These sections are then divided into subsections equivalent to 0.5 minute, which represents approximately an area of 1 km². This area will be equivalent to the system resolution, which will be transformed in the spatial matrix cells, that is, the pixel, which will be the basis for the thematic information INPUT to be stored in the system.

The sets of information plans, representing a section of 30 × 30 minutes, after being geocoded, will be stored by the LISTVAR (Variable List) in the system, becoming suitable for processing in the information system.

This matrix comprises cells (Pixel) in the direction of the rows and of the different information plans which, finally, will be equivalent to the thematic mappings in the matrix columns direction. Each matrix row will be equivalent to a vector trait of that 0.5 minute located in the space, while each matrix column will furnish a spatial distribution reproduction of a specific section (30 minute side). The sequence of two sections will furnish information representative of 1 degree and then, successively, the regions, the state and the whole coastal zone will be covered. The data process is formulated by the aggregation logic, that is, all INPUTS will be measured by 30' × 30' sections. This fact makes the systematization of the system easier and the covering of a wide area such as the Brazilian coastal zone, within the memory limits compatible to microcomputers.

The matrix column represents an information plan which becomes a thematic mapping as it presents each variable in its relative position in the cell. This is accomplished through the interval handling of the thematic data files. This procedure helps the uni- and multi-varied analyses.

As an example of the interaction between the different matrix columns, an environmental scenario is obtained in which various characteristics simultaneously occur.

This product is the result of the Thematic Interfacing programs used for instance, in areas where alluvium soils, sedimentary terrains altitudes below 20 meters and sugar-cane plantation occur simultaneously. It is also the result of the

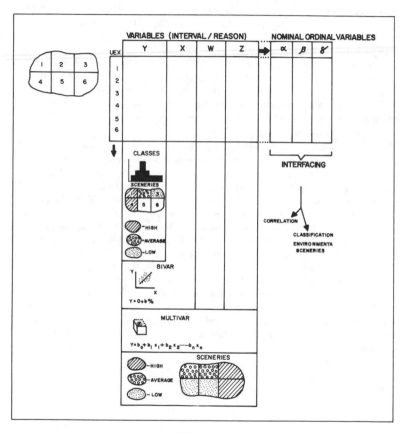

Figure 1:

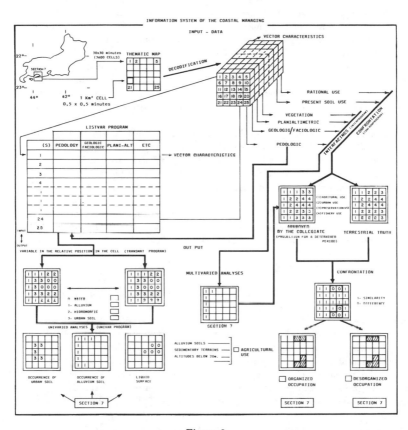

Figure 2:

interfacing of the pedological thematic maps, the geological and plani-altimetric ones, and the maps of agricultural use also. This procedure is essential for coastal space planning. Eventual interactions and the definition of environmental functions can be generated using procedures similar to the ones presented here.

Another potentiality of the SIGECOS methodology is the confrontation between the presently used thematic maps and the projected ones resulting int areas of organized occupation and areas which are undergoing disorganized occupation in relation to the coastal zone planning.

The SIGECOS presents other options for the data processing in the INPUT matrix. This processing is differentiated for the variables measured in the interval and ratio scales and for the variables measured in nominal and ordinal scales.

The analysis of the measured data in the interval and ratio scales permits the use of the parametric and descriptive statistic. The uni- and multi-varied processings, presenting options of correlation and classification, constitutes the basis of this analysis.

In summary, the methodology of the Coastal Management Information System foresees as INPUT information of reports, numerical values as census data and information of thematic maps which are distributed both in areas and in points. As OUTPUT options are offered for the drawing of reports, statements about the measured variables, system procedures, stored information plans and generation of environmental scenarios, essential points for the Coastal Management Plan.

The viability of its utilization is connected to the presence of the geoencoding criterion of a Software developed in BASIC, compatible to the APPLE and PC/XT microcomputers and decoded into Pascal, Fortran and C languages.

3 GEOENCODING CRITERIA

The Coastal Management Information System acts as an important instrument to viabilize the furnishing and following, in a secure, rapid and efficient manner, the Brazilian Coastal area registered information. It is capable of making automatic reproductions of information, of interfacing different data plans, thus generating multiple environmental scenarios, for a single test area, subsidizing the foresight of environmental impact situations estimating their positive and negative effects through the automatic handling of the data stored in its memory. However, to viabilize all these procedures it is necessary to make the present information in the thematic maps compatible to the computer's language. This procedure is denominated GEOENCODING.

Geoencoding is an essential point for the system consistence. Decoding of the information present in the thematic cards into numeric language compatible with the computers use, is, consequently, the key to guarantee the information efficiency. Two basic criteria can be used to attain this result: the cellular and polygonal criteria.

The cellular criterion presents a sweeping structure: the unit of the area in the cell and the procedure is done by cellular aggregation. The polygonal criterion presents a vectorial structure; the unit is formed by coordinated pairs: the procedure is done by the set of ordinates and abscissas which limits the polygonal area.

These two procedures present both advantages and disadvantages. There are no specific studies which systematically analyze their utilization.

The cellular criterion consists of the transformation of the characteristics present in the matrix cell (Pixel) according to the criteria previously established by the project. To illustrate the cellular criterion it was mentioned an environmental mapping of usage and a soil cover having as basis the following legend:

- Urban area: towns, villages, peripheral bogs, industrial zones, plotting, services, institutional areas.

- Farming and raising area: diversified cultures, livestock, plantations, pastures etc.

- Forests: the Mata Atlântica Forests, herbaceous vegetation.

- Humid areas: mangrove swamps, marshes, bogs, flooded fields and meadows, plains, muddy areas.

- Water: all liquid surface such as rivers, coastal lagoons and lakes.

- Barren area: arid land and rocky outcrop such as beaches sandy ridges, dunes, cliffs, scarps, sugar loaves, stone-quarries, etc.

- Accurate Information: ports and terminals, polluting industries, fishing reserves, historical heritage.

Different scales generate different responses not only in cartographic terms but also in the geoencoding criterion. This means that in a large scale in cartographic terms, for instance, the urban areas would be delimited without discriminating if they were towns or villages. In this case, the representative value of the urban areas would be 20. In another more detailed scale, information of the urban occupation type, such as towns, villages, peripheral neighborhoods, etc., would have already been mentioned in the map legend. In this case, the representative values would be all arranged between 21 an 29.

Such being the case, there must be a specific memory bank for each processing scale and the geoencoding must follow a determined uniformity in terms of macroscale (1:100,000). This is based on the fact that, as it is the most ample processing scale, the numbers "Key head" must be tens, hundreds or tens of hundreds, etc. leaving the smaller units to specify the discriminatory characteristics of the major contents.

In the cellular criterion, the smallest unit of information collection is the cell it self or pixel (Picture Elements). In the case of the Coastal Management Plan, this cell will not always represent a square unit for it will be equal to a covered area of $30' \times 30'$.

The data collection representative of each pixel, is based on coverage of the characteristics which are found within its limits. The feature which covers the major portion of the pixel (50%) will be considered as predominant information and as the one to be stored in the Data Bank to be geoprocessed later by the Information System. This shows that when a pixel is totally covered by a feature, the information does not present residual degree and the Data Bank stores a datum free from residue. Obviously, if there are two or more characteristics in the analyzed pixel, the stored datum will be the one which presents the largest area coverage, not mentioning to the Data Bank.

The other characteristics which occur in less proportion in the pixel. However, this residue does not invalidate the processing criterion of the geoencoding for it is directly related to the resolution of the system, that is, to the definitions capacity between two adjacent points.

According to the previously mentioned criteria, the geoencoded data which are compatible with the whole project area, are transported by cells to an information panel. This panel will guide these data to subsequent transposition into the computer memory through a manual digitizing process (by keyboard).

An essential point for a good performance in the geoencoding process consists of making a pattern of the criteria for the transformation of variables into numeric values. One must be alert to the possibility of future use of the same maps in other more complete projects.

In this case, it is necessary to analyze either a geologic or a geomorphologic map keeping in mind the possible rock or relief occurrence in a less restrict or regional area. This procedure will turn viable the standardization of the legends and will also draw attention on interactive analysis between the different cards which cover a single map in case the decoding is done by different groups in distinct periods.

The storage of the data, originated by the geoencoding process of the thematic cards (information plans), can be done in matrix basis having in the rows direction the cells and in the column direction the variables representative of the contents (geologic, geomorphologic, plani-altimetric, vegetal coverage, soil usage etc.). It can also be done in vectorial basis where each information plan constitutes a vector. For didactic effect the first case is more viable (see Fig. 2); nevertheless, it occupies a lot of the computer memory making the process a slow and problematic one when there is a great number of variables. The storage in vectorial basis helps the processing speed and allows the interaction of a greater number of information plans.

The checking of the stored information is a fundamental task for the system's consistence. It has the responsibility of presenting the results with low residue value. Blank cells or digitizing errors, wrong statements, etc. lead to answers which compromise the system's reliability.

4 STRUCTURE OF THE COASTAL MANAGEMENT INFORMATION SYSTEM

The Coastal Management Information System is based on computer logic, which allows to acquire, to store, to match, to analyze and to recover coded information in a spatial manner.

The SIGECOS nature is essentially different from that of a conventional Data Bank. While this works typically with charts, the Information System processes these charts of uni-, bi- and multi-dimensional forms furnishing responses of spatial contents.

Four main functions are identified in the Information System:

1. INPUT
   Consists basically of digital operations associated with the activities of editing, maps, and data base.

2. Data Storage and Recovery
   Creation of the basis for spatial data and modification operations, insertion, deletion, removal, etc...

3. Data Manipulation
   Set of operations which permit to create new information from the inter-relationship of the information present in the data base.

4. OUTPUT
   It can be either in the shape of charts or in spatial shape due to operations, manipulations or recovery.

These functions are done with a software which constitutes the "thinking body" of the Information System. This module confine different programs which integrate themselves forming a harmonic body capable of answering, little by little, the requests which are predicted by the system's logic.

The Coastal Management Information System is an open and interactive system.

Its basic structure was created in such a way that it permits a gradual enlargement, according to the necessities of each group involved in the Coastal Management.

A constant worry at the time of the SIGECOS creation was the possibility of forming state groups including persons who understand the system methodology and which are able to expand it with the addition of new programs. For this reason, the systems must be open and worked on *grey boxes*. The groups which take part in the works connected with coastal management must have in mind the interfacing with other systems and the use of the information already available in other Data Banks. Those who work with open and interactive systems such as the SIGECOS must proceed as the following examples: interfacing with other interactive systems of orbital data processing, Orbital Data Bank, socio-economic Data Bank, etc...

Data processing, in last instance, is used to generate information required by the user. These data are mostly originated from the thematic map. After stored in the system memory, they are used to generate not only automatic reproduction of the information, but also data interfacing, furnishing options of multiple environmental scenarios. This is the foundation for the coastal space management for it permits, in last instance, the follow up of the data in environmental analysis. It also makes easier the behavior evaluation of the present soil usage and the adaptation to its real possibilities.

REFERENCES

[1] Argento, M.S.F. (1987). Mapeamento Ambiental Direcionado ao Gerenciamento de Áreas Deltaicas. UNESP, Rio Claro, 137p.

[2] Bribiesca, E. and R. Avilés (1974). "Codificación en cadens y técnicas de reducción de información para maps y dibujos lineales". Report CCAL-74-7 Centro Científico IBM de América Latina, Mexico.

[3] Bribiesca, E. and A. Guzman (1974). "User's Manual for the geographic data base accessing programs". IBM de Mexico, CCAL-74-17.

[4] Bryan N.; A. Zorrist; and A. Abis (1977). A geographic information system based on digital image processing and image raster data type. *IEEE Transactions on Geoscience Electronics* 15 (3): 152–59.

[5] Correa, E.B. and A.G. Arena (1977). "Manual do Usuário para Exploração de um Banco de Dados Geográficos". Centro Científico da América Latina, IBM, Mexico.

[6] Dias, J.B. and G.A. Sheufler (1985). "Elaboração de carta ambiental através do sistema de processamento geoambiental – SAGA/UFRJ". Cadernos da FEEMA, Série Congressos, no. 28. Rio de Janeiro.

[7] Guzman, A and E. Bribiesca (1974). "Multiple-level geographic data bank for direct access storage". Report CCAL-74-9 Centro Científico IBM de América Latina, Mexico.

[8] Nagy, G. and S. Wagle (1978). Geographic data processing. *ACM Computing Surveys* 11 (2): 139–181.

[9] Nystrom, D.A.; E.W. Bruce; and D.P. Michael (1985). The U.S. Geological Survey (Connecticut Geographic Information System Project – Reston, Virginia). U.S. Geological Survey, 8: 2–13.

[10] Pequet, D.J. (1977). Raster data handling in geographic information systems. *in:* International Symposium on Advanced Data Structures for Geographic Information. Harvard University.

[11] Roqueñi, A.T. and J.O. Vidal (1974). "Localización por computadoras de cuencas lecheras". II Congresso Interamericano de Sistemas e Informatica, Mexico.

[12] Tomlinson, R.F. and R. Boyce (1981). The state of development of systems for handling natural resources inventory data. *Cartographica* 18 (40): 65–95.

[13] Xavier da Silva, J. (1979). O Sistema de Informações Geoambientais do Projeto RADAMBRASIL. Anuário no. 23/79 da Diretoria do S.G.E., p.207–216. Brasília, DF.

[14] Xavier da Silva, J. (1981). "A Geocodificação de Informações Ambientais do Projeto RADAMBRASIL". *Revista Brasileira de Cartografia*, 26: 38–43.

[15] Xavier da Silva, J. (1985). SAGA. Proc. I Congresso Brasileiro de Defesa do Meio Ambiente, vol.II, p. 417–420. Rio de Janeiro.

FOULING AND WOOD-BORING COMMUNITIES DISTRIBUTION ON THE COAST OF RIO DE JANEIRO

Sérgio Henrique G. Silva [1]   Andrea O.R. Junqueira [1]

Maria Julia M. Silva [1]   Ilana R. Zalmon [1]   Helena P. Lavrado [1]

1 INTRODUCTION

Nowadays, it becomes increasingly necessary to manage the natural resources of coastal regions correctly and to determine which human activities are suitable to the characteristics of each area.

Structures such as piers, wharves, bridges or even pipelines of nuclear power plants are always exposed to the action of many different marine organisms, specially fouling and wood-boring ones.

The knowledge of the biological aspects of these organisms becomes important as it provides data which is helpful for the determination of the best use of a coastal area, specially if it is near crowded urban areas such as estuaries, bays or lagoons.

At present, materials such as steel, fiberglass and concrete are used for engineering purposes to increase the durability of marine structures and boats. Nevertheless, the use of wood is still important. This is a traditional and one of the least costly construction materials in countries such as Brazil. However, the presence of fouling and the hard attack of wood-boring mollusks on the wood is intense throughout the year in tropical waters, reducing its durability greatly.

Therefore, it is necessary to find means for the preservation of the wood and to control the activity of these organisms. It is important to understand the biological and ecological effects of these organisms on marine structures regionally in order to design new means of effective control.

The present study of the dynamics of fouling communities and the distribution of wood-boring organisms along the coast of Rio de Janeiro, Brazil, was motivated by the great number of wooden structures usually employed in marinas, wharves, fishing and pleasure crafts, and shipyards.

2 MATERIAL AND METHODS

Experiments were independently carried out in four areas which are described in this study.

---

[1] Departamento de Biologia Marinha, Instituto de Biologia, Universidade Federal do Rio de Janeiro, Rio de Janeiro, RJ 21941, Brazil.

The first one took place at two stations, Portogallo and Piraquara, in Ilha Grande Bay (August, 1982 to July, 1983) (Figure 1-A). The second one took place in the Tijuca Lagoon (September, 1983 to August, 1984). There, five stations were selected according to a decreasing salinity gradient (Figure 1-B).

At Itajuru Inlet (Figure 1-D), the third experiment was conducted, using three stations chosen according to an increasing salinity gradient (January, 1986 to February, 1987).

In Guanabara Bay, two experiments were carried out. The first one took place near the mouth of the bay (August, 1982 to April, 1983), while the second one was based on three stations: the first one near the mouth and the other two placed in the inner parts of the bay (August, 1986 to July, 1987) (Figure 1-C).

The wood-boring organisms were collected using 10 pine-wood sheets (*Araucaria angustifolia*) of 10 × 10 × 0.08 cm each. They were set between two pieces of wood and two pieces of ceramics, the assembly being put together by two brass bolts (Manyak, 1982, modified). In addition, plywood panels were used in order to collect the fouling organisms in Guanabara Bay. The dry weight of these organisms was analyzed in order to give an indication of the general fouling intensity for each area.

3   AREA DESCRIPTION AND RESULTS

3.1   Ilha Grande Bay:

This bay is placed on the southern coast of Rio de Janeiro and can be divided into two areas: one, to the west of Grande Island, with an approximate area of 1,000 km²; the other one to the east, with an area of 300 km². Ilha Grande Bay has two connections with the sea: one, to the east, is 10 km wide and the other, to the west, is 18 km wide. Its waters receive a large amount of wood from the marginal vegetation of Serra do Mar, a mountain range.

Along the margins, there are small towns such as Angra dos Reis, Mangaratiba and Paraty. Nowadays, one of the major problems of this area is the fast and uncontrolled process of soil occupation caused basically by the development of tourist activities and the construction of the BR-101 highway. The local population was transferred to the hillsides without any kind of urban planning. The environmental conditions became increasingly worse as there is a lack of basic sanitation. The estimated population, in 1987, was 108,404 inhabitants, whose organic discharges created a BOD (biochemical oxygen demand) of 1,700 kg/day, considering that part of this domestic effluent was subject to treatment systems and the rest of it was discharged into the sewer and pluvial systems.

Fishing is the most important activity of the primary sector. Angra dos Reis city produces 20–25% of the annual fish catch of Rio de Janeiro State. The major part of the local fishing fleet is formed by wooden crafts.

In the secondary sector, there are two industries: the naval industry, represented by one of the greatest shipyards of Brazil, and the fishing industry. Furthermore, Angra dos Reis has the only nuclear power plant of the country and the largest oil terminal of South America. These are the two major potential sources of pollution in the bay: an accidental oil spill from the terminal and radioactive contamination

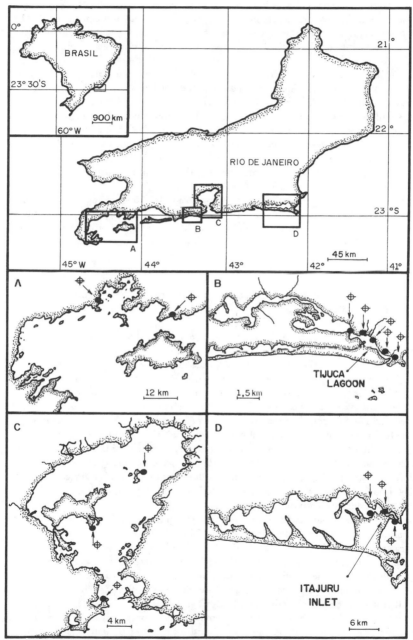

FIGURE 1: MAPS OF THE STUDIED AREAS AND THEIR RESPECTIVE SAMPLING STATIONS (⊕) ALONG THE COAST OF RIO DE JANEIRO STATE. A- ILHA GRANDE BAY. B- JACAREPAGUÁ LAGOON SYSTEM. C- GUANABARA BAY. D-ARARUAMA LAGOON.

of the water, or also thermal pollution caused by the cooling system of the Nuclear station. Despite these problems, Ilha Grande Bay is classified as a non-polluted and an oligotrophic ecosystem, with clean waters and small phytoplanktonic biomass.

The principal environmental parameters analyzed during the experiment are shown in Table I.

Fouling communities showed a rhythm of colonization slower than what is found in other studied areas. The first organisms that settled on the substratum were microalgae, hydroids and encrusting and arborescent ectoprocts. Balanoids, even the small ones, were only found after 4 months. From the sixth month up to the end of the experiment the panels were colonized by a diversified fauna of sponges, tunicates and bivalves. At least 16 species of fouling organisms were identified. A maximum value of biomass was reached after ten months, with 7.0 g/dm^2 in dry weight (Table II). Until the fifth month, the fouling biomass was completely insignificant.

On the other hand, the substratum colonization by wood-boring mollusks was very fast, reaching the maximum density of 460.0 individuals per dm^2 after two months of exposure. In this area, eleven species of wood-boring organisms were identified and the bivalve *Lyrodus floridanus* was the dominant species (Table III).

3.2 Tijuca Lagoon:

This coastal lagoon, together with Camorim and Jacarepagua, constitute the Jacarepagua Lagoon System, situated southwest of the urban zone of Rio de Janeiro, as shown in Fig.1-B.

The Jacarepagua Lagoon System presents a watershed with 13 small tributary rivers which have their sources in the Tijuca and Pedra Branca hills. Only three of these rivers flow into the Tijuca Lagoon, which has an area of 4.8 km^2 and is 6 km long. There is a narrow channel (90 meters wide) connecting the lagoon with the Atlantic Ocean, but it allows for a continuous inflow/outflow of water controlled by the tidal cycle. The adjacent areas of this system are now being submitted to a fast and non-controlled process of soil occupation which causes a great discharge of highly polluted effluents (domestic and industrial ones) into its waters.

According to Medeiros (1982), the estimated population of the drainage basin of this system was 237,657 inhabitants in 1980, based on a demographic census. In 1977, approximately 60% of this population did not have basic sanitary conditions. This probably caused a discharge with a BOD of 54 g/day per capita.

Local industrial activities are very diversified, with approximately 200 companies. The principal products are chemical and pharmaceutic compounds, non-metallic minerals and metallurgic products. These industries produce a great discharge of organic pollutants with a BOD of 3,500 kg/day as well as toxic substances. (phenol, cyanide and heavy metals) (FEEMA, 1984). Besides these activities, fishing continues to be the major source of income for a great number of local residents. The most common species of commercial interest are mullets and robalos. Only small crafts, principally wooden boats, can fish in this lagoon as it is a shallow-water system. As a result, fishing is a small-scale activity and often a mean of subsistence as in the most of the lagoons and estuaries of underdeveloped countries.

Mean salinity values decrease as one proceeds up the lagoon, while tempera-

Table I: Values of environmental parameters analyzed during experiments in the studied areas.

		I. GRANDE BAY		TIJUCA LAGOON		GUANABARA BAY		ITAJURU INLET	
		MIN	MAX	MIN	MAX	MIN	MAX	MIN	MAX
TEMP. (°C)	Mouth	21.0	30.0	20.0	24.3	21.0	27.5	18.0	28.0
	Inner Areas			23.0	30.0	19.5	30.0	21.0	29.0
SAL. (ppt)	Mouth	20.0	36.4	17.2	34.0	27.5	35.0	21.0	37.9
	Inner Areas			5.2	21.3	9.0	31.3	21.0	60.9
D.O. (mg/l)	Mouth	6.0	8.0	–	–	2.8	8.6	4.4	7.7
	Inner Areas			–	–	3.6	15.0	4.1	8.0
BOD (mg/l)	Mouth	0.6	1.6	–	–	1.0	5.5	–	–
	Inner Areas			–	–	1.6	17.0	–	–
TOTAL NITROGEN (μg/l)		56.0	571.0	–	–	149.9	1610.0	–	–
TURBIDITY (m)		5.0	12.5	–	–	0.8	3.7	–	–

Table II: Number of taxa and maximum fouling biomass in the four areas studied.

		I. GRANDE BAY	TIJUCA LAGOON	GUANABARA BAY	ITAJURU INLET
NUMBER OF TAXA	Mouth	16	15	27	27
	Inner Areas		10	10	22
MAXIMUM BIOMASS (g/dm²)	Mouth	7.0	3.0	250.0	10.0
	Inner Areas		30.0	20.0	40.0

Table III: Number of wood-boring species and maximum densities of Teredinidae in the four areas studied.

		I. GRANDE BAY	TIJUCA LAGOON	GUANABARA BAY	ITAJURU INLET
NUMBER OF SPECIES	Mouth	11	8	6	11
	Inner Areas		2		5
MAXIMUM DENSITY (ind/dm²)	Mouth	460.0	50.0	4.0	90.0
	Inner Areas		1.0		50.0

ture values increase. Coelho and Fonseca (1981) classified as *moderate* the level of eutrophication of Tijuca Lagoon and as *high* the eutrophication conditions of Jacarepagua and Camorim lagoons. According to Medeiros (1982), the area which has the highest BOD values is in Camorim Lagoon decreasing towards Jacarepagua and Tijuca lagoons, respectively. The mouth of Tijuca Lagoon shows good water quality conditions despite the discharge of polluted effluents into it, but the conditions become worse as one enters the lagoon system.

The variations of environmental parameters occurred during experiments is shown on Table I.

With regard to fouling communities, the number of species found was greater at the mouth of the lagoon (15 species) than at its inner regions (10 species). Here, the dominant species were balanoids and biomass values were twelve times higher than those found near the mouth of the lagoon. The maximum and minimum values of biomass were 30.0 g/dm^2 and 0.2 g/dm^2, respectively, while biomass values near the mouth varied between 0.4 and 3.0 g/dm^2 (Table II).

The number of wood-boring species decreases as one goes into the lagoon.

Near the mouth, the dominant species was the isopod *Limnoria tripunctata* with a maximum density of 300.0 individuals/dm^2 after a one-year period of exposure. These isopods seemed to compete with teredinids (wood-boring mollusks), especially with *Teredo bartschi*. Its maximum density was of 50.0 individuals per dm^2, after ten months of exposure.

Limnoria tripunctata, the dominant species found in the stations near the ocean, did not occur in areas where salinities were below 17 ppt.

Teredinid density also decreases as one goes into the lagoon. At inner stations, it was found a maximum density of only 1.0 individual per dm^2 after a ten-month period of exposure and *Bankia fimbriatula* was the dominant species. These values were 50 times lower than those found near the mouth of the lagoon (Table III).

3.3 Guanabara Bay:

The approximate area of Guanabara Bay is 381 km^2, including 44 km^2 of small islands. Its watershed has an area of 4,000 km^2 with 35 rivers. None of them is a mighty river but together they provide great freshwater inflow in the bay. The mouth of the bay is 1.8 km wide. It is a system of shallow waters and its maximum depth is of 35 meters. The water circulation is mainly controlled by tides and winds.

With an estimated population of 9,000,000 inhabitants (in 1987), its basin has the second industrial complex of Brazil with more than 10,000 industries, ports, two important oil refineries, and 16 oil terminals. The waters of this bay have many different uses. The primary sector is represented by the fishing of croakers, robalos, sardines and mullets. The secondary activities are performed by industries situated along its margins, using waters of the bay in cooling systems, basically. The tertiary activities are the most important ones comprising not only services such as the ones of harbors and navigation but also leisure and tourist activities. The commercial navigation is intense due to the existence of two ports (Rio de Janeiro and Niterói) and oil terminals situated near Governador Island. The traffic of ships is continuous throughout the year, reaching almost 3,000 ships docking every year at these two ports.

Guanabara Bay is a typical coastal environmental that is subject to a fast process of degradation due mainly to illegal embankments and domestic and industrial discharges. Using data by FEEMA (1987), it is calculated that about 50% of its population does not have any kind of sanitation system. According to this institution, these people produce a discharge of 15.3 m^3/s of domestic 'waste' and only 17% of this sewage is submitted to a secondary treatment corresponding to a BOD of 380 tons per day. Industrial effluents are the principal source of water pollution in Guanabara Bay (50% of organic pollution and almost 100% of chemical pollution). Of 10,000 industries, 5,000 industries pollute significantly the water of this bay (FEEMA, 1987).

As it is a complex system, water quality of Guanabara Bay is not uniform, characterizing regions with different hydrological conditions due basically to water circulation, salinity and discharges of domestic pollutants. In the north-south direction, there is an increasing gradient of salinity. According to FEEMA (1987), from the east to the west of the bay, pollution levels increase gradually, based on the BOD value which varies between 5.0 mg/l and 50.0 mg/l, approximately. Values of organic nitrogen, ammoniacal nitrogen, total phosphorus, chlorophyll a and detergent behave similarly to those of BOD.

The main environmental parameters monitored during experiments are summarized on Table I. We noticed some differences between the hydrological conditions in the mouth and the upper regions of the bay. Regarding to the fouling community, at least 27 species were found near the mouth of the bay, forming many covering layers. The community was dominated by balanoids, ectoprocts (*Bugula neritina*, tunicates (*Styela plicata*) and bivalve mollusks (*Perna perna*). Biomass showed a progressive increase during the experiment and it seemed to be constant after eight months of immersion. The maximum and minimum values of biomass were 250.0 g/dm^2 and 0.5 g/dm^2, respectively (Table II). Competition for space was verified by the settlement of ectoprocts, hydroids and urochordats over balanoids which overgrew on bivalves.

In the upper regions of the bay, it was not found great differences in specific composition of fouling community with time. Ten species among balanoids, spionids and serpulids were identified. Biomass values did not increase significantly either (2.0 to 20.0 g/dm^2), suggesting that there had been an initial limitation of fouling development.

As regards the wood-boring community, only 5 species of Teredinidae and 1 species of Limmoriidae, *Limnoria tripunctata*, which was the dominant species were found. The maximum densities of Limnoriidae and Teredinidae were 23.0 individuals/dm^2 (after 6 months) and 4.0 individuals/dm^2 (after 8 months), respectively (Table III).

3.4 Itajuru Inlet:

Araruama Lagoon, with an area of 200 km^2, is connected to the ocean through Itajuru Inlet. The channel is narrow, 6.5 km long, having an average depth of 2.5 m at the mouth, and the town of Cabo Frio is located along its margins.

The four principal tributary rivers contribute a small volume of freshwater inflow in the lagoon. One of its main characteristics is high salinity values which are related to low rainfall, and high evaporation rates associated to the Northeasterly winds.

The economical basis of Cabo Frio town is the salt production followed by the calcareous extraction from the shells of mollusks that exist in the sediment of the lagoon. In the last 20 years, there has been a progressive development of activities of tertiary sector due mainly to the increase of tourist activities. The primary sector represented by fishing has had a less important expression in the economy of the region. The labor force has been transferred to touristic activities, and the quantity and quality of captured fish has been diminished. This gradual reduction is caused principally by predatory fishing. Cabo Frio is the city in the county with the biggest number of industries (120 units in 1980) including mineral and food industries.

The town of Cabo Frio is now being subjected to a disorganized process of soil occupation, due mainly to the increasing number of house constructions which are occupied only during weekends and holidays. Thus, illegal embankments have been made along Araruama Lagoon and Itajuru Inlet. According to the Demographic Census of 1980, population was of 40,670 inhabitants, but this number could vary during the year. One of the principal problems of the lagoon is the lack of a sewer system. Septic cesspools or even ceramic sewerage pipes are illegally connected to the pluvial drain system that is connected to the lagoon.

Despite its dimension and depth, Itajuru Inlet shows an intense movement of fishing and pleasure boats. There are strong variations of salinity caused principally by tidal cycles. Salinity and temperature increase as one proceeds into the channel. At the mouth, salinity values are similar to the sea ones (35.5 ppt) and tidal influence is maximum. At inner regions of the lagoon, values of up to 60 ppt have been found.

Variations of main environmental parameters monitored are summarized on Table I.

Fouling community presents more species near the mouth than in upper regions of channel. Twenty-seven species were identified, characterizing a community of encrusting and arborescent ectoprocts, colonial tunicates and hydroids. At the farthest station, 22 species were found and the number and size of balanoids increased. Colonies of tunicates also showed greater development in these stations.

The highest value of biomass was found in the regions closer to the end of the channel after a one-year period (40.0 g/dm²), four times higher than that found near the mouth (Table II). The minimum value of biomass was of 3.0 g/dm², near the mouth, and 5.0 g/dm² in the areas close to the end of the channel.

Species diversity and density of wood-boring organisms decrease as one goes into the channel. Near the mouth, 11 species were found, the dominant species being the *Limnoria tripunctata*, which reaches a maximum density of 380.0 individuals/dm² after ten months of exposure. Other species belong to the family of Teredinidae. *Teredo furcifera* was the dominant species of this family with a maximum density of 90.0 individuals/dm² after a 8-month period of immersion. At farthest stations of the channel, five teredinid species were identified. *Teredo furcifera* was also the dominant species with a maximum density of 50.0 individuals/dm² after 8 months (Table III).

The lowest densities of teredinids found along the channel were 20.0 (near the mouth of lagoon) and 7.0 individuals/dm² (at inner stations of the channel).

4 DISCUSSION

The results showed some significant differences among the studied areas with relation to their fouling and wood-boring communities. A low density of wood-boring organisms is very clear in Guanabara Bay. On the other hand, there is a higher biological encrusting activity, here than in Ilha Grande Bay where the maximum value of biomass reached only 7.0 g/dm^2. Guanabara Bay showed fouling biomass 35 times higher than that found in Ilha Grande Bay.

The low incidence of wood-boring organisms in Guanabara Bay is undoubtly related to the great incidence of encrusting organisms covering available substrata. Many previous studies (Clapp, 1946; Weiss, 1948; Nagabhushanan, 1960; Cooke, Grovhoug and Ching, 1980) found a correlation between the fouling biomass and the settlement of wood-boring mollusks. The first ones inhibited the penetration of the second ones into the wooden panels either by acting as a mechanical barrier to the wood-boring larva in settlement stage or by using them as food. Besides, biofouling can influence established wood-boring communities covering the openings of their siphons and thus hindering their respiratory and occasional plankton filtering mechanisms.

Species composition of encrusting epifauna can also be related to wood-boring incidence. Nair and Saraswathy (1971) stated that the balanoids are probably the most efficient organisms in inhibiting settlement of wood-boring mollusks. Cooke et al. (1980) believe that the communities dominated by solitary and colonial tunicates have more marked effects on the larval settlement than those communities dominated by balanoids and serpulids.

Near the mouth of Guanabara Bay, encrusting epifauna is dominated by a considerable density of solitary and colonial tunicates as well as balanoids. Therefore, this bay seems to be an unsuitable area to the development of wood-boring communities. It is important, however, to say that development of a dense and more diversified encrusting fauna only occurs near the mouth of the bay and it is probably related to the moderate eutrophication levels of this area. Rastetter and Cooke (1979) say that nutrient supply influences on fouling communities. According to them, the effect of moderate eutrophication levels is the increase of species diversity due to a greater nutrient availability if it is associated to suitable physical and chemical qualities of water. As a result of this eutrophication, Guanabara Bay waters can maintain a large numbers of filtering organisms which depend directly on plankton and organic suspended matter.

However, moderate eutrophication levels are not found in internal areas of the bay where organic pollution, due to discharges of domestic and industrial pollutants, is so high, that it causes total depletion of dissolved oxygen in some areas and, therefore, hinder the existence of life.

During our experiments, we found the highest BOD, ammonium and nitrate concentrations in these areas and a less diversified fouling community (only 10 species) with maximum biomass value of 20 g/dm^2. Biomass did not increase with time. This suggests that there is a limitation of fouling development. Oil can not be ignored, mainly near Governador Island where there is a permanent oil layer covering substrata. Another factor that can be related to the decrease in fouling diversity is salinity, especially near Paqueta Island where we found salinity values up to 9.0 ppt in the months with the highest precipitation values. Hoagland

(1982), in New Jersey, USA, observed a decrease in number of taxa at the lower salinity stations. However, the decrease in fouling density in internal regions of Guanabara Bay does not involve the development of wood-boring communities as the same factors that limit the fouling development (high organic and oil pollution, low salinity) also limit the wood-boring activity.

In Ilha Grande Bay, due probably to great influence of seawater, there is not large salinity variation as it occurs in upper reaches of Guanabara Bay. Organic and oil pollution are still low despite the lack of suitable systems of sewers and the presence of oil terminals and shipyards in this area.

This bay has oligotrophic waters as it shows low phytoplanktonic biomass. Thus, a small food supply limits the development of fouling. Despite the presence of a significant benthic community in natural substrata, the process of colonization is very slow and this fact benefits the wood-boring organisms which are more independent of marine primary production since they feed basically on terrestrial wood. Densities of 460.0 individuals/dm^2 were found, due probably to the existence of great wood supply in this area. Besides, there are many natural harbors and protected areas dominated by mangroves which are important sources of cellulose.

Values of wood-boring density found in Ilha Grande Bay are among the highest ones cited in literature.

In temperate waters the diversity and sometimes, the density of wood-boring species are very low. Studies carried out by Ghobashy and Hassan (1980), in Suez Canal, considered highly infested wood panels with more than 80 burrows (on each face). This represents an approximate density of only 60 burrows/dm^2. Hoagland (1982) found, after twelve months, a wood-boring community dominated by 3 species with a density of 44 individuals/dm^2 approximately. In Canada, Walden, Allen and Trussell (1967) noticed a maximum density of 34 burrows/dm^2 for *Bankia setacea*. Yet, in Canada, Murray, Dowolcy, Walden and Allen (1967) found densities of up to 100 burrows/dm^2 after 16 weeks in relation to the same species. Comparing this result with the ones found in Ilha Grande Bay we noticed that the process of colonization in this bay is faster, as, after only 8 weeks, densities were four times higher than the ones found by those authors.

Trussell (1967) implies that the number of teredinids increases as latitude decreases.

Hoagland and Turner (1981) believe that it is possible to find 9 sympatric species of Teredinidae in tropical waters. We found exactly 9 species in Ilha Grande Bay, the same number found by Cooke et al. (1980) in Hawaii.

Despite literature citing that wood-boring activity is intense in tropical waters (Southwell e Bultman, 1971) this is not always true. Besides temperature, many factors influence on the wood-boring distribution such as salinity, wood supply, pollution and fouling development.

The principal difference between infestation of tropical and temperate waters is related to seasonal changes. In Ilha Grande Bay, no significant differences in density were detected during a one-year period of experiment. According to Trussell (1967), there is continuous larval production in areas where there are no significant changes in water temperature.

Some studies performed in temperate waters (Schetelma and Truitt, 1954; Kristensen, 1969; Bohn and Walden, 1970; Culliney, 1970; Tsunoda and Nishimoto, 1972; Hoagland and Turner, 1980; and Hoagland, 1982) showed that a raise in temperature is generally the factor that stimulates the process of sexual maturation and spawning of gametes or larvae, leading to a higher density of these organisms when the water temperature is higher. For instance, Tsunoda and Nishimoto (1972) found a density of 550 individuals per dm^2 in the temperate waters of Japan Sea after one month, a value even higher than the one found in Ilha Grande Bay.

Up to now we can notice that fouling and wood-boring communities structure reflect the local environmental conditions and this must be considered when one determines the best use of a coastal area.

Salinity has marked effects on fouling and wood-boring communities in Tijuca Lagoon. Here, species richness diminishes markedly as salinity decreases. However, greater biomass values of fouling organisms were found in the inner regions of the lagoon probably due to the high eutrophication level of its waters. However, the fouling community is only dominated by balanoids. Densities of wood-boring mollusks also diminish according to a decreasing gradient of salinity. Values 50 times higher in the mouth than at inner stations were detected.

A correlation between the low activity of Teredinidae and a decreasing gradient of salinity was also noticed by many studies (Schetelma and Truitt, 1954; Trussell, Greer and Lebrasseur, 1956; Krinstensen, 1969; Culliney, 1970; Rayner, 1979). Most of these studies were carried out in estuaries and they correlated greater incidence of Teredinidae to smaller rainfall, or to greater influence of seawater.

Competition between Teredinidae and Limnoriidae was observed in Tijuca Lagoon where densities of *Limnoria tripunctata* reach up to 380 individuals/dm^2. This biological interaction between these organisms was also studied by Fung and Morton (1976).

Although *Limnoria* densities were numerically higher than Teredinidae ones near the mouth of Tijuca Lagoon, damages caused by the latter ones to wooden structures were greater than those caused by the formed ones. This is due, mainly, to the high average length of teredinids.

Bastida and Torti (1972) and Fung and Morton (1976) emphasize that low salinities can be an environmental barrier to Limnoriidae, explaining the presence of these organisms in areas near the ocean.

Reduction of wood-boring activity in low-salinity areas of Tijuca Lagoon seems to be related to fouling development. In these areas fouling biomass was 10 times greater than the one found in areas near to the ocean and the community was dominated by balanoids. This certainly acts as a limiting factor of the development of a more significant wood-boring community.

High salinity influence on the development of these communities was studied at Itajuru Inlet. There, the number of fouling species found in areas near the ocean was the same as in the mouth of Guanabara Bay (27 species). However, there was a reduction with increasing gradient of salinity but not so steep as it was noticed in Tijuca Lagoon and Guanabara Bay. In Itajuru Inlet, 22 species were found in stations where salinity values reached up to 61 ppt. Nevertheless, biomass values increased four times with increasing salinity.

It seems that the most part of fouling organisms would rather settle on areas near the ocean in Araruama Lagoon. Such behavior is expected to occur in hypersaline lagoons (Emery and Stevenson, 1957, and Friedman, Krumbein, Buyce and Gerdes, 1985).

At the inner part of the channel, a raise in fouling biomass is caused by the development of balanoids, especially *Balanus amphitrite amphitrite*. According to Lacombe and Monteiro (1974), this is a cosmopolitan species which is very resistant to pollution and large variations of temperature or salinity.

The wood-boring isopod *Limnoria tripunctata* dominates in areas near the ocean with a density of 380 individuals/dm^2 which is similar to that found in Tijuca Lagoon. Its distribution is restricted to zones where salinities are similar to the ocean. However, teredinids occur as far as the inner regions of the channel, but its density is reduced in 50%.

As in Tijuca Lagoon, this reduction can also be related not only to salinity but also to a raise in fouling biomass in areas far from the ocean. In Itajuru Inlet, no significant differences between the mouth and the inner areas were observed, probably due to the level of eutrophication which is uniform along this channel.

Unfortunately, there are no available data in literature that relate the wood-boring distribution to high salinity conditions.

In summary, there is a greater development of fouling community, although less diversified and a lower wood-boring activity at the inner areas of Itajuru Inlet and Tijuca Lagoon due mainly to high or low salinities. These results should be taken into account during management of coastal lagoons and estuaries.

Acknowledgements: Funds for this project were granted by the Conselho Nacional de Desenvolvimento Científico e Tecnológico (CNPq) and by the Universidade Federal do Rio de Janeiro (CEPG/UFRJ).

REFERENCES

[1] Bastida, R. and M.R. Torti (1972). Organismos perfurantes de las costas argentinas. La prescncia de *Lyrodus pedicellutus* en el Puerto de Mar del Plata. B. Aires, *Physis* **31** (82): 39–50

[2] Bohn, A. and C.C. Waldcn (1970). Survey of marine borers in Canadian atlantic waters, *J. Fish. Res. Rd. Can.* **27**: 1151–1154.

[3] Clapp, W.F. (1946). Marine borer research committee. New York Harbour. Third Progress Report. 36 pp.

[4] Coelho, V.M.B. and M.R.M.B. Fonseca (1981). Problemas de eutroficação no Estado do Rio de Janeiro. Proc. XI Congresso Brasileiro de Engenharia Sanitária e Ambiental, Fortaleza, pp. 1–55.

[5] Cooke, W.J.; J.G. Grovhoug and P.J.Ching (1980). A survey of marine borrer activity in Hawaiian nearshore waters: effects of environmental conditions and epifauna. Proc. V Congresso Internacional de Corrosion Marina e Incrustaciones, pp. 155–174.

[6] Culliney, R.S. (1970). Larval biology and recruitment of the shipworms *Teredo navalis* and *Bankia gouldi* in the Newport Estuary, North Carolina. Ph.D. Thesis. Dept. Zoology. Duke University. N. Carolina.

[7] Emery, K.D. and R.E. Stevenson (1957). Estuaries and Lagoons (chapter 23) Geol. Soc. America **87** (1): 673–750.

[8] F.E.E.M.A., Fundação Estadual de Engenharia do Meio Ambiente, Rio de Janeiro (1984). Qualidade da água e do ar no Estado do Rio de Janeiro. Relatório de atividades do Departamento de Controle de Poluição da Feema, Rio de Janeiro, R.J.

[9] F.E.E.M.A, Fundação Estadual de Engenharia do Meio Ambiente, Rio de Janeiro (1987). A poluição da Baía de Guanabara: antecedentes e situação atual. Relatório da equipe de Divisão de Projetos (DIPRO).

[10] Friedman, G.M.; W. Krumbein; R. Buyce; and G. Gerdes (1985). Hypersaline ecossystems. The Gavish Sabkha. Ecological Studies Analysis and Synthesis. (53): 540 pp.

[11] Fung, L.F. and B. Morton (1976). Competition between Limnoriids and shipworms in the coastal waters of Hong Kong. Proceedings of the 4th International Congress on Marine Corrosion and Fouling, France, pp. 187–193.

[12] Ghobashy, A.F.A. and A.K. Kassan (1980). Notes on the wood boring in the Suez Canal. Proc. V Congreso Internacional de Corrosion Marina e Incrustaciones, pp. 93–98.

[13] Hoagland, K.E. (1982). Ecological studies on wood boring bivalves in the vicinity of the Oyster Creek Nuclear Generating Station, Report to the U.S. Nuclear Regulatory Research. Washington D.C.

[14] Hoagland, K.E. and R.D. Turner (1980). Range extension of Teredinidae (shipworms) and polychaetes in the vicinity of a temperature zone nuclear generating station. *Marine Biology* 58: 55–64.

[15] Hoagland, K.E. and R.D. Turner (1981). Evolution and adaptive radiation of wood boring bivalves (Pholadacea). *Malacologia* 21 (1-2): 115–148.

[16] Kristensen, I. (1969). Attacks by *T. navalis* L. on inner Danish waters in relation to environmental factors. Vidensk. Meddr. dansk. naturh. Foren. 132: 199–210.

[17] Lacombe, D. and W. Monteiro (1974). Balanideos como indicadores de poluição na Baia de Guanabara. *Rev. Brasil. Biol.* 34 (4): 633–644.

[18] Manyak, D.M. (1982). A device for collecting and study of wood boring molluscs, application to boring rates and boring movements of the shipworm *Bankia gouldi*. *Estuaries* 5 (5): 224–229.

[19] Medeiros, K.L.S. (1982). Um modelo de programação matemática para o controle de poluição em corpos d'água. Aplicação ao Sistema Lagunar de Jacarepaguá. M.Sc. Thesis, Universidade Federal Fluminense. Rio de Janeiro, R.J.

[20] Murray, A.; A.H. Dowsley; C.C. Walden; and I.V.F. Allen (1967). Loses in the pulp yield and quality resulting from "teredo" attack on logs stored in sea water. British Columbia Research Council, Reprint 314.

[21] Nagabhushanam, R. (1960). A note on the inhibition of marine wood boring molluscs by heavy fouling accumulation. *Sci. Cult.* 26: 127–128.

[22] Nair, N.B. and M. Saraswathy (1971). The biology of wood boring Teredinid molluscs. *Adv. Mar. Biol.* 9: 335–209

[23] Rastetter, E.B. and W.J. Cooke (1979). Responses of marine fouling communities to sewage abatement on Kaneohe Bay, Oahu, Hawaii. *Marine Biology* **53** (3): 271–280.

[24] Rayner, S.M. (1979). Comparation of the salinity range tolerated by Teredinids (Mollusca: Teredinidae) under controlled conditions with that observed in an estuary in Papua New Guinea. *Aust. J. Mar. Freshwat. Res.* **30**: 521–533.

[25] Schetelma, R.S. and R.V. Truitt (1954). Ecological factors related to the distribution of *Bankia gouldi* Bartsch in Chesapeake Bay. Chesapeake Biol. Lab. Publ. **100**: 1–31.

[26] Southwell, C.R. and J.D. Bultman (1971). Marine borer resistance of untreated woods over long periods of immersion in tropical waters. *Biotropica* **3**: 81–107.

[27] Trussell, P.C. (1967). Teredine borers (2). *Sea Front.* **13**: 234–243.

[28] Trussell, P.C.; B.A. Greer and R.J. Lebrasseur (1956). Protection of saw logs against marine borers. III. Storage ground study *Pulp. Pap. Can* **57** (2): 77–81.

[29] Tsunoda, K. and K. Nishimoto (1972). Studies on the shipworms. 1. The ocurrence and seasonal settlement of shipworms. *Wood. Res. Kyoto* **53**: 1–8.

[30] Walden, C.C.; I.V.F. Allen and P.C. Trussell (1967). Estimation of marine borer attack on wooden surfaces. *J. Fish. Res. Bd. Can.* **24**: 261–272.

[31] Weiss, C.M. (1948). An observation on the inhibition of marine wood destroyers by heavy fouling accumulation. *Ecology* **19** (1): 120.

THE COASTLINE BETWEEN RIO DE JANEIRO AND CABO FRIO

Dieter Muehe [1]   Carlos H. T. Corrêa [1]

1 INTRODUCTION

The coastline between Rio de Janeiro and Cabo Frio is characterized by successive long beach arcs, oriented in the East-West direction. The beaches are separated by rocky headlands resulting from the erosional retreat of the front scour of the coastal range (Fig. 1). The rectification of the coast was obtained through the building up of barrier beaches, often with double barriers, which locked the river mouth, thus originating a succession of lagoons. The result is an environment with very scenic features. The direction of the barriers, atypical for the Brazilian littoral, is related to the orientation of isobaths along the continental shelf (Kumar et al., 1977), which in turn is a consequence of cenozoic tectonism which affected the region (Asmus and Ferrari, 1978).

The most accepted idea about the evolution of those barrier beaches is that they would have developed by coastwise spit progradation from West to East, enclosing in this process the bays which had been formed by the flooding of fluvial valleys during the holocene transgression (Lamego, 1940, 1945). Recent work, however, tends to consider the evolution of the barriers as having mixed causes, i.e. by a combination of frontal and lateral progradation (Ponçano et al., 1979), and by landward migration according to transgressive oscillations of the relative sea level (Muehe, 1982, 1984; Maia et al., 1984; Coe Neto, 1984; Turq et al., 1986).

The difference in elevation between the older barriers, located further inland and higher, and the more recent ones (Fig. 2), reflects clearly the curves of relative sea level changes established at several locations along the coast between Bahia and Santa Catarina (Fig. 3), presenting a very similar configuration (Suguio et al. 1985). As can be observed, the relative sea level was higher than the present one on two or three occasions, another unusual characteristic, possibly resulting from changes in configuration of the geoid (Suguio and Martin, 1982). Surprisingly, there is evidence that the young barriers would be retreating (Muehe, 1984) and also that sand is being deposited on the top of many of these barriers during storms, whereas the curves of the relative sea level indicate a continuous drop of 1.5 m since 3,500 or 2,600 B.P. The barriers could have retreated at the beginning of the last

---

[1]Departamento de Geografia, Instituto de Geociências, Universidade Federal do Rio de Janeiro, Rio de Janeiro, RJ 21945, Brazil.

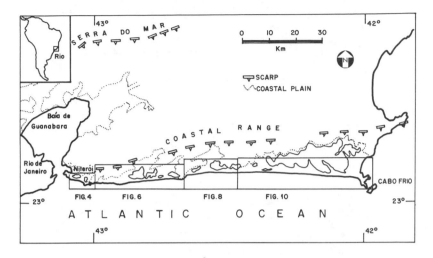

Figure 1: The coastline from Rio to Cabo Frio with the location of studied sections.

transgressive oscillation, but its eventual overwash by storm waves is occurring now and it is typical of a relative sea level rise. It is not clear yet whether these facts result from a possible rise in the sea level, not determined because of the uncertainty of the data of the last centuries, or from an increase in storm severity, or even from a differentiated neotectonic activity relative to other studied areas. Nevertheless, what really matters for the planning of the human occupation of the barrier beaches is the existence of signs of instability which will tend to be reinforced in the future because of an acceleration of eustatic sea level rise due to the greenhouse effect.

Climatic and oceanographical characteristics of the region result from alternation of effects due to the marine tropical anti-cyclone, typical of fair weather, with winds from NE to SE, and the arrival of cold fronts with strong winds from S to SW. Breaking wave heights, usually greater than 0.5 m, may reach 3 to 4 m during storms. Spring tide height is approximately 1.4 m, which causes the coastal processes to be relatively dominated by wave action instead of by the tide.

Occupation of the coastal zone has sharply increased since 1974, as a consequence of better accessibility afforded by the construction of a bridge between Rio de Janeiro and Niterói, as well as the growth of the metropolitan area. Due to lack of an urbanistic plan, the occupation was not always carried out in an adequate way, both in terms of location and from the aesthetic point of view. Since the law requiring that the coastal zone management should integrate federal, state and municipal agencies and the local communities was issued, there has been need for scientific data to prepare integrated thematic maps capable of furnishing the background assistance necessary for developing the management plans.

This work presents a preliminary view of some of the problems occurring along the coast between Niterói and Cabo Frio. These problems become more serious within the next 50 to 150 years, causing highly valued property to be lost as a

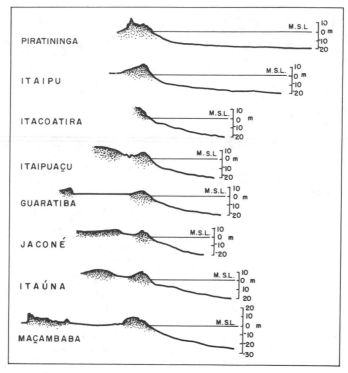

Figure 2: Transverse topographical profiles of barrier beaches of the studied area. Location of profile at the center of respective beach arc. Note the frequent presence of two distinct barriers.

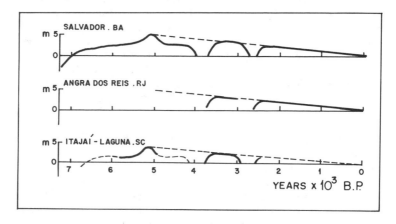

Figure 3: Selected relative sea-level curves for the last 7,000 years for different parts of the Brazilian coast. (After Suguio et al., 1985).

consequence of an already expected rise of the relative sea level.

2 METHODOLOGY

Inexistence of long term observations of relative sea level changes, sediment transport along the beach and historical evolution of the coastline forced the authors to base their conclusions on their own field observations as well as on the interpretation of aerophotographies. The mapping of the coastal zone is limited to the barrier beach, which is classified in terms of its risk level as: em secure, *caution* or *dangerous*, following work by Pilkey *et al.* (1978). This classification takes into account the size of vegetation, presence of dunes causing an increase of the elevation of the barrier, run-up or overwash of the barrier by storm waves, as well as evidence of erosion on the front or in the back side of the barrier. It must be emphasized that no substantial modification of the current erosional processes is expected in the near future, which has already been observed by local residents. However, these processes may become significantly stronger if a relative sea level rise occurs. The borders of each zone are not very precise either, when taking into account the vast extension of the area being studied and the difficulty of access to some points, especially on the Maçambaba barrier beach, between Saquarema and Cabo Frio.

For a clearer cartographic representation, the littoral will be described by segments corresponding to the natural division imposed by the headlands, which isolate different physiographic units, or series of beaches.

3 CHARACTERISTICS OF THE LITTORAL

3.1 Piratininga, Itaipu and Itacoatiara

In this first segment (Fig. 4), Piratininga and Itaipu, where intense urbanization is in progress, represent the first two beaches east of Guanabara Bay. Islands and a headland, the Ponta de Itaipu, protect these beaches from the stronger action of SE waves, though leaving Piratininga and half of Itaipu (also known as Camboinhas Beach) exposed to storm waves, as is the case of Itacoatiara Beach, where the most valued development in the region has been established.

Dunes in the back of Piratininga and Itaipu beaches offer a good protection against marine erosion. However, at the top of the barrier in Piratininga, roads and a sidewalk were built along the beach. In order to protect these works, a sea wall was built in the limit of the back-shore, which disrupted the equilibrium profile, resulting in the destruction of about 1 km of sea-wall, part of the sidewalk on the western half of the beach (Fig. 5), and incipient erosion in the eastern end.

This significant erosional effect is rather the result of inadequate human interference, by interposing an obstacle within the dynamical profile of the beach, than the result of intensification of wave action. For this reason, it can not be said that Piratininga is under erosive processes which may affect the urbanized area. It is worth calling attention to the risk of attempting to fix the top of the beach profile, and that is why this region was classified as *caution zone*. On the other hand, in Itaipu, the gradual elevation of the berm and the increased protection furnished by the islands, allows us to consider this area as a *secure zone*. Itacoatiara, in spite

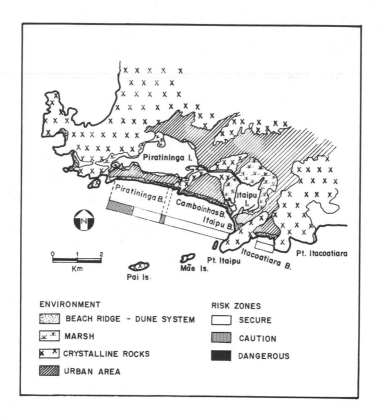

Figure 4: Evaluation of coastline stability from Piratininga beach to Itacoatiara beach.

Figure 5: An example of recovery of the storm profile of the beach submitted to inadequate interference by man at Piratininga beach.

of being more exposed to wave action, may also be considered as *secure* because of the high elevation of the top of the beach, except on its west end, where problems may happen in the future due to constructions which are too close to the front side of the top of the barrier.

3.2 Itaipuaçu and Guaratiba

Itaipuaçu and Guaratiba beaches are located between the Ponta Itacoatiara and Ponta Negra, separated by a cuspated foreland, a result from wave refraction and diffraction by Maricás Islands (Fig. 6). A coarse sand, characteristic of the western half of Itaipuaçu beach, reflects relict sands found in the adjacent inner shelf (Muehe, 1988) and, for its exceptional purity, sorting, and roundness, it is adequate for hydraulic fractioning in oil wells, being extensively exploited. The geomorphological consequence of this coarse grain size is a steep subaereal profile and a narrow surf zone, which, in its turn, reduces wave dissipation. As waves break closer to the shore, the beach offers risks for swimming and is subject to large variations in bottom topography. Wave energy is very high in this region, and quite often waves run up to reach the top of the berm, 7 m above mean sea level, and occasionally, during storms, the beach experiences overwash. Evidence of overwash is found along two thirds of the beach arc, disappearing only from the beginning of the cuspated foreland until Guaratiba Beach, near the Maricá Lagoon. In this portion, the beach sand presents a distribution of diameter appropriate to the formation of small dunes located at the crest of the beach and protecting the barrier beach from erosion. Excluding the western end of Itaipuaçu, very little urbanization has been developed on the most recent barrier. Further east, towards Barra de Maricá, in front of Guaratiba Lagoon, this situation changes, with houses built close to the frontal edge of the barrier beach, showing once again evidence of erosion and wave action effecting the top of the barrier. Barrier overwash is complete immediately to the east of Barra de Maricá, where the back side of the barrier beach is covered

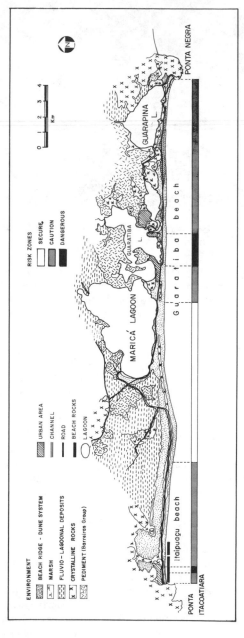

Figure 6: Evaluation of coastline stability from Ponta Itacoatiara to Ponta Negra.

Figure 7: A sand sheet deposited at the back side of the barrier due to overwash in the vicinity of Barra de Maricá.

by a veneer of sand carried by overwash (Fig. 7). Further east, up to Ponta Negra, the presence of dunes and the subsequent elevation of the top of the barrier make this area relatively secure. However, residences built too close to the seaward edge of the barrier, already suffer from the effects of storms, when exceptionally high waves reach the urbanized area.

3.3 Ponta Negra and Saquarema

Between the promontory of Ponta Negra and the town of Saquarema, extends the beach of Jaconé (Fig. 8), whose portion in front of Saquarema Lagoon is also named Saquarema Beach.

In front of the Jaconé Lagoon and up to nearby the middle of the beach arc, human occupation of the younger barrier is still reduced. In most of this part, the elevation of the top of the barrier beach is high enough not to be affected by waves, but at some spots, there is localized erosion of the seaward face of the barrier. Right in front of Jaconé Lagoon, just where a small development has been built, the elevation of the barrier is lower than in the vicinity, and there are verbal accounts and evidence of wave overwash as well as of the existence, in the past, of a tidal inlet. The discontinuous presence of dunes produces an alternation of *secure* and *caution* beach segments, as shown in Fig. 8. Along the rest of the beach arc, located in front of Saquarema Lagoon, there is strong evidence of erosion of the seaward face of the barrier, affecting the road which runs along the top of the barrier (Fig. 9). The small width of the barrier in this section forced the houses to be built too close to the road; the house foundations, usually on piles, were set on the back side of the barrier. With its high density of occupation, the final aspect of this area is aesthetically unpleasant, and at the same time, due to the signs of instability which have been observed, makes it a high risk area if there should be an acceleration of the sea level rise, which will then cause costly property loss.

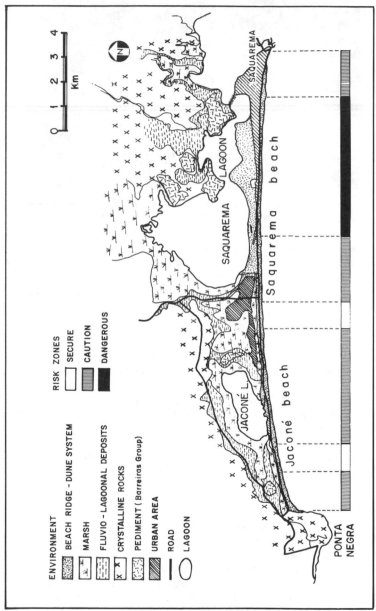

Figure 8: Evaluation of coastline stability from Ponta Negra to Saquarema.

Figure 9: Erosion of the backshore near Saquarema affecting the road built on the top of the barrier.

3.4 Itaúna and Maçambaba

Between Saquarema and Arraial do Cabo, there is a small beach called Itaúna and a 47 km long beach called Maçambaba which encloses the Araruama Lagoon (Fig. 10).

In Itaúna, the small slope of the bottom near the beach causes the breaking waves to be appropriate for surfing, which makes it very popular. The presence of medium size sand, with fractions favorable to the formation of dunes and the occurrence of small rocky islands at the limit between Itaúna and Maçambaba, protects this part of the beach against wave action. Further east, between Itaúna and Vermelha Lagoon, the beach barrier is narrow, and uncovered by either trees or bushes. The storm berm is placed slightly below the top of the barrier, which in turn does not show signs of being overwashed. As in other barrier beaches, there are signs of landward migration, as for instance the disappearance of spits on the backside of the barrier. However, one can not be sure whether this is an ongoing process. Because of the narrowness of the barrier, the lack of dunes and vegetation, the barrier was considered as a *caution zone*, rather because of its potential instability in a scenario of sea level rise than of its present state of stability. Differently from the inner barrier, no residences have been built on the outer barrier, a situation which should be maintained. An intense activity of real estate throughout this region would change this situation very soon.

Between Vermelha Lagoon and the beginning of Gaivotas Bay, inside Araruama Lagoon, the ocean face of the younger barrier seems to be secure. In some portions, the barrier is narrow but the abundance of dunes forms an adequate protection. Nevertheless, it would also be important to refrain from human occupation of areas too close to the ocean border of the barrier. On the back side of the barrier, facing Araruama Lagoon, there is strong evidence of beach erosion. In Figueira Bay, about 200 m of barrier have been lost (Muehe and Corrêa, 1988). A similar process is happening at Tiririca Bay. Roots of trees planted along the margin of the lagoon,

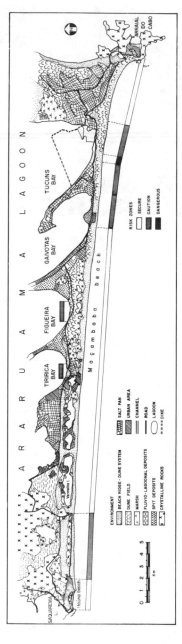

Figure 10: Evaluation of coastline stability from Saquarema to Cabo Frio Is.

Figure 11: Erosion of the backshore at Maçambaba beach.

especially at Figueira Bay, are exposed, evidence of the progress of the erosional process.

Further towards the east, on the portion between Gaivotas Bay and Tucuns Bay, erosion of the sea face of the barrier is strong enough to affect the road that runs along the top of the barrier (Fig. 11). In spite of the presence of dunes, waves occasionally reach the top of the barrier during storms. In front of the Tucuns Bay there is a depression of the terrain which seems to be the result of wind blow out. The older barrier no longer exists along the margin of the lagoon, probably having eroded before the formation of spits in the lagoon. These spits now seem to protect the margin of the lagoon along the Figueira Bay. In Tucuns Bay, dikes constructed to increase salt concentration also give protection to the margin.

At the eastern end, up to the town of Arraial do Cabo, several factors like the Island of Cabo Frio, which gives shelter against waves from SE, the decrease in bottom slope, and the presence of dunes, indicate that this section is better protected from wave action.

4 FINAL CONSIDERATIONS

Barrier beaches are the best protection for the coastal zone against the effects of storms. Because the beach reacts dynamically, its profile and planform adapt to the wave direction and energy, with resulting changes of topography. In case of a sea level rise, the barrier beach tries to maintain its equilibrium by migrating shoreward and increasing its height. Along this process of accommodation, the barrier is eroded on the seaward face and the sea bottom is elevated due to sediment deposition (Bruun 1962). As long as sediment is available, the barrier beach is preserved, although its position moves. Therefore, any human intervention, like sand mining or attempts to stabilize the barrier, may only amplify the effects of coastal erosion.

There is no certainty of the elevation of the sea level due to the greenhouse effect. The expectations within the scientific community, though, favor the opinion of a sea level rise. Therefore, a warning should be made that the occupation of the barrier beaches may become in future an economic as well as a social problem whose solution might be too costly.

It is recommended that, in coastal zone planning, directions should be included which restrict human occupation of higher potential risk areas and also restrict sand mining of these areas.

Acknowledgements: The present work was part of a research project on coastal geomorphology approved by the Program for Geology and Marine Geophysics (PGGM). Financial resources were granted by the Committee for Marine Resources (CIRM) and by the Universidade Federal do Rio de Janeiro (UFRJ).

REFERENCES

[1] Asmus, H.E. and A.L. Ferrari (1978). Hipótese sobre a causa do tectonismo cenozóico na região sudeste do Brasil. *in:* Aspectos estruturais da margem continental leste e sudeste do Brasil. Série Projeto REMAC, n.4, CENPES, PETROBRAS, Rio de Janeiro, p.75–88.

[2] Bruun, P. (1962). Sea level rise as a cause of shore erosion. *J. Waterways and Harbors Div.*, ASCE, **88**: 117–130.

[3] Coe Neto, R. (1984). Algumas considerações sobre a origem do sistema lagunar de Araruama. *in:* "Simposio sobre Restingas Brasileiras", Niterói, Proc., p.61–63.

[4] Kumar, N.; L.A.P. Gamboa; B.C. Schriber; and J. Mascle (1977). Geologic history and origin of São Paulo Plateau (Southeastern Brazilian margin), comparison with the Angola margin and the early evolution of the Northern South Atlantic. *in:* P.R. Supko *et al.*, Initial reports of the deep sea drilling project. U.S. Government Printing Office, v.39, Washington, 1977, p. 927–945.

[5] Lamego, A.R. (1940). Restingas na costa do brasil. Bol. Div. Geologia e Mineralogia, Boletim 96, Rio de Janeiro, 66 pp.

[6] Lamego, A.R. (1945). Ciclo evolutivo das lagunas fluminenses. DNPM, Rio de Janeiro. Boletim 118.

[7] Maia, M.C.A.C.; L. Martin; J.M. Flexor; and E.G.A. Azevedo (1984). Evolução holocênica da planície costeira de Jacarepaguá (RJ). *in:* Congr. Bras. Geologia, 33, SBG. v.1: 105–118.

[8] Muehe, D. (1982). Evidence of landward translation of beach barriers east of Guanabara Bay. Latin American Regional Conference, Rio de Janeiro, 1983. Abstracts. International Geographical Union. p. 91–92.

[9] Muehe, D. (1984). Evidências de recuo dos cordões litorâneos em direção ao continente no litoral do Rio de Janeiro. Proc. Simpósio sobre Restingas Brasileiras, Niterói, 1984, p.75-80

[10] Muehe, D. (1989). Distribuição e caracterização dos sedimentos arenosos da plataforma continental interna entre Niterói e Ponta Negra, RJ. *Rev. Bras. Geoc.* **19** (1). (In press.)

[11] Muehe, D. and C.H.T. Corrêa (1988). Os 'arenitos de restinga' do cordão litorâneo da Maçambaba/Lagoa de Araruama. Cong. Bras. Geol, 35, Belém, SBG, v.2: 553–561.

[12] Pilkey Jr., O.H.; W.J. Neal; O.H. Pilkey; and S.R. Riggs (1978). "From Currituck to Calabash — living with North Carolina barrier islands". Duke University Press. 245 pp.

[13] Ponçano, W.L.; J.V. Fúlfaro; and A.F. Gimenez (1979). Proc. Simpósio Regional de Geologia, 2, Rio Claro, v.1, p. 291–304.

[14] Suguio, K. and L. Martin (1982). Progress in research on Quaternary sea-level changes and coastal evolution in Brazil. Proc. Symp. on Holocene Sea-Level Fluctuations, Magnitude and Causes, 1981, Dept. Geology, USC: 166–181.

[15] Suguio, K.; L. Martin; A.C.S.P. Bittencourt; J.M.L. Dominguez; J-M. Flexor; and A.E.G. Azevedo (1985). Flutuações do nível relativo do mar durante o Quaternário superior ao longo do litoral brasileiro e suas implicações na sedimentação costeira. Rev. Bras. Geoc. 15 (4): 273–286.

[16] Turq, B.; R. Coe; and J.M. Froidefond (1986). Variability of beach ridges on the coast of Maricá (Rio de Janeiro, Brazil). in: J. Barassa (ed.), "Quaternary of South America and Antarctic Peninsula". Rotterdam, A.A. Balkema. v.4: 45–57.

HYDROBIOLOGICAL CHARACTERIZATION OF GUANABARA BAY

Letícia Maria Mayr [1]   Denise Rivera Tenenbaum [1]   Maria Célia Villac [1]

Rodolfo Paranhos [1]   Catarina R. Nogueira [1]   Sérgio L. C. Bonecker [2]

Ana Cristina T. Bonecker [2]

1 INTRODUCTION

Guanabara Bay forms an ecological unity with serious environmental problems derived from an accelerated and unorganized process of urbanization without the necessary support.

The UFRJ/Institute of Biology soon became aware of these problems and since 1985 it has been developing systematic studies about the bay. One of the purposes of such studies is to furnish basic technical information for the project of the gradual recovery of Guanabara Bay, currently in progress at the State environmental agency (FEEMA), which is in accordance with the national coastal zone plan (PNGC). The results of these studies will benefit approximately 10 million people in the metropolitan area of Rio de Janeiro, the second largest urban concentration in Brazil, equal to 80% of the State population (FEEMA, 1988).

Based on data obtained from previous isolated studies, a new project was elaborated so as to establish the systematization and planning of a series of field studies which would finally furnish the hydrobiological characterization of the bay.

2 GENERAL ASPECTS OF GUANABARA BAY

The bay, located in the State of Rio de Janeiro, Brazil (Fig. 1), has a total area of 381 km² and has several islands. The total volume of water is estimated as 2×10^9 m³, and it has a perimeter of 131 km (FEEMA, op. cit.). It is mostly oriented in a N-S direction, has a total extension of 30 km, and the entrance is 1.8 km wide. The region has a tropical humid climate, and its rainy season is during the summer months (December through March) (IBGE, 1977). The watershed of the bay has an approximate area of 4,000 km², and is limited by the mountain range called "Serra do Mar", located at most 20 km from the bay margins. The fresh water contribution is derived not only from the 35 rivers that flow into the bay, none of them of significant discharge (Araujo and Maciel, 1979), but also from

---

[1]Departamento de Biologia Marinha, Instituto de Biologia, Universidade Federal do Rio de Janeiro. Rio de Janeiro, RJ 21941, Brazil.

[2]Departamento de Zoologia, Instituto de Biologia, Universidade Federal do Rio de Janeiro. Rio de Janeiro, RJ 21941, Brazil.

wastes input. Sedimentation along the mouth of those rivers is strong. Tides are semi-diurnal with diurnal inequalities, and their maximum height is 1.4 m.

Hydraulic characteristics should be interpreted considering the balance between fresh water contributions and the tidal prism. Depths are not uniform: along the main channel, which follows the major axis of the bay, depths reach an average of 20 m, whereas near the northwest end the bay is 1 m deep during ebb tide.

This is an extremely important ecosystem considering its multiple uses: recreation, fishing, navigation, water supply, and waste dilution. However, it is also a place undergoing a fast process of degradation, endangering some of these uses.

According to the FEEMA report, 10,000 industries, the Rio de Janeiro Port Authority and 16 oil terminals, 12 shipyards, and 2 oil refineries are found in the area drained by the Guanabara Bay, the second largest industrial concentration in the country. The discharge of organic matter into the bay reaches 465 ton/day, out of which 68 ton/day receive adequate treatment. Industrial liquid wastes are responsible for 25% of the organic material contribution and almost 100% of the pollution caused by toxic substances and heavy metals Cr and Cu proved to be at critical levels in sediment samples (Lacerda et al., 1988). Oil pollution is estimated to be 9.5 ton/day.

Another complex problem is related to urban wastes: about 7,000 ton/day of garbage is thrown out at city dumps, some of them located on the margins of the bay. This practice of increasing the urban area at low cost — aiming basically to solve a much deeper social problem — has several consequences as to the water quality of the bay. For instance, it changes the patterns of tidal induced currents, creates areas of sediment deposition, modifies the nearby bathymetry because of consolidation of the bottom material, besides affecting the water quality itself. Added to the problem of deforestation of the slopes of "Serra do Mar" and the destruction of the mangroves at the inner reaches of the bay, a gradual reduction of depths has been observed in the bay (Amador, 1980).

Therefore, man action has caused serious hazards, both in the ecological and the socio-economic sense: the water of the bay is inappropriate for bathing, the area which was originally covered by mangroves has been reduced by half, fishing activities have been reduced by 90% in the past 20 years, and intense sedimentation has forced an increase of dredging costs for maintaining navigable channels. Land fills have altered patterns of circulation, affecting the ecological balance of some areas in an irreversible way.

Despite its advanced state of degradation, Guanabara Bay plays an important role in the life of the citizens who live around its margins. It is believed that, through actions of environmental control, the total recuperation of the quality of the water may be achieved, as it has happened in other parts of the world. Both corrective and preventive measures should be taken now so that the recuperation and the maintenance of the multiple uses of the bay should succeed in the long term. Therefore, a first step would be the understanding of the dynamics of the bay environment.

Besides water quality studies, the need for the hydrobiological characterization of the Guanabara Bay comes from the fact that it still is a life resource area of great importance. In this sense, planktonic organisms have been widely used as bioindicators, because when they are subjected to the environmental conditions they are unable to maintain their distribution against the movement of water masses (Balech, 1977). Moreover, considering that the plankton is the base line of the food chain in aquatic environments, any severe change in its dynamics will probably reflect on the other trophic levels, including man.

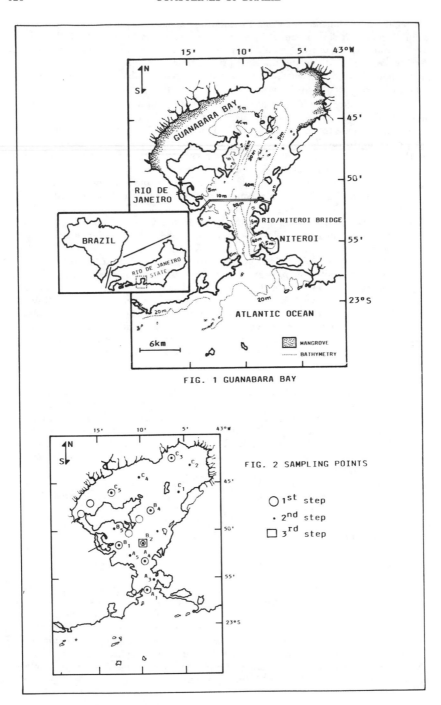

FIG. 1 GUANABARA BAY

FIG. 2 SAMPLING POINTS

○ 1st step
• 2nd step
□ 3rd step

The great importance of the Guanabara Bay as a supplying port was already recognized by the Challenger Expedition (1830), which collected the first plankton samples at its adjacent area. Isolated descriptive studies of the planktonic communities in the bay were developed in the beginning of this century. However, only in 1975 a systematic sampling program was established by FEEMA. At the same time, the Guanabara Bay became the target of academic studies of several university research centers, among them the UFRJ/Institute of Biology which plays an active role in the understanding of the dynamics of this ecosystem.

3 METHODOLOGY

The studies that led to the hydrobiological characterization of Guanabara Bay followed three sequential steps (Fig. 3).

The first step was the compilation of available data. A detailed bibliographic survey was carried out in 1984, as well as personal contacts with Institutes that work in the studied area, and thus untreated data was obtained. Data acquired at FEEMA derived from water samples collected monthly at 13 sampling points (Fig. 2) from 1980 to 1983, and analyzed according to APHA (1980). Temperature and salinity data obtained by PORTOBRAS (The Brazilian Port Authority Holding Company) in 1983 (12 hour sampling in summer and winter, during spring and neap tides), were also taken into consideration.

On a second step, the studies focused on the planktonic communities. The bay was divided into three areas with five sampling points in each one of them (Fig. 2): closer to the entrance to the bay (area A), in the inner reaches of the bay (area C), and an intermediate region (area B). Phytoplankton was sampled with Van Dorn bottle (5m deep), and the zooplankton and the ictioplankton were collected by Hensen nets (horizontal surface hauls) of $200 \mu m$ and $500 \mu m$ mesh sizes, respectively.

The third step intended to evaluate the influence of diel and tidal cycles (on spring tides) during the four seasons (October/86, January, April and July/87). A fixed sampling point was chosen in the main circulation channel (Fig. 2), where field measurements and water samples were taken every three hours, at three different depths: surface ($\approx 0.25m$), midwater (5m) and near the bottom ($\approx 18m$). Following the same time schedule, the zooplankton and ictioplankton were collected by horizontal surface hauls.

The samples were analyzed with the following analytical methodologies: temperature and salinity by a Beckman termosalinometer; dissolved oxygen by Winkler-azide; reactive phosphate by ascorbic acid; nitrite by diazotation; ammonia by indophenol blue; and chlorophyll a by the spectrophotometric method. All of them, except for temperature and salinity, are described by Parsons et al. (1984). The phytoplankton was analyzed by a settling technique (Utermohl, 1958) and total density is expressed in cells.l^{-1}, except for the Cyanophyceae (fil.l^{-1}). Zooplankton and ictioplankton densities are expressed in org.m^{-3}.

Data treatment was performed as follows: 1) the spatial distribution mapping (first step) was achieved by the SYMAP-5.2 System (Dudnik, 1971); 2) species diversity was calculated by the Shannon index (Frontier, 1983); 3) the intervals used for the spatial-time profiles (third step) were established by the Sturge's algorithm (Gerardi and Silva, 1981); and 4) the similarity matrices of samples were constructed based on the Czekanowsky index (second step) and on the Spearman Rank index (third step) and clustered into dendrograms by the WPGMA technique (Legendre and Legendre, 1979).

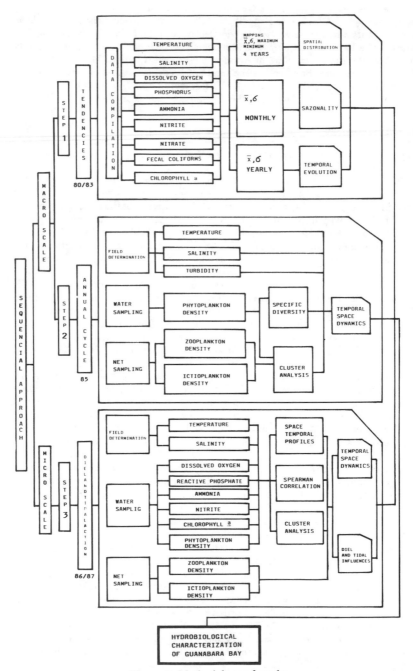

Figure 3: Methodology of study.

4 RESULTS AND DISCUSSION

4.1 First Step

Salinity data, which varied from 13.5 to 36.9, showed, not only the coastal water input, through the highest concentrations in the bottom, but also the freshwater contribution (rivers and wastes), through the lowest concentrations on the surface (Fig. 4a,b). The spatial gradient determined by salinity variations (an amplitude of 10.0 close to the entrance to the bay and of 20.0 in its inner reaches) is less evident for the temperature distribution (Fig. 4c,d). According to Pritchard's (1967) point of view of an estuary, these results confirm the estuarine nature of the studied area.

The parameters related to organic discharge (nutrients, biochemical oxygen demand, and total and fecal coliforms) presented the highest mean values and the highest standard deviations on the northwestern side of the bay. Because of the strong correlation found between total phosphorus and chlorophyll $\underline{a}$ (r=0.920**, Mayr et al., 1986), these parameters were chosen to illustrate the pattern described above (Fig. 4e,f,g). The intense eutrophication of this area results from the great amount of domestic and industrial discharge, associated with the deficient circulation due to several landfills on the shore.

The nutrient ranges (N-NO$_2^-$ = nd–3.5; N-NO$_3^-$ = nd–59.9; N-NH$_3$ = nd–142.0 ; P-PO$_4^{3-}$ = nd–3.2 μM) show a great spatial-time variation in the degree of eutrophication of the bay waters. The same high levels of nutrients are found in other densely urbanized and industrialized places, such as the Todos os Santos Bay (Bahia) in the northeast part of Brazil (SIC,1983), in Tokyo Bay, Japan (Brandini and Aruga, 1983), and in Delaware Bay, USA (Sharp et al., 1982). The variations observed for the nutrients reflect not only the hydrodynamics of the bay (cleaner water along the main circulation channel), but also seasonal changes.

The seasonal evolution of the parameters studied is presented by the variations of temperature and salinity (Fig. 5a), and the consequences of these variations on the other parameters is illustrated by the ammonia and the dissolved oxygen changes (Fig. 5b). The heavy tropical rains in summer surpass the intense evaporation (high temperatures), leading to the dilution of the bay waters during this period of time. As a consequence, the lowest values of salinity and nutrient concentrations are found during the summer. The high nutrient levels found during the winter (dry weather season), may be responsible for the decrease in the dissolved oxygen level, due to its utilization by organic matter decomposition (Head, 1985).

The annual evolution of fecal coliform throughout the studied period (1980–1983) reflects the lack of an urban infrastructure capable of supporting the increasing development of the Rio de Janeiro metropolitan area. The increase of fecal coliforms (Fig. 6a) is also observed in the ammonia levels (Fig. 6b), while the dissolved oxygen concentrations is decreasing as time goes by (Fig. 6c).

4.2 Second Step

Temperature and salinity variations confirm the spatial-time distribution found on the first step. The hot rainy season (January–April) and the dry colder weather (June–August) caused the variations found in water temperature (18.0 – 30.0°C) and salinity (21.0 – 36.0) during 1985. Turbidity data demonstrate the influence of the coastal water in area A (clearer water), as well as the assessment of the amount of debris from rivers and wastes on areas B and C (Fig. 7). Both influences also affect the salinity distribution. The planktonic organisms reflected the environment conditions.

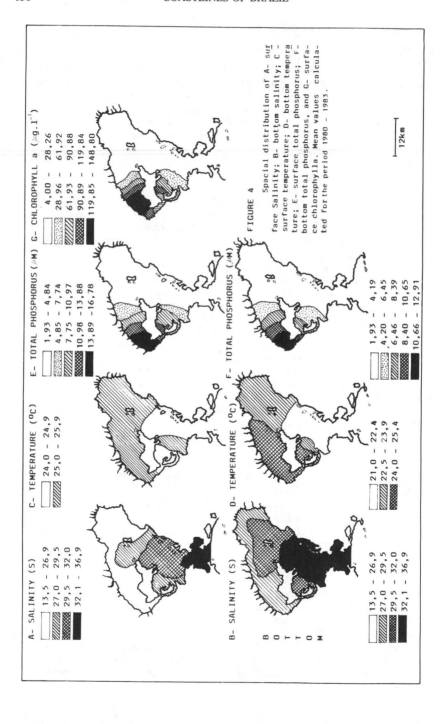

A- SALINITY (S)

13,5 – 26,9
27,0 – 29,5
29,5 – 32,0
32,1 – 36,9

C- TEMPERATURE (°C)

24,0 – 24,9
25,0 – 25,9

E- TOTAL PHOSPHORUS (μM)

1,93 – 4,84
4,85 – 7,74
7,75 –10,97
10,98 –13,88
13,89 –16,78

G- CHLOROPHYLL a (μg.l⁻¹)

4,00 – 28,26
28,96 – 61,92
61,93 – 90,88
90,89 – 119,84
119,85 – 148,80

B- SALINITY (S)

BOTTOM

13,5 – 26,9
27,0 – 29,5
29,5 – 32,0
32,1 – 36,9

D- TEMPERATURE (°C)

21,0 – 22,4
22,5 – 23,9
24,0 – 25,4

F- TOTAL PHOSPHORUS (μM)

1,93 – 4,19
4,20 – 6,45
6,46 – 8,39
8,40 – 10,65
10,66 – 12,91

12km

FIGURE 4

Spacial distribution of A- surface Salinity; B- bottom salinity; C - surface temperature; D- bottom temperature; E- surface total phosphorus; F- bottom total phosphorus, and G- surface chlorophylla. Mean values calculated for the period 1980 – 1983.

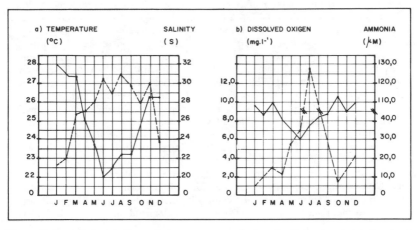

Figure 5: Seasonal variations of a) temperature (—) and salinity (- - -), b) dissolved oxygen (—) and ammonia (- - -). Mean values of surface data for each month from 1980 to 1983.

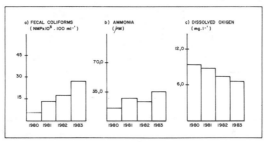

Figure 6: Temporal variations of a) fecal coliforms, b) ammonia, and c) dissolved oxygen. Mean values of surface data for each year from 1980 to 1983.

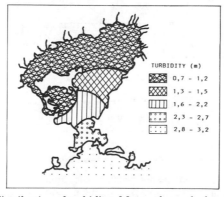

Figure 7: Spatial distribution of turbidity. Mean values calculated for each sampling point for 1985.

An unexpected high phytoplanktonic variability (170 taxa) is opposed to low species diversity index values (50% $\leq$ 2.0 bits.cel^{-1}). Signs of environmental stress are caused by blooms of several species: *Skeletonema costatum* Greville (an opportunistic species), *Eutreptia lanowii* Steuer (an indication of organic matter), and *Protoperidinium trochoideum* (Stein) Lemmerman (known to cause red tides) (Villac, 1988). The high Cyanophyceae density (10^6 fil.l^{-1}), characteristic of eutrophicated waters (Carr and Whitton, 1982), reaches outstanding concentrations during the summer period and in area C, probably due to the well defined freshwater request of this group (Fogg *et al.*,1973). The same intense phytoplanktonic growth ($10^5 - 10^7$ cells.l^{-1}) has already been found and can be understood as a consequence of the fertilizing effect of the organic matter (Sevrin-Reyssac *et al.*, 1979).

The cluster analysis (Fig. 8) shows the following spatial-time trend for the phytoplankton: the summer populations (group I) stand out from the rest of the year (group II); the most significant groups (pairs) show different populations for areas A and C, and mixed populations for area B. This pattern is due to qualitative changes in the phytoplankton specific composition, mainly detected by variations in the diatom community, a group that has strict ecological limits (Bourrelly, 1968).

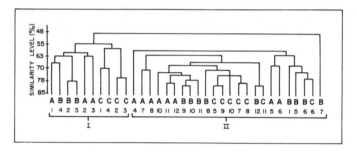

Figure 8: Display of samples derived from the similarity matrix using the Czekanovsky index. Variables: 170 taxa of phytoplankton. Observations: mean values of the organisms calculated for each area (A,B,C) for every month (numbers).

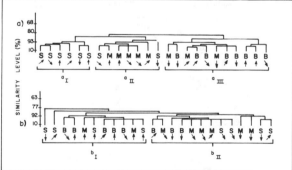

Figure 9: Cluster display of samples derived from the similarity matrix using Spearman Rank index for January (a) and July (b): S (surface), M (midwater), B (bottom), ↑ (high water), ↓ (low water), ↗ (flood tide), and ↘ (ebb tide).

The same spatial-time distribution is found in the zooplankton and ictioplankton, though in this case the quantitative variations outweigh the qualitative changes. Area A presented the highest densities of organisms $(1.4 \times 10^3 - 2.4 \times 10^4$ org.m$^{-3})$, mainly in summer time. Copepoda were the dominant group (*Acartia lilljeborghi* Geisbrecht and *Paracalanus parvus* Claus) followed by Cladocera and Crustacea larvae. High densities of *Muggiaea kocki* Wild and *Thalia democratica* Forskal demonstrate the coastal water contribution in area A (Boltovskoy, 1981). In area B, organism densities varied from 2.2×10^3 to 6.9×10^3 org.m^{-3}, where Copepoda dominance was followed by Appendicularia and fish eggs. Area C presented the lowest densities $(300 - 700$ org.m$^{-3})$, with the predominance of Copepoda and Appendicularia.

The results obtained in the first and second steps allow for the understanding of the hydrobiology of the bay in a macro-scale view. However, the significant changes that occur in micro-scale bases have not yet been detected. Thus, the influences of diel and tidal cycles are investigated in the third step.

4.3 Third Step

The results presented in this step have been analyzed by using the most representative information.

January (summer) and July (winter) have been chosen as sampling periods to illustrate both diel and tidal influences, because these months show the seasonal pattern found before (Fig. 10a,b). The ictioplankton also indicates a seasonal trend, through outstanding densities of eggs of the Engraulidae family in July: cold winter waters and plenty feeding resources allow for favorable conditions for the natural reproductive cycle of this group in this period of the year.

Diel influence can be noticed mainly on surface samples. A slight increase in temperature values during daytime is followed by greater phytoplankton, chlorophyll a, and dissolved oxygen concentrations, probably due to the intense photosynthesis of daylight (Parsons *et al.*, 1977). The high zooplanktonic density found during the night suggests a migration pattern, although this hypothesis will only be confirmed when the identification of the organisms is completed.

Considering the water column as a whole, during ebb tides the increase in the organic matter input is responsible for high nutrient levels and therefore responsible for the oxygen consumption, despite the higher concentrations of chlorophyll a and of phytoplankton. Higher salinity of coastal waters influence the bay waters near the bottom, mainly on flood tides. This influence is confirmed by lower concentrations of chlorophyll a and of phytoplankton, accompanied by species of strictly marine habitat:*Doliolum nationalis* Borgert (Boltovskoy,*op.cit.*), *Rhizosolenia alta* f. *gracillima* (Cleve) Grunow and *R. styliformis* Brightwell (Navarro, 1981), and *Thalassiothrix mediterranea* Pavillard (Navarro, 1983).

Tidal action is directly influenced by the degree of the water column thermal stratification. The temperature vertical profile in January shows a stratification pattern reflected in the cluster analysis (Fig. 9a): surface (group a_I), midwater (group a_{II}), and bottom (group a_{III}). Tidal influence in January can only be identified by the negative correlation between dissolved oxygen and nutrients (P-PO$_4^{3-}$: $r = -.572$**; N-NH$_3$: $r = -.872$**), as well as by the negative correlations between salinity and chlorophyll a ($r = -0.801$**), and between salinity and phytoplankton density ($r = -0.738$**). The lack of thermal stratification in July (Fig. 10b) allows for water column homogeneity, mainly in high waters and low waters. The cluster analysis shows that in July (Fig. 9b) both flood and ebb tide conditions (groups b_I

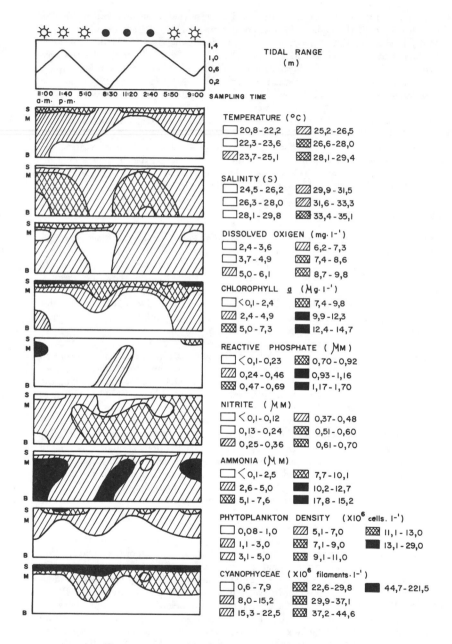

Figure 10: A: Isolines graphs for January/87.

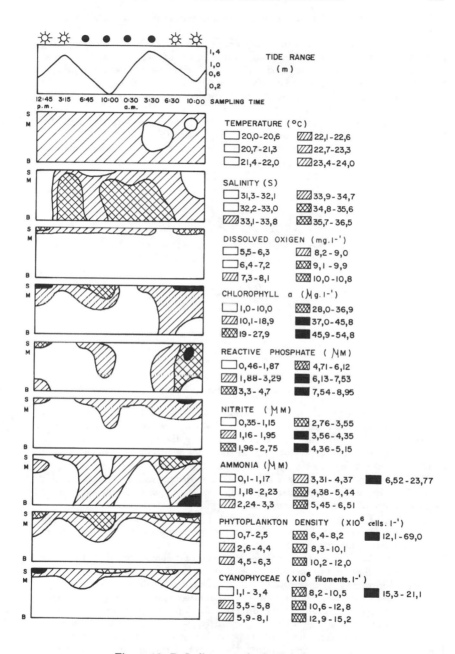

Figure 10: B: Isolines graphs for July/87.

and b_{II}, respectively) influence the distribution of all parameters along the water column as a whole.

The results obtained in the third step are representative for this sole sampling point, for its strategic localization demonstrates, in average, the best and the worst water quality conditions, as far as eutrophication is concerned. In order to achieve the full understanding of diel and tidal actions in the hydrobiology dynamics of the bay, the same 24 hour sampling program is being carried out at other fixed sampling points.

Based on the results obtained, we propose to divide Guanabara Bay into sections, according to their hydrobiological characteristics. Five distinct sections are evinced, in which natural and anthropic factors act in a differentiated manner (Fig. 11).

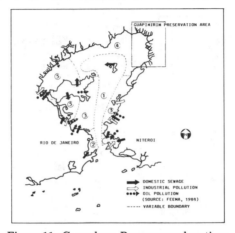

Figure 11: Guanabara Bay proposed sections.

Section 1. Defined by the main circulation channel, where the best environmental conditions are found due to the more effective sea water contribution.

Section 2. Although near the entrance of the bay, the coves of this section are subjected to strong organic pollution from the cities of Rio de Janeiro (west side) and Niterói (east side), the two most developed urban centers of this region.

Section 3. Characterized by a high level of environmental deterioration, this section is influenced by domestic sewage, industrial wastes, and oil pollution, added to the presence of the harbour and several shipyards.

Section 4. The northern section is directly influenced by the drainage network of less deteriorated rivers. The Guapimirim preservation area stands out as one of the few remaining mangroves.

Section 5. Located on the northwestern side, and characterized as the most deteriorated region, due to several sources of pollution. Landfills in this area also increase deterioration, by making local circulation more deficient.

From what we have presented, we believe that Guanabara Bay is at an unstable balance. Both pollution sources and hydrodynamics determine critical areas, as well as areas that are still capable of absorbing disturbances. Thus, in order to establish a monitoring program consistent with its peculiarities, we must consider the space gradients of environmental deterioration. Moreover, if the micro-scale variations related to diel and tidal cycles are not taken into consideration, the interpretations of the results may be misguided.

5 CONCLUSIONS AND RECOMMENDATIONS

The high complexity of the Guanabara Bay environment difficults the study of its intricate hydrobiology. However, considering the sequential approach adopted, some conclusions and recommendations are presented.

The physical and chemical parameters used reflected the environmental variations, to which planktonic organisms showed very significant responses. The spatial gradient determined by the estuarine nature of the bay, as well as seasonal changes, subject the planktonic dynamics, according to the ecological limits of the organisms found.

The low water quality, accompanied by high Cyanophyceae concentrations and frequent phytoplanktonic blooms, indicates that the bay undergoes severe environmental stress. Fortunately, the renewal of the bay waters due to its tidal cycle guarantees its auto-depurating potential. Considering that it differs from place to place, depending on both the pollution focuses and the circulation pattern, we believe that very strict and urgent measures should be taken in order to control pollution sources, as well as the maintenance of the free surface area of the bay.

The great social-economic importance of Guanabara Bay justifies the high investments necessary for its recuperation. The universities have the responsibility of forming qualified human resources as well as of obtaining basic information for environmental studies. Thus, governmental agencies will be able to develop, establish and control environmental policies which would guarantee a good quality of life for future generations. To us, it remains a question and a challenge: what will be the future of Guanabara Bay?

Acknowledgements: Financial support for this project was granted by CNPq, FUJB and CEPG-UFRJ.

REFERENCES

[1] APHA (1980). "Standard Methods for the Examination of Water and Wastewater". 15th. ed. APHA, AWWA, WPCF, Washington D.C., 1134 pp.

[2] Amador, E.S. (1980). Assoreamento da Baía de Guanabara – taxas de sedimentação. *An. Acad. Bras. Cienc.* **52** (4): 723–742.

[3] Araujo, D.S.; N.C. Maciel (1979). "Os manguezais do recôncavo da Baía de Guanabara". Cadernos FEEMA, ser. tec., 10/79.

[4] Balesh, E. (1977). "Introduction al Fitoplancton Marino". Ed. Univ. Buenos Aires, 211 pp.

[5] Boltovskoy, D. (ed.) (1981). "Atlas del Zooplancton del Atantico Sudoccidental". UNIDEP, Argentina.

[6] Bourrelly, P. (1968). "Les algues d'eau douce – algues jeunes et brunes". Editions N. Boubee e Cia.: 243–258.

[7] Brandini, F.P. and Y. Aruga (1983). Phytoplankton biomass and photosynthesis in relation to the environmental conditions in Tokyo Bay. *Jap. J. Phycol.* **31**: 129–143.

[8] Carr. N.G. and B.A. Whitton (eds.) (1982). "The Biology of Cyanobacteria". Blackwell Sci. Public., Botanical monographs, 19.

[9] DHN (1976). "Roteiro da Costa Sul – Brasil". Ministério da Marinha: 49–75.

[10] Dudnik, E.E. (1971). "SYMAP user's reference manual". Dep. of Archit., Illinois Univ., Rep. no. 71-1.

[11] FEEMA (1988). "Projeto de recuperação gradual do ecossistema da Baía de Guanabara". Sec. Est. do Meio Ambiente, Gov. Est. do Rio de Janeiro.

[12] Fogg, G.E. *et alli.* (1973). "The Blue-green Algae". Acad. Press, 459 pp.

[13] Frontier, S. (1973). L'échantillonage de la diversité spécifique,*in* Pérès, J.-M. (ed.), "Stratégies d'echantillonage en écologie". Les Presses de L'Univ. Laval Québec: 417–436.

[14] Gerardi, L.H.O. and B.C.N. Silva (1981). "Quantificação em Geografia". São Paulo:DIFEL, 161 pp.

[15] Head, P.C. (1985). Data presentation and interpretation, *in* Head, P.C. (ed.), "Practical Estuarine Chemistry: a Handbook". Camb. Univ. Press: 278–330.

[16] IBGE (1977). "Geografia do Brasil - Região Sudeste". 3: 1–89.

[17] Lacerda, L.D.; C.M.M.Souza and M.H.D.Pestana. (1988). Geochemical distribution of Cd, Cu, Cr and Pb in sediments of estuarine areas,along the southeastern Brazilian coasts, *in* Seeliger, U. *et alli.* (eds.), "Metals in Coastal Environments of Latin America". Springer-Verlag: 86–99.

[18] Legendre, L. and P. Legendre (1979). "Écologie numérique, tome 2: la structure des données écologiques". Coll. d'Écologie, no. 12, Masson, Paris et Pul., Quebec, XIV.

[19] Mayr, L.M. *et alli.* (1986). Temporal-space analysis of the Guanabara Bay (RJ-Brazil): plankton and its inter-relation with physical-chemical parameters. *Wat. Sci. Tech.* 18: 332.

[20] Navarro, J.N. (1981). A survey of the marine diatoms of Puerto Rico I. Suborders Coscinodiscineae and Rhizosoleniineae. *Botanica Marina* 24: 427–439.

[21] Navarro, J.N. (1983). A survey of the marine diatoms of Puerto Rico VII. Suborder Raphidineae: Families Auriculaceae, Epithemiaceae, Nitzschiaceae and Surirellaceae. *Botanica Marina* 26: 393–408.

[22] Parsons, T.R.; M. Takahashi and B. Hargrave (1977). "Biological oceanographic processes" (2^{nd}ed.). Pergamon Press, Oxford, 322 pp.

[23] Parsons, T.R.; Y. Maita and C.M. Lalli (1984). "A manual of chemical and biological methods for seawater analysis". Pergamon Press, Oxford, 173 pp.

[24] Pritchard, D.W. (1967). Observations of circulation in coastal plain estuaries, *in* Lauff, G.H.(ed.), "Estuaries". A.A.A.S.: 37–44.

[25] Sevrin-Reyssac, J. *et alli.* (1979). Biomasse et production du phytoplankton de la Baie de Guanabara (État de Rio de Janeiro, Brésil) et du secteur óceanique adjacent. Variation de mai à juillet 1978. *Bull. Mus. Natn. Hist. Nat.*, Paris, 4ème série, 1(B), 4: 329–354.

[26] Sharp, J.H., C.M. Culberson and T.M. Church (1982). The chemistry of the Delaware estuary. General conditions. *Limnol. Ocean.* 27 (6): 1015–1028.

[27] S.I.C. (1983). "Diagnose ecológica da Baía de Aratu". Sec. Ind. Com., Governo da Bahia.

[28] Utermohl, H. (1958). Perfeccionamento del metodo cuantitativo del fitoplancton. Ass. Int. Limnol. Teórica y Aplicada, *Com. mét. limnol.* 9: 1–39.

[29] Villac, M.C. (1988). O fitoplancton da Baía de Guanabara (RJ, Brasil): dinâmica da população a 5m, durante 1985. CNPq, rep. no. 822785-86.2 AP.

VERTICAL DISTRIBUTION OF BARNACLES OF THE INTERTIDAL ROCKY SHORES OF GUANABARA BAY, RJ, BRAZIL

Iva Nilce da Silva Brum [1]   Ricardo Silva Absalão [2]

1 INTRODUCTION

Investigations about the ecology of communities which live in the intertidal region have been concentrated to temperate areas while the tropical and subtropical areas have received, comparatively, little attention. Guanabara Bay is not an exception despite its social and economic importance and the risk of the increasing environmental degradation that it has been undergoing in the last 50 years. If such process is not interrupted and corrected, the recovery of the ecosystem will become too costly.

Although barnacles are not typically used as biological indicators of pollution, they present some of the properties mentioned by Barbaro et al. (1978) such as: organisms that do not move by themselves, plentiful in the environment, lifetime superior to one year and they are easily collected on several natural and artificial substrata.

Among those who have studied the vertical zonation of intertidal organisms in Brazil, only Oliveira (1947) and Costa (1962) were interested in the Balanomorpha of Guanabara Bay. However, these authors found neither quantitative data nor details about models for the vertical zonation of this species.

Lacombe and Monteiro (1974) made reference to B. a. amphitrite as a biological indicator of pollution in their study about the distribution of the Balanomorpha in Guanabara Bay, because of its extreme abundance in the polluted areas of the bay with low index of species diversity.

Experimental works (Barbaro et al., 1978; Weerelt, 1982) confirmed the capacity of B. a. amphitrite for concentrating pollutants in its soft tissues, once these elements are released in the environment.

This paper aims to give a quantitative analysis, using the belt-transect method, to describe the Balanomorpha species vertical zonation models of the intertidal in the rocky beaches of Guanabara Bay. Community aspects such as: composition in species, and their numerical abundance and dominance, were examined and the results were compared according to the degree of protection inside the bay.

---

[1]Departamento de Invertebrados, Museu Nacional, Universidade Federal do Rio de Janeiro, Quinta da Boa Vista, Rio de Janeiro, RJ 21942, Brazil.

[2]Departamento de Zoologia, Instituto de Biologia, Universidade Federal do Rio de Janeiro, Rio de Janeiro, RJ 21941, Brazil.

2 DESCRIPTION OF THE AREA

Guanabara Bay is located in the Southern region of Brazil (Rio de Janeiro State) and it is the second in size along the Brazilian littoral. It is located within latitudes 22°57' and 22°41' S and longitudes 43°02' and 43°16' W (Fig. 1). It has an area of 381 km², including 44 km² of islands and islets. Its approximate perimeter is of 140 km, the width at the mouth is about 1.8 km, and the maximum depth is almost 30 m. The watershed of the bay has an area of approximately 4,000 km² including 35 main rivers which contribute to the fresh water flow and the solid load arrival (Coelho and Fonseca, 1976; FEEMA, 1987).

According to Amador (1980b), it is possible to observe on the margin and islands of Guanabara Bay, the presence of primary rocks such as granites, granitic gneiss, and migmatites, the most common minerals of these rocks being feldspars, biotite and quartz.

Currents in the bay are generated by tide and wind; tides are semi-diurnal with maximum amplitude of 1.4 m.

The climate is tropical humid with temperature around 25 °C and practically two seasons: one more humid, from November to April, and another one drier from May to November. In the first one there are storms, high temperatures (monthly average from 27 °C to 30 °C), and high speed winds, while in the second season the temperature is mild and the pluviometric indexes are low (FIDERJ, 1978).

The Guanabara Bay, because of its position and orientation, is subject to winds that blow in several directions and is affected practically during all the year by moving polar anticyclones and its winds from the south hemisphere (Coelho and Fonseca, 1976).

The salinity of the surface water varies in the several regions of the Guanabara Bay. From 1979 to 1983 the highest average values (32 ppt) were detected at the entrance of the bay, and the lowest ones (27 ppt) in regions near the river inlets at the inner parts of the bay (Mayr et al., 1984).

The surface water temperature (Mayr op.cit.) increases gradually from 20 °C to 30 °C towards the interior parts of the Bay, the highest values being found at the end and on the west side of the middle of the Bay.

Dissolved oxygen (DO), pH, and biochemical oxygen demand (BOD) are normal at the mouth and in areas near the Bay entrance. At the end and in the west side of the Bay, where water circulation is weak, it is possible to observe the broad variability of dissolved oxygen, which goes from zero to more than 15 mg/l (Coelho and Fonseca, op.cit.).

The principal sources of pollution in the Guanabara Bay are domestic sewage, the liquid effluents of the industries, and oil and garbage disposal (Coelho, 1987). According to this author the heavy metals originated from industrial sources are deposited mainly in the Guanabara Bay sediments. The levels of heavy metals in the water are relatively low, the highest values being for Cu, Zn, Hg and Pb.

3 MATERIAL AND METHODS

After the initial recognition of the rocky beaches of Guanabara Bay, 16 stations (Fig. 1) were selected for the present study. Only in three, the transects were made in continuous wild coasts without boulders (São João Beach, Boa Viagem Island

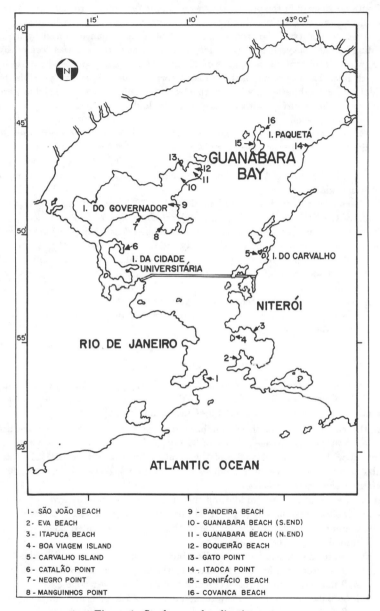

Figure 1: Study area localization.

and Ponta do Negro); in the others, they were placed on isolated rocks. The choice of stations was subject to the following criteria: bigger representativity of barnacles, easy access, regularity of the rock surface, and little disturbance caused by man. According to the rocky surface extension examined, the transect was formed by one or two ranks of contiguous squares of 20 cm × 20 cm placed perpendicularly to the beach line. The beginning of the transect corresponded, whenever possible, to the tidal zero extending up to where barnacles were visible. The tide heights were marked on the rock surface with the use of a 2 m high ruler marked every 10 cm and with a water level.

The barnacles were directly counted in each square. When it was not possible to identify the species in the place, they were taken to the laboratory in order to be examined and identified. When the transect was formed by two ranks of squares, it was taken the average of the number of individuals in the corresponding squares and of same tidal elevation.

The barnacles collected were fixed in alcohol at 70% and put in the crustacea collection of the National Museum of the Federal University of Rio de Janeiro.

The similarity among all the squares was established considering the occurrences of the species as attributes, by the similarity index of Sorensen (1948). Faunistic zones, which were considered as indicators of the verical distributional patterns of the species or associations of species, were then established by the Cluster Analysis (UPGMA Method).

Time variations was observed in two stations: Eva Beach (July and October, 1987; January and May, 1988), and Ponta do Negro (July and November, 1987; February and May, 1988).

4 RESULTS

Ten species of Balanomorpha were identified (Table I) in the 22 investigated transects of the Guanabara Bay from July 1987 to May 1988. Balanidae was the dominating taxon (6 species) followed by Chthamalidae (3 species).

At the entrance area of the Guanabara Bay, at places exposed to wave action, clear waters and average salinity of 34 ppt, *C.bisinuatus* and *T.s.stalactifera* dominated with 95.33% and 4.09% of the total number of individuals (21,435.5, cumulative average number of individuals in all stations), respectively, while *B.a. amphitrite* was very rare (0.03%).

At inner areas of the bay (middle and end of the Bay), with weak hydrodynamic effects, variable average salinity (9 ppt to 33 ppt), and muddy waters, *B.a.amphitrite* was the dominant species. In the middle of the Bay it represented 83.43% of the total of individuals (13,068.5) and 83.72

In relation to the vertical pattern of distribution of species it is possible to notice that there is a strong tendency in the area of the Bay entrance to the formation of three well marked faunistic zones (Figs. 2 and 3). The lower zone extends from the tide level 0.0 m up to 0.84 m (average value of 0.45 ± 0.26 m) and is characterized by *B.a.amphirite*, *B.improvisus* and *B.trigonus* species which are, however, not abundant. The intermediate zone placed between the tide levels 0.29 m and 1.29 m (average value of 0.98 ± 0.29 m), is mainly characterized by *T.stalactifera* and *C.proteus* species, the first being more abundant. The upper zone is located

Table I: Species of Balanomorpha collected in the intertidal region during the study of the rocky beaches of Guanabara Bay in the period of July/87 to May/88.

FAMILIES	SPECIES
Chthamalidae	*Euraphia rhizophorae* (Oliveira, 1940)
	Chthamalus bisinuatus (Pilsbry, 1916)
	Chthamalus proteus (Dando and Southward, 1980)
Tetraclitidae	*Tetraclita stalactifera stalactifera* (Lamarck, 1818)
	Fistulobalanus citerosum (Henry, 1974)
	Balanus amphitrite amphitrite (Darwin, 1854)
Balanidae	*Balanus eburneus* (Gould, 1841)
	Balanus improvisus (Darwin, 1854)
	Balanus trigonus (Darwin, 1854)
	Megabalanus coccopoma (Darwin, 1854)

between the tide levels 0.58 m and 1.75 m (average value of 1.44 ± 0.22 m) and is characterized by *C.bisinuatus*.

Among the four beaches which were studied in this area, only Itapuca did not show a lower faunistic zone. The intermediate zone extends between tide levels 0.00 m and 1.35 m (average value 0.89 ± 0.41 m) and is characterized by an abundance of *T.s.stalactifera* and *C.proteus*, and few *B.a.amphitrite* individuals. The upper zone, between levels 0.58 m and 1.60 m (average value 1.41 ± 0.24 m), is characterized by *C.bisinuatus*.

In the middle of the Bay, 8 of the 11 investigated transects did not present an intermediate faunistic zone. Where the intermediate zone occurred (Figs. 4 and 5), the three faunistic zones were characterized by the following tide levels and species: a) lower zone: 0.44 ± 0.21 m, with *B.a.amphitrite*, *B.eburneus*, *B.improvisus* and *F.citerosum*; b) intermediate zone: 0.86 ± 0.22 m, with *B.a.amphitrite*, *C.proteus* and *C.bisinuatus*; c) upper zone: 1.23 ± 0.35 m, with *bisinuatus* more abundant than in the intermediate zone.

In places where only two faunistic zones were observed (Figs. 6 and 7), the lower zone is characterized by the tide level 0.82 ± 0.18 m and by *F.citerosum*, *B.eburneus*, *B.improvisus* and *B.trigonus* species, while the upper zone is characterized by the tide level 1.44 ± 0.20 m and for presenting abundance of *B.a.amphitrite*.

At the innermost areas of the Bay, the intermediate faunistic zone was not observed in any of the investigated places (Figs. 8 and 9). In the region, the lower zone is characterized for extending itself up to the tide level 0.79 ± 0.22 m and by *F.citerosum*, *B.eburneus*, *B.improvisus* and *B.trigonus* species. The extension of the upper zone reaches the tide level 1.22 m ± 0.20 m with the abundance of

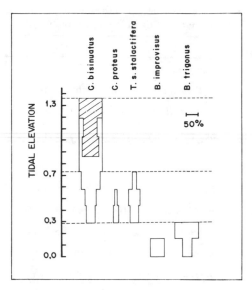

Figure 2: Eva Beach. Dominance of Balanomorpha species which are present along the transect, related to the populational density. Scale proportional to the dominance.

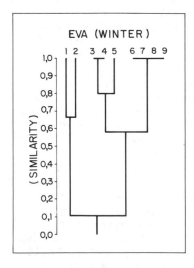

Figure 3: Eva Beach. Dendrogram of the cluster analysis of the different points of the transect based on the presence-absence of the species. Sorensen index.

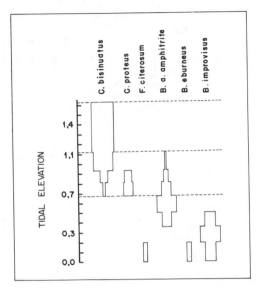

Figure 4: Ponta do Negro (Winter). Dominance of Balanomorpha species which are present along the transect. Scale proportional to the dominance.

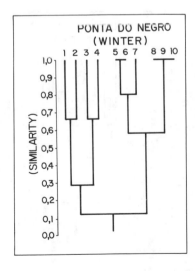

Figure 5: Ponta do Negro (Winter). Dendrogram of the cluster analysis of the different points of the transect based on the presence-absence of the specials. Lorensen index.

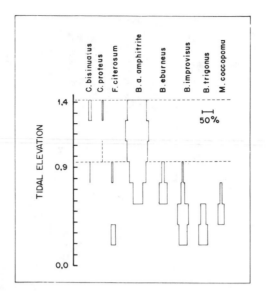

Figure 6: End of Guanabara Beack (Winter). Dominance of Balanomorpha species which are present along the transect. Scale proportional to the dominance.

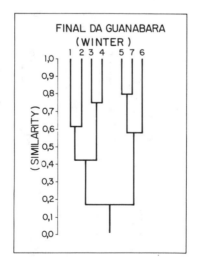

Figure 7: End of Guanabara Beach (Winter). Dendrogram of the cluster analysis of the different points of the transect based on presence and absence of species. Lorensen index.

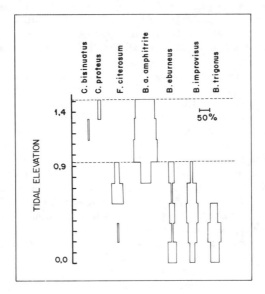

Figure 8: José Bonifácio Beach (Winter). Dominance of Balanomorpha species which are present along the transect. Scale proportional to the dominance.

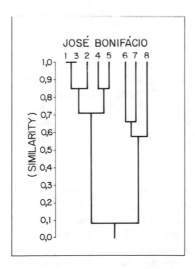

Figure 9: José Bonifácio (Winter). Dendrogram of the cluster analysis of the different points of the transect based on presence and absence of species. Lorensen index.

B.a.amphitrite and also the presence of *E.rhizophorae* and *C.bisinuatus*.

The relation of the faunistic zones with the tide levels determined for each location is presented on Table II. For all the stations in each area of the Bay, the average values and standard deviations of tide levels were also computed and are indicated on Tables III.

Eva Beach, in the area closer to the Bay mouth, presented three well defined faunistic zones in the winter and in the summer, and only two zones in the other seasons. The organisms showed a slight move towards the supralittoral fringe in spring while, in winter, they moved towards the infralittoral.

The composition of the population of barnacles varied only in the lower zone. Among the Balanidae, *B.improvisus* was the species most found in that zone, occurring both in winter and summer.

Populational density was larger in autumn (1.5698 ind/cm^2) and smaller in spring (0.5032 ind/cm^2). The increase of barnacle population in autumn was due to the large number of young individuals (base diameter $\leq$ 2 mm) of *C.bisinuatus* which had recently established. This species was dominant during the four seasons.

Shannon index computed for Eva Beach in the four seasons showed the largest diversity during winter (0.0839) and the smallest during spring (0.0584). Mortality rate for the species was not significant in any of the seasons.

Ponta do Negro, in the mid-Bay area, presented three faunistic zones in winter and two in the other seasons. During spring, the upper limit of the organisms distribution rose towards the supralittoral fringe. The composition of the population varied only in the lower zone. Among the Balanidae, *B.a.amphitrite*, *B.eburneus*, *B.improvisus* and *F.citerosum* were species most frequently found, *B.a.amphitrite* being the dominant species in this zone in all seasons.

As regards the total area of the transect on the upper zone, *C.bisinuatus* was dominant in winter, spring and summer, while *B.a.amphitrite* was dominant in autumn.

Populational density of the Balanomorpha was larger in autumn (1.2752 ind/cm^2) and smaller in summer (0.0331 ind/cm^2). The increase observed during autumn is due to the large number of young individuals of *B.a.amphitrite* and *B.improvisus* that had been recently settled. Mortality rate for Balanidae was smaller in autumn ($\leq$ 19.50%) and larger in summer ($\geq$ 66.67%). For Chtamalidae, mortality rate was not significant ($\leq$ 3.48%). The largest diversity of species at Ponta do Negro happened in spring (0.5878) and the smallest in autumn (0.2591).

5 DISCUSSION

The presence of *T.s.stalactifera*, restricted to the bay entrance, has been already recorded by Oliveira (1947). As regards its vertical distribution, Oliveira (*op.cit.*) found the species position in the lower midlittoral, below the *Chthamalus* zone, and positioned, in an imprecise way, *B.a.amphitrite* above the two previously mentioned species. Our observations indicate that *B.a.amphitrite* is a common element of the lower faunistic zone in this area of the Bay, which agrees with the records of Costa (1962) in which *B.a.amphitrite* and *Bunodosoma caissarum* actinean mark the beginning of the infralittoral.

With the interiorization of the collect stations, those placed in the middle and in the end of the Bay show the suppression of the intermediate faunistic zone and

Table II: Elevation (in meters) of the faunistic zones at each studied site.

	Location	Date	Faunistic Zones		
			Upper	Intermediate	Lower
	São João Bch.	11-21-87	1.75 – 1.29	1.29 – 0.84	0.84 – 0.00
	Eva Bch. (wi.)	07-25-87	1.36 – 0.73	0.73 – 0.29	0.29 – 0.00
	Eva Bch. (sp.)	10-23-87	1.52 – 0.73	—	0.73 – 0.29
Ent.	Eva Bch. (su.)	01-22-88	1.19 – 0.73	0.73 – 0.29	0.29 – 0.00
	Eva Bch. (au.)	05-03-88	1.19 – 0.58	—	0.58 – 0.00
	Itapuca Bch.	07-23-87	1.60 – 1.35	—	1.35 – 0.18
	Boa Viagem Bch.	07-24-87	1.34 – 1.15	1.15 – 0.38	0.38 – 0.13
	Carvalho Is.	09-23-87	0.98 – 0.72	0.72 – 0.37	0.37 – 0.00
	Catalão Pt.	07-27-87	1.15 – 0.57	—	0.57 – 0.00
	Negro Pt. (wi.)	07-09-87	1.63 – 1.12	1.12 – 0.67	0.67 – 0.00
	Negro Pt. (sp.)	11-05-87	1.63 – 0.82	—	0.82 – 0.00
	Negro Pt. (su.)	02-04-88	1.46 – 0.82	—	0.82 – 0.19
Mid.	Negro Pt. (au.)	05-16-88	1.46 – 0.67	—	0.67 – 0.00
	Manguinhos Pt.	09-22-87	1.07 – 0.75	0.75 – 0.27	0.27 – 0.00
	Bandeira Bch.	07-10-87	1.15 – 0.69	—	0.69 – 0.10
	Guanabara Bch. (S)	07-11-87	1.50 – 0.93	—	0.93 – 0.18
	Guanabara Bch. (N)	07-13-87	1.52 – 0.95	—	0.95 – 0.19
	Boqueirão Bch.	08-10-87	1.69 – 1.13	—	1.13 – 0.00
	Gato Pt.	08-12-87	1.19 – 0.73	—	—
	Itaoca Pt.	08-26-87	1.06 – 0.91	—	0.91 – 0.10
End	José Bonifácio Bch.	08-25-87	1.51 – 0.93	—	0.93 – 0.00
	Covanca Bch.	08-11-87	1.11 – 0.54	—	0.54 – 0.00

Note: (wi.) = winter; (sp.) = spring; (su.) = summer; (au.) = autumn.

Table III: Average values of tide levels of the faunistic zones in the three areas of Guanabara Bay.

Areas of the Bay	Tide levels (m) average values ± stand. dev.		
	Upper Zone	Intermediate Zone	Lower Zone
Entrance	1.44 ± 0.22	0.98 ± 0.29	0.45 ± 0.26
	1.41 ± 0.24	0.89 ± 0.41	—
Middle	1.23 ± 0.35	0.86 ± 0.22	0.44 ± 0.21
	1.44 ± 0.20	—	0.82 ± 0.18
End	1.22 ± 0.20	—	0.79 ± 0.22

the disappearance of *T.s.stalactifera*. In this situation, *B.a.amphitrite* extends its vertical distribution to the higher/drier levels, becoming the main element of the upper faunistic zone replacing the *C.bisinuatus*, characteristic of this zone, in the area of the Bay entrance.

This increase in the vertical distribution of *B.a.amphitrite* in higher levels, indicates that the species is relatively resistant to desiccation. On the other hand, the disappearance of *T.s.stalactifera* from the intermediate zone and *C.bisinuatus* from the upper one, suggests that both species are sensitive to larger variations of salinity and/or to the water pollution. Oliveira (1947) considered *T.s.stalactifera* as characteristic of waters with average salinity between 34 ppt and 32 ppt, requiring a moderate action of waves to grow.

The presence of *B.a.amphitrite* in all the investigated stations and in other places of Guanabara Bay (personal observation), in which salinity varies from 34 ppt to 9 ppt confirms the eurihalinity of the species described by other authors (Nilsson-Cantell, 1948; Shatoury, 1958; Newman, 1967). Although we have registered a significant mortality in some stations at the middle and at the end of Guanabara Bay, the species is still abundant in these parts of the bay. For its resistance to pollution (Barbaro *et al.*, 1978; Weerelt, 1982) it can be used as bioindicator in an environmental monitoring program. The mortality verified in the lower levels of intertidal might be attributed to the almost complete cover of bryozoans that blossom in polluted water.

According to interiorization in Guanabara Bay, the change of elevation of the faunistic zones suggests that, when considering the three zones, the upper limit of the lower faunistic zone can be determined by interspecies competition among the species of this zone and those of the intermediate one. This would be a competition for the rocky substratum since in the rocky intertidal regions, space for settling and growing is frequently very limited.

As stated in Table III it is possible to notice that the tide height, characteristic of the lower faunistic zone, changes from 0.45 m (Bay entrance with three faunistic zones) to 0.79 m at the end of the Bay where only two faunistic zones are present. Because of the weak hydrodynamic action at the end of the Bay, the vertical extension of the lower faunistic zone should be restrict and not be larger than 30 cm. This is an indication of a local amplification of the tide. A similar pattern is also observed between the stations with two and three faunistic zones of the middle of the Bay region, changing from 0.44 m in the stations with three zones to 0.82 m in the stations with two faunistic zones.

Connell (1961) shows the predatory effect of *Chthamalus stellatus* on *Thais* and the effect of the competition with *Balanus balanoides* to establish the lower limit of the vertical distribution of *Chthamalus stellatus*; its upper limit is guided by the species resistance to desiccation. In this case, *Balanus a. amphitrite* was restricted to the lower faunistic zone, where three zones were present, as near the Bay entrance. However, at places where only two faunistic zones existed, the species extended largely the upper limit of its vertical distribution. This situation is related to the absence of *T.s.stalactifera* as a characteristic specie of this intermediate faunistic zone, not present in the inner areas of the Bay. Thus, the authors are able to suppose that the competition between these two species would impose an upper limit for the occurrence of *B.a.amphitrite* in the Bay entrance area; however the different requirements concerning the salinity could also influence or even partially explain this situation. Thus, it would be necessary further studies about the possible competition between *B.a.amphitrite* and *T.s.stalactifera* and between *B.a.amphitrite* and *C.bisinuatus* to support the above hypothesis.

Comparison between Balanomorpha found at Eva Beach (Bay entrance) and Ponta do Negro (mid-Bay) confirmed the well known fact that the extension of the zones of vertical distribution of organisms increases with the degree of exposition to wave action (Stephenson and Stephenson, 1949 and 1972; Lewis, 1964).

The basic sequence of Balanomorpha: Chthamalidae, Tetraclitidae and Balanidae, common in tropical to warm temperate beaches (Foster, 1978) was observed at Eva Beach in July (winter) and January (summer), at São João Beach (spring) and at Boa Viagem Island (winter).

6 CONCLUSION

The structure and species composition of the Balanomorpha assemblages was studied in 16 stations throughout Guanabara Bay. Barnacles could be used as monitors of environmental conditions, since for each area of the Bay (with its salinity regime and pollution degree) there would be a structure and own composition among the barnacles.

For a better characterization of the sazonality of the distribution of these animals, it would be necessary monthly observations as well as correlations with other physical parameters such as meteorological events, wave conditions and tidal variations. The authors recommend that, in a comprehensive study of Guanabara Bay, biological studies like the one presented here be associated with models of water quality and circulation.

Acknowledgements: The authors wish to thank the biologists Edina Maria Pereira Martins and Celia Maria de Souza Sampaio for their help in the field work.

This work was based on the D.Sc. dissertation of the first author, submitted in December 1988 to the Zoology Department of the "Instituto de Biociências da Universidade de São Paulo".

REFERENCES

[1] Amador, E.S. (1980). Assoreamento da Baía de Guanabara — Taxas de Sedimentação. *An. Acad. Brasil. Ciênc.* **52** (4): 723–742.

[2] Barbaro, A.; Polo, B. Francescon; and M. Bilio (1978). *Balanus amphitrite* (Cirripedia: Thoracica) - A Potencial Indicator of Fluoride, Cooper, Lead, Chromium and Mercury in North Adriatic Lagoons. *Mar. Biol.* **46**: 247–257.

[3] Boudouresque, C.F. (1971). Méthodes d'études qualitative et quantitative du benthos (en particulier du phytobentos). *Thetis*, France, **3** (1): 79–104.

[4] Coelho, V.M.B., (coord.) (1987). A poluição da Baía de Guanabara: Antecedentes e Situação Atual. FEEMA, Departamento de Estudos e Projetos (D.E.P.): 1–21.

[5] Coelho, V.M.B. and M.R.M. de B. Fonseca (1976). Estudo do Caso de Poluição nas Águas da Baía de Guanabara: Sistema de Estuário Tropical Úmido. Relatório FEEMA: 4–55.

[6] Connell, J.H. (1961). The influence of interspecific competition and others factors on the distribution of the barnacle *Chthamalus stellatus*. *Ecology* **42** (4): 710–723.

[7] Costa, H.R. (1962). Nota preliminar sobre a fauna de substrato duro no litoral dos Estados do Rio de Janeiro e Guanabara. *C. Est. Zool.* Fac. Nac. Filos. Univ. Brasil, Av. no. 15: 1–11.

[8] F.E.E.M.A., Fundação Estadual de Engenharia do Meio Ambiente, Rio de Janeiro (1987). Qualidade das Águas no Estado do Rio de Janeiro. Seleção de Estudos de Qualidade de Corpos D'Água. Divisão de Planejamento Ambiental (DIPLAM): 1–15.

[9] F.I.D.E.R.J., Fundação Instituto de Desenvolvimento Econômico e Social do Rio de Janeiro. Diretoria de Geografia e Estatística (1978). Indicadores Climatológicos do Estado do Rio de Janeiro. Sistema de Informações para o Planejamento Estadual (S.I.P.E.): 1–156.

[10] Foster, B.A. (1978). The marine fauna of New Zealand: Barnacles (Cirripedia-Thoracica). *New Zealand Oc. Inst. Memoir* **69**: 1–160.

[11] Lacombe, D. and W. Monteiro (1974). Balanídeos como Indicadores de Poluição na Baía de Guanabara, *Rev. Bras. Biol.*, Rio de Janeiro; **34** (4): 633–644.

[12] Lewis, J.R. (1964). "The Ecology of rocky shores", London, 322 pp.

[13] Mayr, L.; M.C. de Biase; and P.M.L. Martins (1984). Análise espaço-temporal de parâmetros físico-químicos da Baía de Guanabara. Simpósio Brasileiro sobre Recursos do Mar, Rio de Janeiro, RJ, 15 a 19 de outubro de 1984, 15 pp.

[14] Newman, W.A. (1967). On the physiology and behaviour of estuarine barnacles. Proc. Symp. Crustacea - III. *Mar. Biol. Ass. India*: 1038–1066.

[15] Nilsson-Cantell, C.A. (1948). The Armstrong College Zool. Exped. to Siwa Oasis (Lybian Desert) 1935. Notes on a *Balanus* from the saline lake Birkel el Gessabaia (Exabaia). *Proc. Egypt. Acad. Sci.* 4: 43–44.

[16] Oliveira, L.P.H. (1947). Distribuição Geográfica da Fauna e Flora da Baía de Guanabara. *Mem. Inst. Oswaldo Cruz.* Rio de Janeiro, **45** (3): 709–735.

[17] Shatoury, H.H.A. (1958). A freshwater mutant of *Balanus amphitrite*. *Nature* **181**: 790–791.

[18] Sorensen, T. (1948). A method of establishing groups of equal amplitude in plant sociology based on similarity of species content. *Biol. Skr.* **5** (4): 1–34.

[19] Sthephenson, T.A. and A. Sthephenson (1949). The universal features of zonation between tide marks on rocky coasts. *J. Ecol.* **38**: 289–305.

[20] Sthephenson, T.A. and A. Sthephenson (1972). "Life between on rocky shores". W.H. Freeman, San Francisco, 425 pp.

[21] Weerelt, M.D.M. van, (1982). Níveis de Cromo no Estuário do Rio Irajá (Baía de Guanabara) e Incorporação Experimental de Cr em cracas (*Balanus sp.*). M.Sc. Thesis, Universidade Federal do Rio de Janeiro. 80 pp.

SULFATED POLYSACCHARIDES FROM MARINE INVERTEBRATES

Ricardo P. Vieira[1]   Rodolpho M. Albano[1]   Mauro S.G. Pavão[1]

Paulo A.S. Mourão [1]

1 POLYSACCHARIDES AS STRUCTURAL COMPONENTS OF LIVING TISSUES

Polysaccharides are the most abundant structural macromolecules in living tissues. They impart shape, protection, support, elasticity and rigidity to plant and animal tissues. For example, chitin, a homopolymer of N-acetyl-glucosamine, is the major macromolecule in the exoskeleton of Arthropods. The most abundant structural polysaccharide in plants is cellulose, a linear polymer of glucose.

A distinctive group of structural polysaccharides is found in marine algae (Percival and McDowell, 1967; Painter, 1983) and vertebrate connective tissue (Rodén, 1981). The presence of sulfate ester greatly increases their water binding capacity, therefore contributing to the resilience of the tissue. This property is fundamental for the function and nutrition of several structural tissues, such as the articular cartilages.

The sulfated polysaccharides found in marine algae comprise a variety of molecular species. The most abundant are the carrageenan and fucoidan, which are isolated from red algae (Rhodophyta) and brown algae (Phaeophyta), respectively.

Carrageenans are linear chains of galactose residues. Additional complexities of these polysaccharides arise as the presence of sulfate ester, methyl group and in the partial conversion of galactose into 3,6-anhydrogalactose. Fucoidan is a polysaccharide formed mainly by fucose residues sulfated at position 4 (Percival and McDowell, 1967; Painter, 1983).

The glycosaminoglycans of animal tissue are composed of disaccharide units, in which one of the sugars is always an aminosugar and the other sugar is a hexuronic acid or a neutral hexose (mainly galactose) (Rodén, 1981). The most abundant glycosaminoglycan in animal tissue is chondroitin 4/6-sulfate, composed of repeating units of N-acetyl-galactosamine and glucuronic acid. The sulfate can be present in position 4 or in position 6 of the aminosugar.

[1]Departamento de Bioquímica, Instituto de Ciências Biomédicas, Universidade Federal do Rio de Janeiro, Caixa Postal 68041, Rio de Janeiro, RJ 21910, Brazil.

2 BINDING PROPERTIES OF THE SULFATED POLYSACCHARIDES

Glycosaminoglycans and sulfated polysaccharides from marine algae are highly hydrophilic and polyanionic, which enables them to attract water and cationic material.

The glycosaminoglycans interact with various classes of molecules. For example, plasma proteins, such as lipoproteins, protease inhibitors, a variety of complement factors, as well as proteins derived from cell surfaces and the extracellular matrix. The binding between these macromolecules has, in each case, a physiological implication. Binding of heparin, a highly anionic glycosaminoglycan, is responsible for the anticoagulant property of this molecule (Lindahl and Hook, 1978).

The algal polysaccharides have the ability to form gels in which polymer strands of ordered conformation bind to each other (Lindahl and Hook, 1978).

3 THE IMPORTANCE OF DETERMINING THE CHEMICAL STRUCTURE OF MOLECULES

Our Laboratory is involved in the chemical and structural determination of sulfated polysaccharides from different sources. The main purpose of such studies is to compare these molecules with others previously known and relate their structure with physicochemical and biological properties.

Invertebrate and vertebrate connective tissues have been compared in relation to function and chemical composition (Mathews, 1975). We have found high amounts of sulfated polysaccharides in two classes of marine invertebrates that revealed interesting features. These tissues from marine invertebrates are the tunic of ascidian (Chordata-Tunicata) and the body wall of sea cucumber (Echinodermata-Holothuroidea), see Figures 1 and 2.

In this work we describe the procedures for the isolation, purification and chemical characterization of the sulfated polysaccharides from the tunic of ascidian and the body wall of sea cucumber.

4 SULFATED POLYSACCHARIDES FROM THE TUNIC OF ASCIDIANS

4.1 Morphology of the ascidian tunic:

The tunic of ascidians is an external supportive and protective skeleton (Barnes, 1980). It consists of dense bundles of fibrillar material embedded in a loose network of fine fibrils (unpublished observations), an organization reminiscent of the vertebrate cartilage.

4.2 Extraction of the sulfated polysaccharides:

The ascidian *Styela plicata* was collected from the Guanabara bay , Rio de Janeiro. The tunic was carefully separated from other tissues, immersed immediately in acetone, and kept for 24 hr at 4°C. The sulfated polysaccharides were extracted from the dried tissue by papain digestion, as previously described (Albano and Mourão, 1983; 1986). Alternatively, the sulfated polysaccharides can be extracted from the tunic by guanidine hydrochloride solutions (Albano and Mourão, 1986).

Figure 1: *Styela plicata*, a tropical ascidian frequently found in the eutrophic water of Guanabara Bay. Note the hard tunic with two siphons, which are the main feature of this group of animals (Chordata-Tunicata).

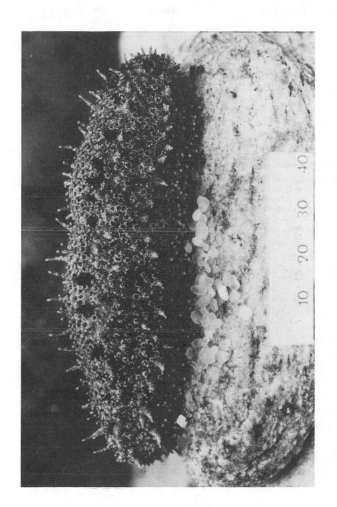

Figure 2: *Ludwigothurea grisea*, a very frequent specie of sea cucumber of the eutrophic waters of Guanabara Bay.

Table I: Chemical composition, specific optical rotation, and average molecular mass of the different sulfated polysaccharides from the tunic of *S.plicata*.

Fraction	Molar Ratios				Sulfate/	$[\alpha]_D^{20°C}$	M.M.
	Gal	Glc	Man	HexN	Total Sugar		
					mol/mol		KDa
Total	0.49	0.32	0.04	0.15	0.95	-79°	
F-1	0.82	0.14	n.d.	0.04	0.66	-119°	>1000
F-2-A	0.20	0.57	n.d.	0.23^a	0.73	-32°	20
F-2-B	0.31	0.27	0.12	0.40^a	0.67	-13°	8

(^{a}) About 85% of the hexosamine is glucosamine.
M.M. Molecular Mass; n.d., not detected.

4.3 Purification of the sulfated polysaccharides:

The sulfated polysaccharides from the ascidian tunic were purified by DEAE-cellulose, Sepharose CL-4B and Sephadex G-200 columns (Fig.3). The DEAE-cellulose column separated most of the hexoses from the ultraviolet absorbing materials (nucleic acids and protein), which were eluted before or at the beginning of the salt gradient (Fig.3A).

The DEAE-cellulose purified polysaccharides were fractioned, according to their molecular weight, by gel chromatography on Sepharose CL-4B and Sephadex G-200. The sulfated polysaccharides were separated into three fractions, designated as F-1, F-2-A and F-2-B (see Fig.3 B/C and Albano and Mourão (1986)).

Fig. 4 shows the electrophoretic mobilities of the purified polysaccharides on agarose and polyacrylamide gel. Fraction F-1 did not migrate into the polyacrylamide gel due to its high molecular weight (Fig.4B) while F-2-A and F-2-B showed an average molecular weight of 20,000 and 8,000 daltons, respectively. Electrophoresis on agarose gel confirmed the homogeneity of the fractions (Fig.4A).

Table I shows the chemical analysis, optical rotation and average molecular weight of the three fractions of sulfated polysaccharides from the tunic of *S.plicata*. The F-1 fraction has a high galactose content, and the hexosamine content increases as the molecular weight decreases. F-2-A has the highest content of glucose, whereas mannose is present only in the F-2-B fraction. All fractions have a high content of sulfate.

4.4 Chemical structure of fraction F-1:

The strong negative optical rotation of fraction F-1 suggests the presence of either β-D-galactofuranosyl or α-L-galactopyranosyl. These possibilities were further investigated using chemical and enzymatic methods. We determined that the galactose occurs entirely in the L-enantiomeric form (Mourão and Perlin, 1987; Pavão, Albano and Mourão, in press).

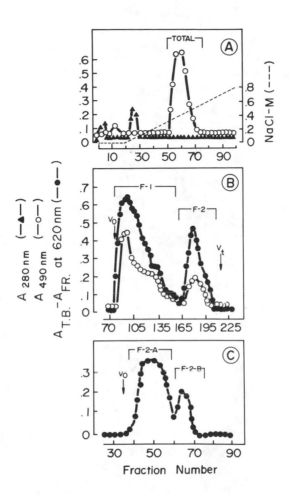

Figure 3: Purification of the polysaccharides extracted from the tunic of *S.plicata*. A, DEAE-cellulose column of the polysaccharides from *S.plicata*. B, Sepharose CL-4B column of the sulfated polysaccharides. C, Sephadex G-200 of fraction F-2 obtained from Sepharose CL-4B column. The fractions were assayed for their metachromatic properties (-o-), hexoses contents by the DuBois reaction (-o-) and their ultraviolet-absorbing material (-Δ-). For other details see Albano and Mourão (1986).

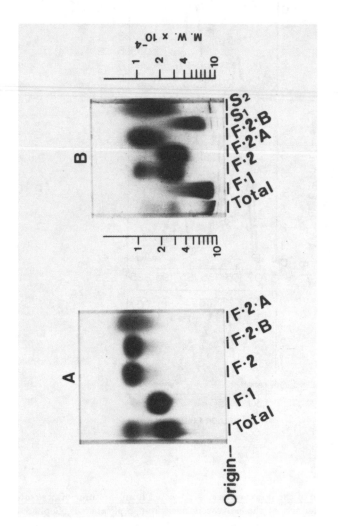

Figure 4: Electrophoresis of the purified sulfated polysaccharides from *S. plicata*. A, agarose gel electrophoresis. B, polyacrylamide gel electrophoresis.

The structure of the fraction F-1 was determined using a vast array of techniques. The nature of their glycosidic linkages and the position of sulfate were determined by methylation (Mourão and Perlin, 1987). They were confirmed by periodate oxidation (Albano and Mourão, 1986) and nuclear magnetic resonance spectroscopy (Mourão and Perlin, 1987). F-1 fraction from *S.plicata* was then determined to consist of a central core of 1→4 glycosidicaly linked α-l-galactopyranose residues, sulfated at position 3, bearing numerous non-sulfated L-galactopyranose branches (Fig.5A).

4.5 Comparison between fraction F-1 and other galactose-rich polysaccharides:

The structure of fraction F-1 from ascidians is unique among previously described sulfated glycans. The main galactose-rich sulfated polysaccharides described in living tissues are keratan sulfate and carrageenans. Keratan sulfate (Fig.5B), which occurs mainly in mammalian cartilages and corneas, is composed of β-D-galactopyranose units 1→4 glycosidically linked to N-acetyl-D-glucosamine 6-sulfate. The algal carrageenans present a more heterogeneous structure (Fig. 5C). They have a linear chain of β-D-galactopyranose residues linked glycosidically through position 1→3 to α-galactopyranose. The α-galactopyranose can occur in D or L form, or can be partly converted to 3,6-anydro forms. The sulfate ester may occur at position 2, 4 or 6 of the galactose residues.

The fraction F-1 from the ascidians differs from these previously described sulfated polysaccharides not only in the type of linkages and position of sulfation, but also in the extensive branching, while both keratan sulfate and carrageenans are linear polysaccharides. Furthermore, the ascidian glycans are the first polysaccharides that contain large amounts of L-galactose and not its D-isomer.

5 SULFATED POLYSACCHARIDES FROM THE BODY WALL OF SEA CUCUMBER

5.1 Morphology of the sea cucumber body wall:

The body wall of the sea cucumber is formed mainly by collagen fibers embedded in an amorphous matrix. Small irregular microfibrils, which resemble the proteoglycans of mammalian connective tissue, form bridges between the collagen fibers. Small cells, characterized by a dense nucleus surrounded by alcian blue-stained secretory granules, is observed irregularly between the collagen fibers (Junqueira *et al.*, 1980).

5.2 Extraction of the sulfated polysaccharides:

The body wall of the sea cucumber *Ludwigothurea grisea* was carefully separated from other tissues, immersed immediately in acetone, and kept for 24 hr at 4°C. The sulfated polysaccharides were extracted from the dried tissue by papain digestion, as previously described (Mourão and Bastos, 1987).

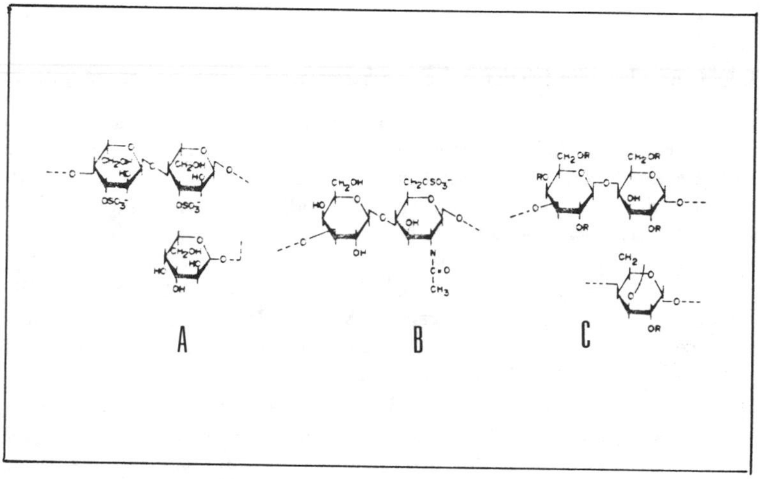

Figure 5: <u>Structure of the galactose-rich sulfated polysaccharides present in living tissues in comparison with fraction F-1 of ascidians polysaccharides.</u>   The main structure features of fraction F-1 from *S.plicata* (A), the reapeating disaccharides unit of keratan sulfate (B) and the main units of algal carrageenans (C).

Table II: Chemical composition, specific optical rotation, and average molecular mass of the purified fractions of sulfated polysaccharides from *L.grisea*.

Fraction	Molar Ratios					Sulfate/	$[\alpha]_D^{20°C}$	M.M
	Fuc	GlcUA	GalNH	GlcNH	Gal	Total Sugar		ranges[a]
								KDa
F-1-x	0.68	<0.01	0.04	0.11	0.17	0.50	-93°	>100
F-1-y	1.00	<0.01	<0.01	<0.01	<0.01	0.55	-158°	8–50
F-2	0.32	0.30	0.33	<0.01	0.05	0.88	-30°	20–40

([a]) Molecular mass ranges compared with glycosaminoglycan standards.

5.3 Purification of the sulfated polysaccharides:

The sulfated polysaccharides from *L.grisea* were purified by DEAE-cellulose and Sepharose CL-4B columns (Mourão and Bastos, 1987; Vieira and Mourão, in press). Fig. 6 shows the electrophoretic mobilities of the purified polysaccharides on agarose and polyacrylamide gel. Fraction F-1-x did not migrate into the polyacrylamide gel due to its high molecular weight, while F-1-y showed a broad band. Fraction F-2 had a single band on the polyacrylamide gel with an average molecular weight of 35,000 daltons (Fig.6A). Electrophoresis on agarose gel confirmed the homogeneity of the fractions (Fig.6B).

The chemical analysis and the specific optical rotation of the purified fractions of sulfated polysaccharides is shown in table II. Fucose and sulfate are detected in all fractions; however, the proportions of these components vary from one fraction to another. F-1-y is a single sulfated fucan, while hexosamines and galactose are found in F-1-x. Fraction F-2 has approximately equimolar proportions of fucose, glucuronic acid and galactosamine.

The strongly negative optical rotation of F-1-x and F-1-y (-93° and -158°, respectively) is compatible with residues of α-L-fucopyranosyl. This structure type is supported by the finding that the fucose obtained by acid hydrolysis of these fractions is exclusively of L- configuration (Vieira and Mourão, in press).

5.4 Chemical structure of fraction F-2:

The structure of fraction F-2 was determined by methylation, ^{13}C-NMR, periodate oxidation and degradation with specific enzymes (Vieira and Mourão, in press). This fraction is a branched polysaccharide containing a central core of repeating disaccharide units of β-D-glucuronic acid 1→3 glycosidically linked to N-acetyl-β-D-galactosamine, which are partially sulfated at carbon 6 of the hexosamine moiety. The methylation studies (Vieira and Mourão, in press) indicate that approximately half of the glucuronic acid is substituted by disaccharide units formed by fucose linked glycosidically through position 1→2 (Fig.7B) or 1→4 (Fig.7C). The other glucuronic acid residues are not fucosylated (Fig.7A).

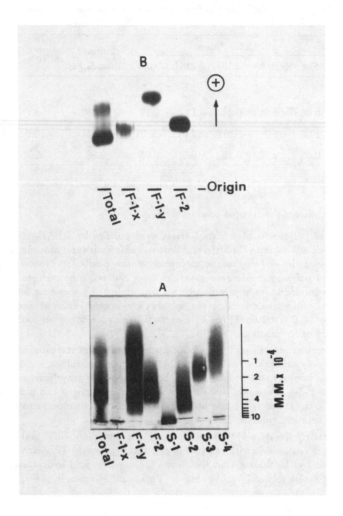

Figure 6: Electrophoresis of the purified polysaccharides from *L.grisea*. A, poly-acrylamide gel electrophoresis. B, agarose gel electrophoresis. Details about the fractionation of these polysaccharides are described in Vieira and Mourão (in press).

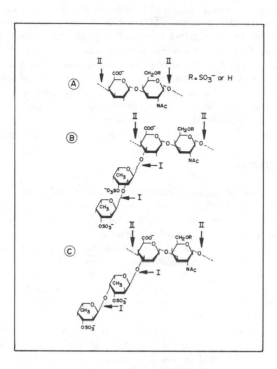

Figure 7: <u>Hypothetical structure for the major components of fraction F-2.</u> Fraction F-2 is composed of a chondroitin sulfate-like core, containing branches of sulfated fucose. After partial acid hydrolysis (I), which removes the fucose branches, the polymer is degraded by chondroitinase AC or ABC (II), forming unsaturated disaccharides (see Fig. 8). Half of the glucuronic acid residues are not fucosylated (A), while the other half are substituted by disaccharide units of fucose 1→2 (B) or 1→4 (C) glycosidically linked.

Partial acid hydrolysis of fraction F-2 produces mainly sulfated fucose and an acidic oligosaccharide composed of equimolecular proportions of D-glucuronic acid and N-acetyl-D-galactosamine (Vieira and Mourão, in press). This acidic oligosaccharide is degraded by chondroitinase AC or ABC forming non-sulfated and 6-sulfated disaccharides, while the intact fraction F-2 is resistant to both chondroitinases (Fig.8). Therefore, the presence of sulfated fucose branches obstructs the access of the chondroitinases to the chondroitin sulfate core of fraction F-2. However, after partial acid hydrolysis, which removes the sulfate fucose residues from the polymer, the acidic oligosaccharide obtained is degraded by both chondroitinases. The function of the sulfated fucose branches in this unique chondroitin sulfate is a matter of speculation. Possibly, these branches may render the glycosaminoglycans chain more resistant to degradation by endogenous and/or exogenous glycosidases.

6 MAIN CONCLUSIONS

In our studies we found a high concentration of sulfated polysaccharides in the body wall of a sea cucumber and in the tunic of an ascidian. These two tissues of marine invertebrates possess structural function, have small amounts of cells and high amounts of extracellular matrix. Therefore, they are comparable to the connective tissue of vertebrates in their function and morphological characteristics. Interestingly, the high amounts of sulfated polysaccharides found in these tissues resemble the great quantities of glycosaminoglycans that are characteristic of the vertebrate connective tissues. Possibly, these sulfated glycans may be essential for maintaining the structural integrity of the connective-like tissues of invertebrates.

The chemical structure of these polysaccharides are unique among all previously described sulfated glycans. However, they show some characteristics that resemble the sulfated polysaccharides from marine algae and others that resemble the glycosaminoglycans from animal tissues. For example, fraction F-2 from the body wall of sea cucumber, composed of a central core of chondroitin sulfate, resembles the animal glycosaminoglycans. On the other hand, fraction F-1-y from the same invertebrate reminds us of the marine algae fucoidan, since both polysaccharides are made up of sulfated α-L-fucopyranose units. Similarly, the F-1 fraction from the ascidian tunic, which is composed mainly of L-galactose residues, resembles the marine algae carrageenan.

In this paper we reported the methods used for the extraction, purification and structural characterization of the sulfated polysaccharides obtained from two marine invertebrates which occur abundantly in the eutrophic waters of Guanabara bay. These studies are of great importance both in academic research and in sugar polymers biotechnology, since these polysaccharides share several structural features with the carrageenans, fucoidans and glycosaminoglycans. Therefore, the sulfated polysaccharides from ascidians and sea cucumbers may have anticoagulant and antihemostatic activities as the sulfated glycosaminoglycans. In the same way, these polymers may also have the gel formation properties and the ability of forming a viscous solution as in the case of algal sulfated polysaccharides. In this case, ascidians and sea cucumbers could be used as alternative sources for these kind of polymers, provided a rational way for the exploitation can be devised. The enterprise would thus require the concurrent support from the Marine Biology disciplines in order to ensure the correct management of living resources.

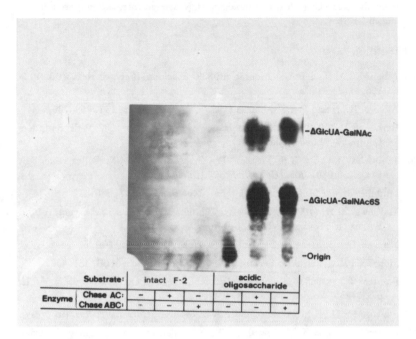

Figure 8: Paper chromatography of the products formed by the action of chondroitinase AC or ABC on intact fraction F-2 and on the acidic oligosaccharide. The products formed by chondroitinase were separated by paper chromatography in isobutyric acid: 1.0M NH4OH (5:3,v/v) for 24 hr, and localized by silver nitrate staining. Observe that intact fraction F-2 is resistant to both enzymes while the acidic oligosaccharides is degraded forming unsaturated 6-sulfated disaccharides (^GlcUA-GalNAc 6S) and unsaturated non-sulfated disaccharides (^GlcUA-GalNAC).

Acknowledgements: The authors would like to thank Luiz Eduardo de Macedo Cardoso for the help in the preparation of this manuscript. This work was supported by grants from Financiadora de Estudos e Projetos (FINEP), Conselho Nacional de Desenvolvimento Científico e Tecnológico (CNPq) and International Foundation for Science (IFS).

REFERENCES

[1] Albano, R.M. and P.A.S. Mourão (1983). *Biochim. Biophys. Acta* **760**, 192–196.

[2] Albano, R.M. and P.A.S. Mourão (1986). *J. Biol. Chem.* **261**, 758–765.

[3] Barnes, R.D. (1980). *in:* "Invertebrate Zoology", p.1030–1032, W.B. Saunders Company, Philadelphia.

[4] Junqueira, L.C.U.; G.S. Montes; P.A.S. Mourão; L.M.N. Salles; and S.S. Bonetti (1980). *Rev. Can. Biol.* **39**, 157–164.

[5] Lindahl, U. and M. Hook (1978). *Ann. Rev. Biochem.* **47**, 385–417.

[6] Mathews, M.B. (1975). "Connective Tissue. Macromolecular Structure and Evolution", Springer-Verlag, Berlin.

[7] Mourão, P.A.S. and I.G. Bastos (1987). *Eur. J. Biochem.* **166**, 639–645.

[8] Mourão, P.A.S. and A.S. Perlin (1987). *Eur. J. Biochem.* **166**, 431–436.

[9] Painter, T.J. (1983). *in:* "The Polysaccharides", G.O. Aspinall (ed.) Vol.II, p.195–285, Academic Press, New York.

[10] Pavão, M.S.G.; R.M. Albano; and P.A.S. Mourão. *Carbohydr. Res.* (in press).

[11] Percival, E. and R.H. McDowell (1967). "Chemistry and Enzymology of Marine Algal Polysaccharides, Academic Press, New York.

[12] Rodén, L. (1981). *in:* "The Biochemistry of Glycoproteins and Proteoglycans", W.J. Lennarz (ed.), p.267–371, Plenum Publishing Corp., New York.

[13] Vieira, R.P. and P.A.S. Mourão. *J. Biol. Chem.* (in press).

ENVIRONMENTAL IMPACT OF THE STRANDING OF A FREIGHTER SHIP IN THE "PARQUE NACIONAL MARINHO DOS ABROLHOS", BAHIA, BRAZIL

J. Gonchorosky [1]   G. Sales [1]   M.C.P. Oliveira [1]

1 INTRODUCTION

The Abrolhos Marine National Park was created by presidential decree no. 88,218 of April 6, 1983 encompassing two distinct areas of the southern coast of the State of Bahia, Brazil, with a total area of approximately 266 square nautical miles. However, the actual implementation only began in August of 1987 with the hiring of the current project coordinators. During this time the "Golden Unity" ecological accident occurred. The cargo vessel, after crossing over Abrolhos shoal, got stuck on some reefs near Santa Barbara Island in the Abrolhos Archipelago.

The removal of the "Golden Unity", which remained stranded for 20 days, was followed by a direct visual study of the destruction caused by the cargo vessel as well as photographic documentation. As a result of the accident, three legal proceedings were opened but none has, to this moment, had any positive results in terms of punishment for those responsible or reimbursement to the Park.

2 LOCATION

On the southern coast of the State of Bahia, between parallels 17° and 20° S, the continental shelf extends to 240 miles from the coast to the beginning of the ramp, in contrast to the average distance of 40 miles along the eastern and northeastern coast of Brazil. This formation is called the Abrolhos bank.

On the northern portion of this bank and adjacent coastline, between parallels 17°23′ and 18°10′ one encounters a group of coral reefs, island outcrops of sedimentary rocks, mangroves and inlets. The reefs form two arcs: one closer to the coast and the other further away and more extensive.

The Abrolhos archipelago is formed by the islands: Santa Barbara, Redonda, Siriba, Sueste and Guarita, and is located approximately 40 nautical miles from the Caravelas river shoals and 1 mile west of the Abrolhos shoal. In this same physiographic context is located the Abrolhos Marine National Park ("Parque Nacional Marinho de Abrolhos") that is subdivided in two distinct areas. The first encompasses the shoal and archipelago with 233.6 square nautical miles and the

---

[1]Parque Nacional Marinho dos Abrolhos, Rua Sete de Setembro 234, Caravelas, BA 45900, Brazil.

second the Timbebas reefs with 32.35 square nautical miles located in front of the city of Alcobaça, approximately 10 miles away.

The richness of coral formations was the dominant factor for the creation of the Park. Although this richness includes only eight varieties of corals, one can find in this region endemic species found only in Brazil such as *Mussimilia brasiliensis*, *Mussimilia harttii* and *Millepora brasiliensis*.

The reefs in the Abrolhos shoal grow in columns from the seabed to the surface, many times appearing above water. They are called "capoeirões" and have the format of mushrooms reaching a height of 25 meters and widths of 50 meters.

These formations were first described by Hart (1870) and recently studied by Leão (1982). The formation is unique in the world and can be grossly compared to the algae chalices described by Ginburg *et al.* (1973) in the Bermudas.

In addition the region is an important feeding ground for marine turtles and is frequented in winter and spring (August and November) by schools of jubart (*Megaptera novaeangliae*) whales.

3 HISTORY OF THE ACCIDENT

On the morning of July 28, 1987, the cargo vessel "Golden Unity" of panamanian flag entered the park area leaving its normal route near the Abrolhos shoal. The ship had 130 m in length, weighed 18,000 ton and was loaded with sugar. The ship crossed the shoal on an east-west direction colliding constantly against the capoeirões, refusing to maintain radio contact and to accept orientation from a pleasure boat that was on location.

The "Golden Unity" sailed 3 nautical miles over the shoal, destroying the capoeirões in an area of over 110,000 sq.mts. In addition it got stranded twice on the coral fringe of Santa Barbara Island, disfiguring more than 300 linear meters of corals. The fauna and flora of these areas were seriously compromised.

The successive strikes against the island led to the rupture of its hull and the leaking of 6 tons of sugar and the ship fuel oil. The "Golden Unity" remained for 20 days trying to free itself and was finally towed by a Brazilian Navy ship to the port of Salvador.

The damage was evaluated by three oceanographers and registered *in loco* by a marine photographer during 5 days aboard the Albatroz; the equipment used was for dependent diving (compressed air) and autonomous (cylinders). A report was filed and sent to the authorities in mid-september of the same year.

These facts led to three legal proceedings: one contavencional, another compensatory through the State of Bahia Federal Courts, and the third was by the navy court located in the State of Rio de Janeiro.

The Federal Courts condemned the accused, the ship commander to three months detention and payment of costs for violation of Article 26 letter *d* of law no. 4771 that foresees a fine of up to 100 minimum wage (approximately US$ 4,000 in February/89 values).

However, the compensatory proceedings brought against Golden Unity Marine SA, owners of the vessel were cancelled.

The Navy Court proceedings are still under way with no results up to the present moment.

The accusation of the ship commander was in default since he was freed by Brazilian authorities and returned to his native country right after the accident.

4 CONCLUSION AND COMMENTS

This accident coincided with the start of effective work on the implementation of the Park, the only one of its kind in the country (marine), and therefore it did not have the necessary infrastructure to accompany the recovery (and recolonization) of the damaged reefs. However, the presence of technicians on location and during the proceedings were able to disclose the following:

- This accident was clearly the largest ecological disaster in the Marine National Park of Abrolhos.

- Part of the damage is irreversible since the climatic environment that made these formations possible are currently non-existent.

- Although condemned the ship commander did not have to pay any compensation or fine and the park remained with no indemnity for the damages.

- The inefficiency and disorganization of the authorities responsible for environmental matters in Brazil is flagrant since a criminal accident of these proportions led to no punitive action against those involved.

- The financial expenses for the creation and implementation of the Marine Park are enormous and the resources that could have raised from any compensation would not solve or repair the environmental damage; however, they would be extremely for studies of environmental and even more so to help in the creation of the necessary infrastructure to manage and help avoid accidents and aggressions against the Marine National Park of Abrolhos.

REFERENCES

[1] Ginsburg, R.N. and J.H. Schroeder (1973). Growth and submarine fossilization of algal cup reefs, Bermuda. *Sedimentology* 20: 575–614.

[2] Hart, C.F. (1870). "Geology and Physical Geography of Brazil". Boston, Fields, Osgood & Co.: 174–273.

[3] Leão, Z.M.A.N. (1982). Morphology, geology and developmental history of the southernmost coral reefs of Western Atlantic, Abrolhos Bank, Brazil. Ph.D. Dissertation. Rosenstiel School of Marine Atmospheric Sciences, University of Miami, 218 pp.

MANAGEMENT OF FISHERIES IN THE STATE OF RIO DE JANEIRO, BRAZIL

Sergio Roberto P. Annibal [1]

1 INTRODUCTION

The fisheries resources management implies an integrated knowledge which can be divided into two subjects: Multiple Uses of Hydric Resources, and Fisheries Resources Evaluation and Management.

Management aspects of hydric resources are considered worldwidely by authors such as Vaillant (1977), Heikoff (1980), and discussed in symposia such as the International Symposium on Utilization of Coastal Ecosystem (1985).

There are many FAO documents related to evaluation and management of fisheries resources (Welcome and Henderson, 1977; Panayoton, 1982; Christy, 1983; Troadec, 1984; Caddy and Sharp, 1986). In Brazil there are also important synthesis of fisheries stock evaluation performed by some groups (PDP-SUDEPE/FAO, 1974 and 1985) and many technical documents by SUDEPE ("Superintendência do Desenvolvimento da Pesca").

The difficulty for the integration of this knowledge is caused by the multidisciplinary subjects and the incomplete diagnoses that provide many unrealistic alternatives of management.

To improve the interdisciplinary knowledge and to subdivide the problem in bio-ecological sectors, international committees recommend the development of integrated evaluation groups (Bakum et alli., 1982). On the other hand, some regional management strategies have been developed with good results in some countries such as Japan (Asada et alli., 1983) and the Philippines (Smith and Panayoton, 1984).

In Brazil, our experience in this field (Annibal, 1985; Annibal and Oliveira, 1985; and Annibal, 1986) shows the need for regionalism and multidisciplinarity.

Our subject, placed in the State of Rio de Janeiro, tries to illustrate a type of regional management. The main idea is to speed the solutions of the problems of the fisheries production as well as the aquatic environmental quality.

Our main objective is to bring forward the discussion of the subject "management" analyzing some important aspect.

[1]Departamento de Biologia Marinha, Instituto de Biologia, Universidade Federal do Rio de Janeiro, Rio de Janeiro, RJ 21941, Brazil.

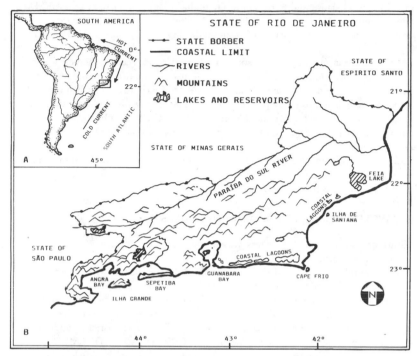

Figure 1: Location and geographical diversity of the State of Rio de Janeiro. A –
General oceanographical circulation: Brazil current (warm) and Malvinas current
(cold). B – Main geographical sites.

2 FISHERIES RESOURCES AND CONSERVATION

The State of Rio de Janeiro is localized along the convergence zone of the hot and
cold oceanic currents (Fig. 1A), where a strong inflection of the coast takes place,
and where "upwelling" occurs seasonally (Silva, 1977; and Rodrigues, 1977).

Geographically, Rio de Janeiro is a State rich in coastal and continental hydric resources. Besides its subtropical climate, topographical and phytoecological
heterogeneity determine a great aquatic environmental diversity (Fig. 1B).

On the other hand, in our densely populated state (288.40 hab/km², FIBGE,
1985), the harmful effect of human activities in the environment are becoming more
and more intense, due to urbanization and to agricultural projects. The dynamics
of environmental management is almost always carried out without an appropriate plan, affecting directly flora and fauna where fisheries resources are included
(Fig. 2). Abundance and quality of fisheries resources in each place are clear indicators of the environmental quality, representing a practical aspect that can mobilize
communities as well as public and private institutions, in order to achieve a conservation ideology and a planned management. The consciousness of the problem was
recently shown in the symposium "A Pesca, o Lazer e a Poluição na Baia de Guan-

abara" (Fishing, Leisure and Pollution in Guanabara Bay), sponsored by FEEMA (Fundaçcão Estadual de Engenharia do Meio Ambiente) — the State environmental agency — and ABES (Associação Brasileira de Engenharia Sanitária) (FEEMA, 1988).

The interconnection of fisheries resources information represents the basic point in up-to-date management, rural or urban. The use of aquatic environment promotes a sportive, commercial or regional fishery's production and can bring social and economical benefits to many places. To obtain it, maintenance of aquatic environmental quality is very important, so much so, that SUDEPE published one issue of the "Jornal da Pesca) (no. 15-88) to discuss the contamination of the Brazilian rivers.

Thus, the development of fisheries resources production, resulting from orientation about fishery and aquaculture activities, could provide conservationist attitudes, if there is appropriate management.

3   ECOSYSTEM'S DIVERSITY AND MULTIPLE USES

The State of Rio de Janeiro presents varied water resources, both in continental and in marine environments.

In continental areas we find the Paraíba do Sul river basin, with a potential which must be studied so that its resources could be exploited in the future. There is also a great number of small rivers that descend Serra do Mar and Serra das Araras — mountain ridges that follow roughly parallel to the coast — some reservoirs (Funil Dam, in Resende, and Ribeirão das Lages Dam, in Rio Claro), small ponds and Lagoa Feia, important lake to the northern area of Rio de Janeiro (Fig. 3).

The coastal lagoons represent another group of resources with different forms, dimensions and some interesting characteristics. There are also three major bays — Guanabara, Sepetiba, and Ilha Grande – which are well protected environments, showing many estuarine and marine characteristics (Fig. 3).

Finally, there are many oceanic beaches which present different hydrodynamical conditions, insular ecosystems such as Ilha Grande, Ilha de Cabo Frio and Ilha de Santana, and open oceanic areas.

The spatial gradients of depth, temperature, salinity and turbidity, presented in Fig. 3, indicate basic aspects of the environmental diversity found in the littoral of Rio de Janeiro.

There are many important factors for each area and type of fishery resource such as: capture, processing, and commerce. These factors provide many levels of fishery activities and generate different administrative strategies and legislative reforms. Besides, in an aquatic ecosystem, it may occur simultaneous uses that will bring out other aspects that should be considered. In the Guanabara Bay, for example, one finds seaside resorts, sportive and nautical activities, military areas, industrial and domestic sewage disposal (pollution) and fisheries. Some of these activities are antagonistic although they share the same space. This fact implies many kinds of rules, administrative strategies and programs which can only be set up by well done evaluation of available information.

The complexity of the interaction among these elements shows that the first objective of management must be the division of information in ecosystem, making

Figure 2: Schematic view of the relations between natural habitats of the fisheries resources and coastal development. Environmental impacts: 1 – pesticides; 2 – industrial and domestic wastes; 3 – shoreline changes; 4 – extermination of the ecosystem.

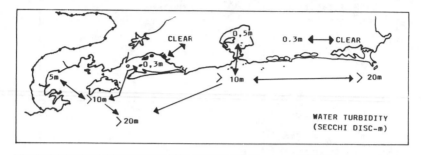

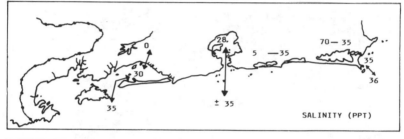

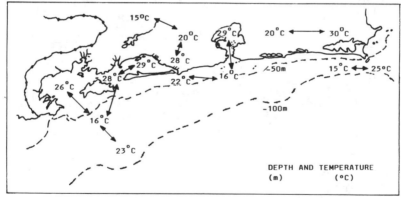

Figure 3: Spatial gradients of water turbidity, salinity, depth and temperature in the southern littoral of Rio de Janeiro.

easy the analysis of the qualitative and quantitative conditions of available fisheries resources.

4 FISHERIES RESOURCES AND EVALUATION

The selected fisheries resource populations include: natural aquatic ecosystems communities (*fishery*); or artificial systems (*aquaculture*). Anyway, each species should be observed in all aspects of bioecology and of specific fisheries techniques, considering the diagnoses about market.

We can consider, generically, that the fishery resource varies specially in the level presented in Fig. 4 (adapted from Mc Connell, 1987).

In the State of Rio de Janeiro the total fish yield represented 100,000 ton/year, approximately 10% of the national yield, but it has a 300,000 ton/year potential (FIPERJ, 1988). The distribution zone of the principal resources can be observed in Fig. 5.

However, the State of Rio de Janeiro, as well as other States in Brazil, do not have a good assessment data system. Most of the information, when available, is diffuse, confused and discontinuous. As a result, it becomes difficult to achieve the good performance of an administrative strategy of fisheries.

It is necessary to prepare an information program that will integrate environmental characterization, stock evaluation and fisheries statistics in order to perform an appropriate management. Nevertheless, some questions arrive: what is the best way to perform this program? which institutional structure is available?

5 INSTITUTIONAL RESPONSIBILITIES

Despite many laws or decrees, it is very difficult to control or to punish any kind of environmental destruction. The public institutions which are responsible for it can not act efficiently due to lack of funds and also to problems that are generated by incompetence. For instance, in the book "Directrizes – Objetivos Básicos e Estratégias para o Desenvolvimento da Pesca" (SUDEPE 1975/1980), about basic objectives and strategies for fiseries development, the fishery sector is divided into 20 activities and 19 responsible institutions.

As an example the responsible agents for the "Manpower Training Program" are: SUDEPE, Universities, State Governments, the Navy, EMATER (Empresa de Assistência Técnica e Extensão Rural), private industries, Ministry of Education. Obviously, such large number of institutions cause a significant diffusion of funds in order to perform this activity. Further, it becomes difficult to define the training programs and, as a general consequence, it results in low efficiency in manpower specialization.

On the other hand, public institutions always shape management structures in sectors or departments that subdivide their responsibilities. It is often difficult, though, to determine precisely which activities or responsibilities a department has. This is due to the instability of technical criteria as regards the objectives and also to the excess of functions carried out by each institution at the same time. SUDEPE, for example, accumulates 19 activities in fishery's sector, generating an institutional deficiency.

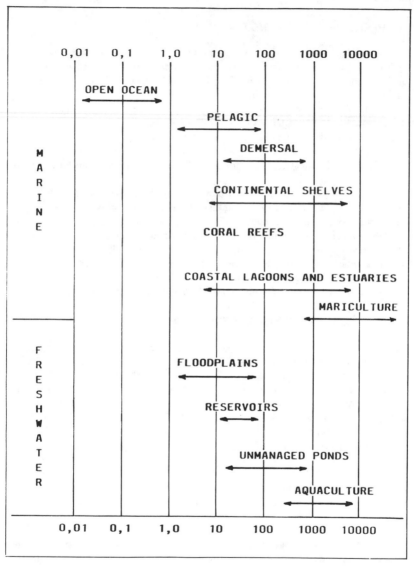

Figure 4: Comparative fish yields in tropical ecosystems (adapted from McConnel, 1987).

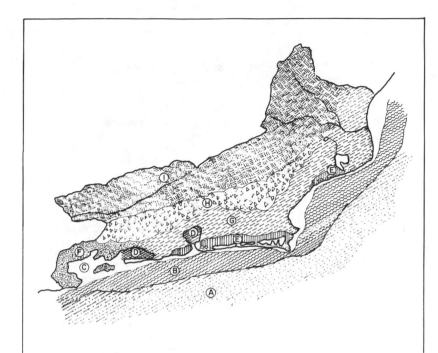

ENVIRONMENT		FISHERIES RESOURCE		ABUNDANCE ZONE								
HABITAT		DIVERSITY		A	B	C	D	E	F	G	H	I
MARINE												
	PELAGIC	SCOMBRID		●	◑							
		CLUPEID		◑	●	◑						
		"SQUIDS"		◑	●	◑						
		CARANGID		◑	●	◑						
	BENTHONIC DEMERSAL	SCIAENID		◑	●	◑						
		ARIID		◑	●	◑						
		SOLEID		◑	●	◑						
	ROCK REEFS	PENEID			●	●	◑					
		SERRANID			●	●	◑					
		LUTJANID			●	●						

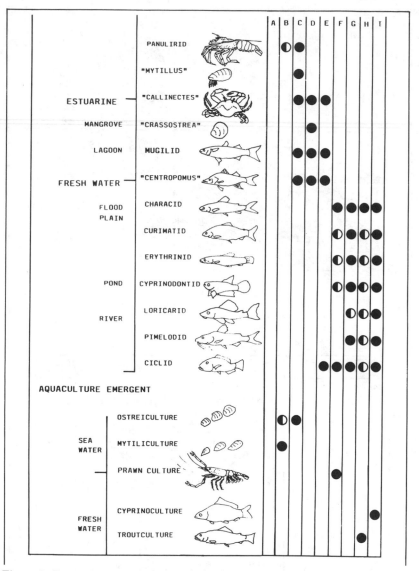

Figure 5: Zones of distribution of the main fisheries resources found in the State of Rio de Janeiro.

The management made for objectives or projects which are developed by multidisciplinary commissions, can be effective because there is technical and political credibility, and because group members are acquainted with the problem.

The multidisciplinary aspect, the dimensions and the heterogeneity of our country prevent commissions from solving the problems. Members of CIRM (Comissão Interministerial para os Recursos do Mar) which has already contributed to the development of some general activities, can not know the details of all regional problems and their solutions may not be the appropriate ones. On the other hand, FIPERJ (Fundação Instituto da Pesca do Rio de Janeiro) although starting its first work program now, can provide very good results, if it studies real regional problems and classifies the specific information in order to find effective solutions.

Whatever the level of commissions or work group, there must be a basic idea: the members should be the executors of the evaluation and up to date diagnosis. It should be computed in the diagnosis all technical information and social-economical needs of local communities.

Responsibilities and competence of public institutions must be well determined and improved. Nevertheless conservation of fisheries resources can only be effective when communities and state governments work together in a process of regional management.

6 REGIONAL MANAGEMENT

Control group laws or police inspection are not enough to determine guiding norms for the aquatic resources management system. It is necessary good relationship between communities and fishery colonies. In this case, regionalization is also important because local communities can observe and react against harmful actions to the environment.

Of course it is not easy to provoke reactions as it involves three basic mechanisms: local environmental education, municipal political representation and frequent communication between the communities and the federal or state public institutions.

Local environmental education would have the following objective: to introduce more knowledge about the ecological situation in schools and other educational media in the municipality in order to generate an ecological awareness based in local and natural conditions.

The municipal political representation would be embodied by environmental secretaries, established according to the regional fishery conditions. Angra dos Reis County, for example, has a municipal fishery secretary since 1986, and Arraial do Cabo County since 1987 has a coastal management secretary which is mostly concerned with fishery resources. These are isolated examples among the 20 coastal counties in the State.

The federal or state departments, consultive or legislative, would be responsible for elaboration of technical, scientific and juridical reports according to each situation.

We use a figurative scheme to describe the mechanisms of regional diagnosis (Fig. 6), where one big cube represents the ecological situation and one cylinder represents the communities and institutional agencies.

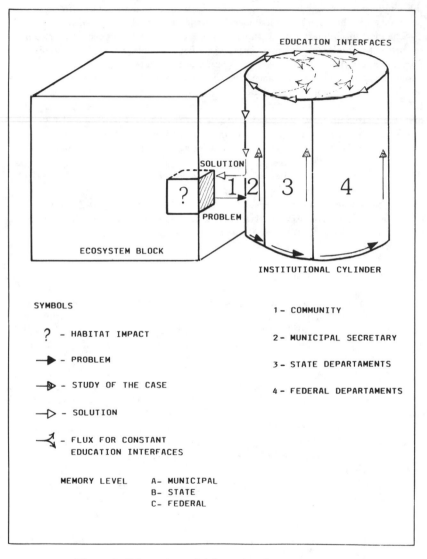

Figure 6: Schematic model for regional management.

From a local problem inside the *Ecosystem Block* the community of a fishery colony (1) has a straight relationship shown at the *Institutional Cylinder*. This possibly makes the municipal secretary (2) study the case and/or send it to state departments or federal agencies in order to find a solution. Then, rules and criteria are explained to the communities. All solutions flow into the *Institutional Cylinder Content* generating *constant education interfaces* and memory for management analysis in many levels (A – Municipal; B – State; C – Federal).

It is not very easy to implement in its totality these programs but it must begin in one place or another, not only to acquire experience in fishery management, but also to develop the general coastal management.

7 CONCLUSIONS

Nowadays, in the State of Rio de Janeiro there are reasons to believe that a program for management of the fisheries resources can be started, mainly because many sectors of the communities and technical institutions are interested on it.

However, it is important to emphasize the need for regionalized knowledge as regards fisheries resources and their evaluation, considering different ecosystems.

Each municipal community should be able to require access to all information about environmental conditions and harmful actions to the environment. A harmonious relationship between man and environment will only be possible if there is awareness and knowledge about these problems in order to find the best solutions.

REFERENCES

[1] Annibal, S.R.P. (1985). Pêche et hydrologie en Amazonie Centrale. *Verh. Internat. in Limnol.* **22**: 2692–2697.

[2] Annibal, S.R.P. (1986). Programa de Pesquisa sobre Recursos Pesqueiros no Estado do Rio de Janeiro: Avaliação e Manejo. Int. Report, Dep. Biologia Marinha, UFRJ.

[3] Annibal, S.R.P. and J.F.D. Oliveira (1985). Situação dos Recursos Pesqueiros da Amazônia Ocidental. *in:* Relatório da 2a. Reunião do Grupo de Trabalho e Treinamento em Avaliação de Estoque. FAO/SUDEPE. SUDEPE/PDP Série Documentos Técnicos, no. 34.

[4] Asada, Y; Y. Hirasawa; and F. Nagasaki (1983). La ordenación pesquera en Japón. FAO – Doc. Tec. Pesca, 238, 25 pp.

[5] Bakum, A.; J. Beyer; D. Pauly; J.G. Pope; and G.D. Sharp (1982). Ocean sciences in relation to living resources. *Can. J. Fish. Aquat. Sci.* **39**: 1059–1070.

[6] Chac, N.L. and W.K. Smith (eds.) (1985). International Symposium on Utilization of Coastal Ecosystems: Planning, Pollution and Productivity. Rio Grande, 1982. 496 pp.

[7] Caddy, J.F. and G.D. Sharp (1985). An ecological framework for marine fishery investigations. FAO Fish. Tech. Pap. 238, 152 pp.

[8] Christy Jr., F.T. (1983). Derechos de uso territorial en las pesquerias marítimas: definiciones y condiciones. FAO Doc. Les. Pesca 227, 11 pp.

[9] FAO (1983). Reunión Preparatoria para la Conferencia Mundial de la FAO sobre Ordenación y Desarollo Pesqueros. April 11–15, 1983, Rome. FAO Inf. Pesca 293, 189 pp.

[10] FEEMA – Fundação Estadual de Engenharia do Meio Ambiente (1988). Projeto de Recuperação Gradual do Ecossistema da Baía de Guanabara. (doc. preliminar). SEMA, Gov. Est. Rio de Janeiro, 140 pp.

[11] FIPERJ – Fundação Instituto de Pesca do Estado do Rio de Janeiro (1988). Work Propose of the FIPERJ 1989–1990. Tech. Paper no. 1, 37 pp.

[12] Heikoff, J.M. (1980). "Marine and shoreland resources management". Ann Arbor Science, 214 pp.

[13] McConnell, R.H. (1987). "Ecological Studies in Tropical Fish Communities", Cambridge Univ. Press, 382 pp.

[14] Pannayoton, T. (1982). Management concepts for small scale fisheries: economic and social aspects. FAO Fish. Lec. Pap. 228, 53 pp.

[15] Rodrigues, R.F. (1977). Evolução da massa d'água durante a ressurgência em Cabo Frio. Inst. Pesq. Marinha, Min. Marinha, Rio de Janeiro, no. 115, 31 pp.

[16] Silva, P.C.M. (1977). Upwelling and its biological effects in Southern Brazil. Inst. Pesq. Marinha, Min. Marinha, Rio de Janeiro, no. 112, 6 pp.

[17] Smith, I.R. and T. Pannayoton (1984). Derechos de uso territorial y eficiencia economica: el caso de las cocesiones pesqueras en Filipinas. FAO Doc. Tec. Pesca 245, 18 pp.

[18] SUDEPE – Superintendência do Desenvolvimento da Pesca (1980). Diretrizes, objetivos básicos e estratégia para o desenvolvimento pesqueiro 1975, 23 pp.

[19] SUDEPE – Superintendência do Desenvolvimento da Pesca (1988). Jornal da Pesca. Min. Agricultura, Brasília, DF, no. 15, set/out. 12 pp.

[20] SUDEPE / FAO (1974). Relatório da Primeira Reunião do Grupo de Trabalho e Treinamento (G.T.T.) sobre Avaliação de Estoques, Brasília. SUDEPE/PDP Ser. Doc. Tec. no. 7, 149 pp.

[21] SUDEPE / FAO (1985). Relatório da Segunda Reunião do Grupo de Trabalho e Treinamento (G.T.T.) sobre Avaliação de Estoques, Brasília. SUDEPE/PDP Ser. Doc. Tec. no. 34, 439 pp.

[22] Troadec, J.P. (1984). Introdución a la ordenación pesquera: su importancia, dificuldades y metodos principales. FAO Doc. Tec. Pesca AA4, 60 pp.

[23] Vaillant, J.R. (1977). "Accroissement et Gestion des Resources en l'Eau". Ed. Eyrolles, Paris, 246 pp.

[24] Welcome, R.L. and H.F. Henderson (1977). Aspectos de la ordenación de las aguas continentales para la pesca. FAO Doc. Tec. Pesca, 161, 36 pp.

IMPORTANCE, ESTABLISHMENT AND MANAGEMENT PLAN OF THE "PARQUE NACIONAL MARINHO DOS ABROLHOS", BRAZIL

Julio Gonchorosky[1]   Gilberto Sales [1]   Maria Julia C. Belém[2]

Clovis B. Castro [2]

1 THE ABROLHOS AREA

The largest coral reef complex in the South Atlantic Ocean lies off the southern coast of Bahia State, Brazil, between latitudes 17°20′ S and 18°10′ S. The Abrolhos area, as cited in this paper, follows the definition set forth by Leão (1982). It includes a few small islands (Abrolhos Archipelago) and a group of coral reefs. The Eastern Brazilian Continental Shelf is usually narrow (approximately 50 km wide), but it widens in the Abrolhos area, extending up to 200 km where the Abrolhos Archipelago is located. Sea depth in the islands and reefs rarely exceeds 25 m.

The Abrolhos Archipelago comprises five small volcanic islands (Santa Bárbara, Sueste, Siriba, Redonda, and Guarita). These islands have embryonic fringing reefs (Pitombo et al., in press), which are not constructions where corals play a remarkable building role (Laborel, 1970a; Leão, 1982). They present reef organisms growing in a hard substrate formed mainly by coralline algae and other organisms.

The real coral reefs are placed in two "arcs", which are approximately parallel to the coast. The inner arc presents a series of large reef structures formed by the coalescence of patch reefs, as well as isolated patch reefs. The larger of these structures is the "Parcel das Paredes", which is 20 km long and 10 km wide. The top of these reefs are usually exposed during low tides. A drilling in a small island in the middle of one of the southernmost of these reefs ("Recife da Coroa Vermelha") showed the presence of coral through most of the drilling (15.2 m deep) and the top of the pre-Holocene sequence was attained at 12.7 m from the surface of the island (which is approximately 1.5 m above sea level) (Leão, 1982). The drilling did not reach the basis of coral reef structures.

The outer arc ("Parcel dos Abrolhos") which is close to the archipelago is concentric with the inner arc, and separated from this arc by a channel 11–15 km wide and 20–29 m deep. In the Parcel dos Abrolhos, the reefs are deeper and the uppermost pinnacles are exposed only during low tides. In the outer part of this Parcel,

---

[1]Parque Nacional Marinho dos Abrolhos (Coordinators) – R. Sete de Setembro, 234, Caravelas, BA 45900, Brazil.

[2]Museu Nacional, Universidade Federal do Rio de Janeiro, Quinta da Boa Vista, São Cristóvão, Rio de Janeiro, RJ 20942, Brazil.

the top of the reefs are almost never exposed. These reefs are discontinuous (like a cluster of patch reefs). These are the richest coral reefs off the Brazilian coast (Laborel, 1970a; Belém et al., 1986).

The coast is lined with mangroves or sand beaches.

The main cities in this area are: Caravelas, Alcobaça, Prado (to the North), and Nova Viçosa (to the South). They are small (circa 15,000 inhabitants each) and access to them through land is made on unpaved roads — one has to drive approximately 50 km from the nearest paved road (BR-101). Their economy is mainly based on fishing (shrimp), cocoa, manioc, papaya plantations and cattle raising. In the mangrove, crabs, fishes, oysters, and other organisms, provide extra sources of food and jobs to the poorer population.

A study of the diversity of fishes in the area showed that the reefs (including the islands) and the coast (mangroves and shore) have almost completely different groupings of fish species — three common species among the 95 recorded in the whole area (Nunan, 1979).

According to Laborel (1970a), the diversity of coral species decreases in a gradient from the outer side of the "Parcel dos Abrolhos" to the inner side of the "Parcel das Paredes" (inner arc reef). He affirms this probably occurs due to increasing turbidity in the waters closer to the shoreline.

In 1981, one of the authors (Castro) was invited by the "Instituto Brasileiro de Desenvolvimento Florestal" (IBDF), the Brazilian conservation agency, to evaluate the area of Abrolhos as a potential conservation unit (Castro and Secchin, 1982). In the few dives performed during this short visit, it was confirmed that the local fauna is both rich and unknown, as evidenced by two lots among the collected specimens — a new record of one family in the South Atlantic and a new species (Belém et al., 1982; Castro, in press) — both with large specimens (> 30 cm high).

It is important to note that these reefs show a small number of scleractinian corals and octocorals when compared to the richest Caribbean reefs. In Abrolhos, 16 scleractinian species (Laborel, 1970b) and 6 octocoral species (Castro, 1986) were recorded up to now. In the Northern American tropical region, up to 62 scleractinian corals were recorded in a single area (for discussion see Glynn, 1973). Moreover, more than a dozen octocoral species (up to 38 species) occurring in reef habitat [1], at a depth of less than 25 fathoms, were recorded in areas of the Caribbean (see Bayer, 1961). Nevertheless, it should be noted that both Laborel (1970a, 1970b) and Castro (1986) state that more detailed surveys will probably add new records to the coral and octocoral fauna of Abrolhos. On the other hand, although there are few species in Abrolhos, many are endemic either to the Brazilian coast or to the Abrolhos area itself.

During part of winter and of spring (July through November), humpback whales (Megaptera novaeangliae) visit the area, usually with several of their young following their mothers. In the 1988 season, over 30 whales were observed. In summer, a few loggerhead sea turtles (Caretta caretta) and green sea turtles (Chelonia midas) lay eggs on the sand beaches of the islands. The islands of the archipelago are also used for nesting by several species of sea birds.

Several authors agree that the reefs of the area are unique when compared to

---

[1] Carijoa riisei (= Telesto riisei) was counted, although Bayer (1961) marks it as not occurring in reef habitat, because it was included in the number of species recorded in Abrolhos by Castro (1986).

reefs along the Brazilian coast, as well as to other regions in the world, (Belém *et al.*, 1986; Castro and Secchin, 1982; Laborel, 1970a; Leão, 1982; Nunan, 1979).

2 CREATION OF THE PARK AND HISTORICAL BACKGROUND

The first proposal to establish a national marine park in Abrolhos came from researchers from the "Universidade de São Paulo" (Joly *et al.*, 1969). It was discussed during a symposium on environmental conservation held in Rio de Janeiro in 1968. These authors described the exploitation of the reefs by the use of dynamite during low tides. According to them, "fishermen" (the quote is theirs) removed blocks of coral to be transformed and used as mortar on the mainland. They believed the most adequate area to be transformed into a park was the Archipelago and the surrounding areas of coral banks, including the "Parcel das Paredes" and the "Parcel dos Abrolhos". The park should consist of a single continuous quadrilateral area with vertices on the following points:

point	latitude	longitude
A	18°02'00" S	039°20'30" W
B	17°38'30" S	039°00'00" W
C	17°45'00" S	038°38'30" W
D	18°08'00" S	038°39'30" W

Furthermore, they believed the park administration should be part of the "Departamento de Hidrografia e Navegação" of the Brazilian Navy (which controlled the whole area before the establishment of the Park). Although such task would be completely out of the jurisdiction of that institution, we shall see that, initially, the transfer of control of the area brought some problems to its conservation.

The seventies saw a "boom" of new Brazilian National Parks, with the creation (but not the implantation) of several terrestrial units. The first federal marine conservation unit was created in 1979, the "Reserva Biológica do Atol das Rocas".

On April 6th, 1983, the "Parque Nacional Marinho dos Abrolhos" (PARNA) was created by a decree of the Brazilian Presidency, under the jurisdiction of IBDF. In this decree, a provision was inserted to keep Navy activities in the area independent of the IBDF. The "Ilha de Santa Bárbara" was excluded from the PARNA, staying under the jurisdiction and the control of the Brazilian Navy. Moreover, the IBDF should organize the PARNA in "agreement with the Navy". The decree established a 180 days term (October, 1983) after its publication for an official Management Plan to be prepared. Up to now (January, 1989), the IBDF has not shown an official Management Plan.

The PARNA was established with two distinct areas: one centered in the "Parcel dos Abrolhos"; and the other in one of the inner reefs (the "Recife das Timbebas") (Fig. 1).

The area centered in the "Parcel dos Abrolhos" includes this reef and the Archipelago. It has approximately 233.60 square nautical miles (801.23 km²) and it is delimited by the following four vertices:

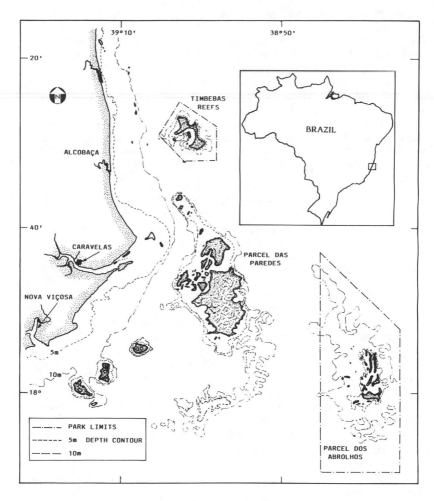

Figure 1: Localization of the Park.

point	latitude	longitude
A	17°43′ S	038°45′ W
B	17°54′ S	038°33.5′ W
C	18°09′ S	038°33.5′ W
D	18°09′ S	038°45′ W

The "Recife das Timbebas" is the farthest from the coast among the inner arc reefs. It is separated from the shore by depths of up to 20 m, while most of the other inner reefs are in depths of 8–10 m. Its protected area has approximately 32.35 square nautical miles (110.96 km²). It is enclosed in a pentagon with vertices on the following points:

point	latitude	longitude
A	17°25′ S	039°02.7′ W
B	17°28′ S	038°58′ W
C	17°32′ S	038°58′ W
D	17°32′ S	039°02′ W
E	17°29′ S	039°05.4′ W

Thus, the area of the whole park is almost 265.95 square nautical miles (912.19 km²).

3 PROBLEMS WHEN CREATING THE PARK

The small area included in the PARNA (approximately 910 km²), when compared to the one suggested by Joly *et al.* (1969) (approximately 2900 km²), was a compromise between conservation needs and the needs of economic activities. The Abrolhos area (in and out of the PARNA) has been traditionally used for fishing. Nevertheless, although there are many fishing boats registered in nearby coastal cities, most of them are restricted to shrimp fisheries. This kind of fisheries occurs close to the coastline and does not interfere directly with park activities. Larger boats, usually from Vitória and Conceição da Barra (both cities in Espírito Santo State), fish in the reef area. They use three main strategies: bottom lines, the commonest, capturing benthonic fishes — groupers, basses, jewfishes, and other carnivores; midwater depth fishing nets — they are left drifting in deeper places and capture mainly sharks, rays, and travelling fishes; and, more recently, spear fishing using compressors pumping air from the surface, the latter kind is illegal in Brazil.

The creation of the PARNA brought some immediate problems to the conservation of the area. The Navy no longer restricted visitors and the IBDF did not start to organize the PARNA for several years, although visits were prohibited. The publicity created by articles in magazines, newspapers, and television increased the number of visitors that had neither instructions, nor control on their action in the PARNA.

The increasing market of sea aquariums and decoration objects from the sea in Brazilian large cities brought another problem to the preservation of the area. Although there are no official estimates, it is common knowledge in the area that large quantities of fire-coral (*Millepora spp.*), scleractinian corals, gorgonians, and mollusks are collected by divers. In the Abrolhos Archipelago, Pitombo *et al.* (in press) state that a "*Millepora* zone" described by Laborel (1970a) one meter below low low tide level in both sites they studied was not observed during their work.

Although three species of *Millepora* occur in Abrolhos, Pitombo *et al.* (in press) report that only *Millepora alcicornis* was found and, even so, in low densities (relative coverage: 1.5, 2.8, and 11%). According to these authors, "possibly these absences may be due to human impact since Laborel's visit, with emphasis on the predatory action of tourists and coral dealers".

This situation continued until August, 1987, when an agreement between the IBDF and the "Fundação Brasileira para a Conservação da Natureza" (FBCN) started the implantation of the PARNA. This agreement was responsible for the hiring of personnel to coordinate the foundation of the Park.

4 IMPLANTATION

The first months (August–December) after the beginning of the agreement were used by the coordinators in contacts in the nearby shore cities. During this period, an accident ocurred with the ship "Golden Unit", damaging circa 100,000 m² of reefs in the "Parcel dos Abrolhos" and the Archipelago (see Gonchorosky *et al.*).

During this period, an office was opened, with the help of the Alcobaça City Hall, and the renovation of an abandoned house at Santa Bárbara Island, given up by the Navy, was begun. This office was later transferred to a house in Caravelas, donated by the Caravelas City Hall.

The tourist season in Abrolhos is from December to March, due to the fact that at this time the weather is better, with weaker winds (usually 4–15 knots NE winds), consequently clearer and warmer waters (27–28 °C) (Diretoria de Hidrografia e Navegação, 1974 *apud* Leão, 1982). This period also coincides with school summer vacations. Most visits to the area occur in this period.

The number of tourists per year is still small, due to the difficulty of reaching the area. During the first year of implantation 3,000 persons per year were estimated.

During the summer season, there was the permanent presence of Park personnel — although limited to two persons — in the house of Santa Bárbara Island. Control activities and tourist orientation services were started near the Archipelago. Graduate and undergraduate students in Biology and Oceanography helped in these activities as volunteers — the Park provided only transportation and food.

Contacts with visitors, and with tourist boat captains and crews were very satisfactory, although there were severe logistic restraints to this work. There were no adequate boats, not even people with documents that enabled them to enforce park regulations. Nevertheless, almost all boats respected and supported the Park personnel activities. During summer, spear guns were gathered during the visits to the area, and returned to their owners when the boats were leaving it.

An administration problem for managers of the PARNA is the large number of institutions involved in the area. The Brazilian Navy keeps control of Santa Bárbara Island, the only one which is inhabited in the Archipelago. The IBDF coordinates the implantation and future management of the Park through the "Departamento de Parques Nacionais e Reservas Equivalentes" (DN), in Brasília. Funding comes from the DN, through the FBCN, which is located in Rio de Janeiro. In Brazil, control of fisheries belongs to the "Superintendência do Desenvolvimento da Pesca" (SUDEPE) and the Navy (boats). On the other hand, the IBDF should also have control, as it is responsible for the conservation unit. A regulation or redefinition of the role of each institution in the area is urgently needed. This necessity is aggravated by the absence of an official management plan.

By the end of 1988, the PARNA had some more logistical support to develop its activities. Headquarters installed at Santa Bárbara Island, an office at Caravelas, and a visitor center under construction at Caravelas (Kitongo); three boats: an adapted fishing boat (43 feet) for long range surveillance and transportation to and from the Archipelago, a fast "patrol" boat (18 feet) for short range use, and a small motor boat (9 feet) for ship inspection at at Santa Bárbara Island.

The Park also hired (although not permanently) two more persons to help in the control/orientation activities.

5 A THREE YEAR "MANAGEMENT PLAN"

In order to accelerate and regulate the implantation of the PARNA, a management proposal was prepared by the implantation coordinators, under the guidance of the DN/IBDF. However, the financial situation of environmental institutions in Brazil is such that they cannot supply even the most urgent needs of the Conservation Units, much less implant the large number of recently created units. Thus, this proposal was submitted to several private industries, asking for financial support. This procedure is facilitated by Law number 7505, July 2nd, 1986 – "Lei Sarney", which supports donations for cultural projects by fiscal incentives. This sort of scheme has been successfully set up in other conservation projects.

A Triennial Plan (1989–1991) was prepared based on the experience of the first fifteen months of implantation activities. It is based on the development of five "basic" programs. These plans can be divided into three main lines of action and two "support" programs.

A first main line of action is environmental protection. Three main factors increased the exploitation of reefs in Abrolhos. Shrimp fishing is now periodically prohibited in the area by SUDEPE. This makes local fishermen develop their activities in the reef area (bottom lines) — although it must be stressed that there are reefs off the Park area. Disclosure of the rich fauna of the region, uncontrolled for several years, increased the number tourists interested in spear fishing, and ornamental fish hunters who took great quantities from the Park area.

Two different actions were proposed to deal with the problem of reef exploitation. Park personnel, helped by graduate and undergraduate students (interns), will inform tourists arriving at the Archipelago about the reef ecosystem and of rules and regulations of the PARNA. Visitors will be informed where diving and landing is permitted, and measures will be taken to prevent damages to PARNA. On the other hand, IBDF accredited agents, in an agreement with the Brazilian Navy, will patrol the outer limits of the Park, bringing law-breakers to the Navy Port Authority and to the IBDF State Headquarters. There must be a Support Office at Alcobaça, which is closer to the "Recife das Timbebas", in order to facilitate its control.

The second line of action is environmental education: the developing of a consciousness in the Southern Bahia population, particularly among fishermen, of the importance of not disturbing the area marked for preservation. This program is very important. It will certainly be difficult and time consuming to change some habits of the local population. Although organized fisheries deal mainly with shrimp, for centuries the fishery resources of the whole area have been used without any limitation. The fishermen's associations and colonies are being contacted and several aspects of management are being discussed with them. This includes the possibility of rotation of fishing areas, restriction of periods and total fisheries prohibition. Their needs have to be included in any conservation plan for the area. Basic preservation ideas are being introduced in these meetings — initially regarding coral reefs, mangroves, and sea turtles.

Although present fisheries communities are being contacted, the major emphasis will be given to contacts with elementary schools (above 5th grade [2]). A plan has to be prepared so as to give these students an environmental education. As the children grow up, ecological consciousness will be developed in the population. A professional is to be hiredto lecture in local schools, fishermen's associations, etc.

The third line of action deals with stimuli and support for scientific research and interchange, in order to know the fauna and flora of the coral reef complex, to study the relationship of marine and land systems in the area, to study the possibility of delimiting areas and seasons in which unskilled fisheries could be permitted, etc. This is the hardest program to be accomplished. The volume of financial support which is necessary to develop all of these research objectives is a large one for Brazilian conservation units standards. Thus only logistical support is intended and contacting Universities to encourage the development of studies in the area. At this moment (January, 1989), the following subjects are being investigated: reef zonation and inventory (Museu Nacional, Universidade Federal do Rio de Janeiro); sea turtles (IBDF); humpback whales (Núcleo de Educação e Monitoramento Ambiental - NEMA); and mollusks (Museu Oceanográfico/Fundação Universidade do Rio Grande).

Besides these three lines of action, two other support programs are necessary: an administrative program to coordinate the actions of all other programs, and a maintenance program for installations and equipments in order to keep logistical support working properly.

6 DISCUSSION

A management plan of the PARNA, including the zoning of restricted activities, has two main factors that lead, at least initially, to a restrictive policy. This policy would be different from the one indicated in the case of the Great Barrier Reef Marine Park, in Australia (see Kelleher and Kenchington, 1982). There, a huge reef area is included in the Park, the Zoning Plan is elaborated with great public participation, and regulation is kept to a minimum.

In Brazil, the area covered by reefs in Southern Bahia is relatively small when compared to other reef regions in the world and, even so, only a small part of the reefs were included in the Park. Also, Southern Bahia is one of the poorest and less developed regions of Brazil. The local population has been using reef resources without any restrictions for centuries and did not participate in the decisions which resulted on the change of status of the area. In this case, a "simpler" situation, a few restricted reefs (the Park) and "open" reefs (out of Park area), is probably easier to be assimilated by local inhabitants and by tourists, as well as to control.

---

[2]In Brazil, education is divided in elementary school (8 years), secondary (3 years), and undergraduate studies).

The areas which are most used by tourists nowadays — a wreck in the "Parcel dos Abrolhos" and the Archipelago — are here indicated as the only visiting areas, at least initially. They could be included in a three nautical mile radius area around the Santa Bárbara Island Lighthouse. The outer limits of such area is approximately 1 hour from the Archipelago in local boats.

The reefs in the Park, especially the "Parcel dos Abrolhos, attract commercial fishermen because they are among the best fishing grounds in the region. Several boats come from other states to catch large quantitites of "noble" fish (groupers, basses, etc.). Nevertheless, we believe that all modalities of fishing should be prohibited within the limits of the Park. This is not as radical as it seems for several reasons. The Park includes a small part of reefs in the Abrolhos area and there are "non-Park" reefs a few miles away from the Park. Fishing grounds closer to the mainland than the "Parcel dos Abrolhos" are overfished and it is not desired to let this situation happen in Park reefs, which should be kept as recruitment grounds only.

Research should be supported in three lines: to describe organisms and the reef in space (horizontal and vertical distribution) and time (season, growth and reproduction); to help in the management of the park (human impact — effects of boats, visitors, pollution, etc. on park reefs); and to acknowledge the fauna and flora of the area. All research should be oriented to cause minimal disturbance in the environment (e.g. collecting by divers, instead of using trawlings).

Unfortunately mangrove areas are not included in the Park, as relation between the different biotas in the region is not yet understood. Actually, there is no study dealing with this subject in the Abrolhos area. In Brazil, there are specific laws to protect mangroves, but enforcement is certainly not as effective as it would be desired. Several mangroves in Brazil are in danger because of the extraction of wood, pollution, urban expansion etc. Nowadays, a major concern is the risk of industrial pollution. There are cellulose (Mucuri river) and alcohol plants (Mucuri river and Caravelas river) along rivers that drain to the Abrolhos area. There are oil drillings in the largest local mangrove area (Exploração Petróleo Cassumbá, 60,000 liters/day). It is current Park policy to encourage local City Halls to develop Coastal Management Plans.

Acknowledgements : Activities in the Abrolhos area of the "Setor de Celenterologia" of Museu Nacional/UFRJ were supported by "Conselho Nacional de Desenvolvimento Científico e Tecnológico" (CNPq), "Fundação Universitária José Bonifácio" (FUJB), and "Conselho de Ensino para Graduados" (CEPG/UFRJ).

REFERENCES

[1] Bayer, F. M. (1961). The shallow-water Octocorallia of the West Indian region. A manual for marine biologists. The Hague, Martinus Nijhoff. pp. 1-373.

[2] Belém, M. J. C.; C.B. Castro and C. Rohlfs (1982). Notas sobre *Solanderia gracilis* Duchassaing and Michelin, 1846, do Parcel dos Abrolhos, BA. Primeira ocorrência de Solanderiidae (Cnidaria, Hydrozoa) no litoral brasileiro. *An. Acad. Brasil. Ciênc.*, Rio de Janeiro, **54** (3): 585–588, 3 figs.

[3] Belém, M.J.C.; C. Rohlfs; D. O. Pires; C.B. Castro and P.S. Young (1986). S.O.S. Corais. *Ciência-Hoje*, Rio de Janeiro, 5 (26): 34–42.

[4] Castro, C. B. A new species of *Plexaurella* Valenciennes, 1855 (Coelenterata, Octocorallia), from the Abrolhos Reefs, Bahia, Brazil. *Rev. Brasil. Biol.*, Rio de Janeiro, 49 (1). (In press.)

[5] Castro, C. B. and C. A. Secchin (1982). Um Parque Nacional para Abrolhos. *Ciência-Hoje*, Rio de Janeiro, 1 (2): 38- -43.

[6] Glynn, P. W. (1973). Aspects of the ecology of coral reefs in the Western Atlantic Region. p.271-324. In: Jones, O.A. and R. Endean. Biology and Geology of Coral Reefs. Volume II: Biologia 1. Academic Press, New York. 480 pp.

[7] Gonchorosky, J.; G. Sales and M. C. P. Oliveira. Environmental impact of the stranding of a freighter ship in the "Parque Nacional Marinho dos Abrolhos", Bahia, Brazil. In: The Sixth Symposium on Coastal and Ocean Management, July 11–14, 1989. Charleston. (Abstract. Paper Reference Number 371.)

[8] Joly, A. B.; E. C. Oliveira Filho and W. Narchi (1969). Projeto de Criação de um Parque Nacional Marinho na Região de Abrolhos, Bahia. *An. Acad. Brasil. Ciênc.*, Rio de Janeiro, 41 (Suplemento): 247–251, 1 fig.

[9] Kelleher, G. G. and R. A. Kenchington (1982). Australia's Great Barrier Reef Marine Park: Making development compatible with conservation. *Ambio*, Stockolm, 11 (5): 262–267.

[10] Laborel, J. (1970a). Les peuplements de madréporaires des côtes tropicales du Brésil. *Ann. l'Univ. Abidjan* (E) 2 (3): 1–260.

[11] Laborel, J. (1970b). Madréporaires et Hydrocoralliaires récifaux de cotes brésiliennes. Systématique, Écologie, Répartition verticale et géographique. *Ann. Inst. Océan.*, Paris, 47: 171–229.

[12] Leão, Z. M. A. N. (1982). Morphology, geology, and developmental history of the southernmost coral reefs of Western Atlantic, Abrolhos Bank, Brazil. Coral Gables, Florida, University of Miami. Ph.D. Dissertation. 216 pp.

[13] Nunan, G. W. (1979). The zoogeographic significance of the Abrolhos area as evidenced by fishes. Coral Gables, Florida, University of Miami. M.Sc. Thesis. 146 pp.

[14] Pitombo, F. B.; C. C. Ratto; and M. J. C. Belém. Species diversity and zonation pattern of hermatypic corals at two fringing reefs of Abrolhos Archipelago, Brazil. In: Proceedings of the Sixth International Coral Reef Symposium. Townsville, 8-12 August, 1988. (In press.)

AN ANALYTICAL SYNOPTIC-DYNAMIC STUDY ABOUT THE SEVERE
WEATHER EVENT OVER THE CITY OF RIO DE JANEIRO ON JANUARY 2, 1987

Fábio de Alcantara [1]   Dulce Cardoso Washington [1]

1 INTRODUCTION

Bad weather conditions have been observed in Brazil, associated with patterns that lead to classify such events as severe weather. Such weather systems may cause violent impacts on coastal installations, offshore oil platforms, harbors and terminals (e.g. fishing, oil and ore). The event described in this work took place at the anchorage area of the Port of Rio de Janeiro. Other events could also be mentioned: storms near the Maricás Islands and Cabo Frio, and the storm surge happened in August 1988, which destroyed the sewage line along Leblon beach, Rio de Janeiro. (This event is described by Rosman and Valentini, elsewhere in this conference.)

Due to the lack of effective coastal management program, the damaging effects of the storm could not be avoided. However, because of their fast development and small spatial scale, the monitoring of such weather systems can not be performed on a synoptic scale analysis. Consequently, observation stations should have equipments for quick apprehension of the genesis of the storm such as meteorological radars coupled with observation from satellite images. With these means, material property and human lives could be protected against such events.

In the more developed countries severe weather conditions have deserved attention of researchers among others Zehr (1986), Rodgers (1984) and Fernandez (1973), House (1960).

In Brazil, Lage and Silva Dias (1984) have conducted studies in the area of convective systems occurred over São Paulo.

Nevertheless some incertitude still exists on the aspects of thermodynamic development which causes the intensification of the convective systems. Consequently the present study is important in order to present bases for further knowledge of these systems.

The present work aims to review the synoptic parameters that lead to the severe weather occurred on January 2, 1987 over the city of Rio de Janeiro. The pattern of this weather was reported on the newspapers as strong wind (40 – 50 knots) lasting one and a half hour and 20 minutes of heavy showers. Severe damages on

[1]Departamento de Meteorologia, Instituto de Geociências, Universidade Federal do Rio de Janeiro, Rio de Janeiro, RJ 21945, Brazil.

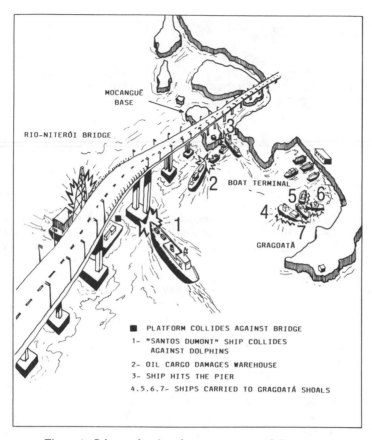

PLATFORM COLLIDES AGAINST BRIDGE
1- "SANTOS DUMONT" SHIP COLLIDES
   AGAINST DOLPHINS
2- OIL CARGO DAMAGES WAREHOUSE
3- SHIP HITS THE PIER
4.5.6.7- SHIPS CARRIED TO GRAGOATÁ SHOALS

Figure 1: Scheme showing the consequences of the storm.

ships in the Guanabara Bay were reported, including crash of an offshore platform (Fig. 1) against the Rio-Niterói Bridge.

For nearly 30 years the mesoscale has been used to study the magnitude of the meteorological entities like the ones involved in this storm. However, the relationship of spatial magnitude of the involved physical variables have not yet been definitely established. Nowadays the atmospheric disturbances characteristic of these mesoscale systems frequently vary from 4 to 400 km length, Fugita (1981). Observational studies have showed that this mesoscale vortex is frequently associated with strong winds, which, however, do not reach the intensity of cyclostrophics storms, like tornados, dowbrushers or microbrushers.

Modelling and observational studies about such systems that have been developed have not arrived yet at desirable performance; thus, they do not offer complete knowledge of the physical mechanisms, dynamical or thermodynamical, that govern the interactions between the macrocyclones and the misocyclones.

2 SOURCE OF DATA AND METHODS

The meteorological data used in this study, as synoptic reports (00/12/18:00 GMT), upper air soundings (12:00 GMT) from the International Airport of Rio de Janeiro (Galeão), and data from climatological stations of Rio de Janeiro area, sponsored by the Instituto Nacional de Meteorologia. The satellite GOES image came from the Instituto de Pesquisas Espaciais (INPE), therefore, not very good for our purpose because the GOES W was not in its position in the period of the event.

Objective Analysis Program was used in order to optimize the quantification of the dynamic and thermodynamic parameters involved in the event. To obtain the contribution of these parameters for the development of the system, Sutcliffe Development Theory was used, which is formulated by the expression (Pettersen, 1956):

$$\frac{\partial \xi_a}{\partial t} = -\mathbf{v} \cdot \nabla \xi_a - \frac{R}{f}\nabla^2 \left[\frac{g}{R}\mathbf{v} \cdot \nabla T + \log\left(\frac{p}{p_0}\right)\overline{w(\Gamma_a - \Gamma)} + \log\left(\frac{p}{p_0}\right)\frac{1}{c_p}\frac{d\overline{w}}{dt} \right]$$

where:

ξ_a = absolute vorticity in the lower layer;

$-\mathbf{v} \cdot \nabla \xi_a$ = vorticity advection in the level of nondivergence;

$\mathbf{v} \cdot \nabla T$ = thickness or temperature advection;

$\log\left(\dfrac{p}{p_0}\right)\overline{w(\Gamma_a - \Gamma)}$ = representative term of the adiabatic changes

in the relationship with vertical motions;

$\log\left(\dfrac{p}{p_0}\right)\dfrac{1}{c_p}\dfrac{d\overline{w}}{dt}$ = warming term.

Such terms allowed us to judge the participation of heating in the development of the system and the dynamic expressed by the vorticity advection, which determined the intensity achieved by the storm.

3 OBSERVATIONAL ANALYTIC STUDIES

The characteristics of the basic state of the synoptic conditions showed successive quasi-stationary cold fronts over the north of the state of Rio de Janeiro blocked by the subtropical South Atlantic High Pressure cellula. Such fronts were associated with strong macrocyclone spreading across the coastline, Fig. 2, showing the temperature field under it, 30°C e RH = 50% (Fig. 3).

The evolution of the synoptic system is detected after six hours in the 18:00 GMT chart showing the macrocyclones amplified, reaching about 2,500 km in the meridional axis and 2,000 km in the longitudinal axis, spreading from the 20° to 40°S and from the 30° to 55°W.

The vertical structure showed consistently a real hydrostatic and a pattern of true dynamic macrocyclone going to the 100 hPa level where the Dines Compensation is revealed, represented by the necessary presence of an anticyclone - 300 mb (Fig. 4 e 5).

The vertical time cross section (Fig. 6) taken from Galeão, Rio de Janeiro, shows:

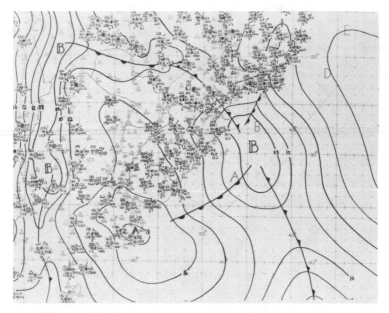

Figure 2: Surface chart at 1200 GMT, on January 2, 1987.

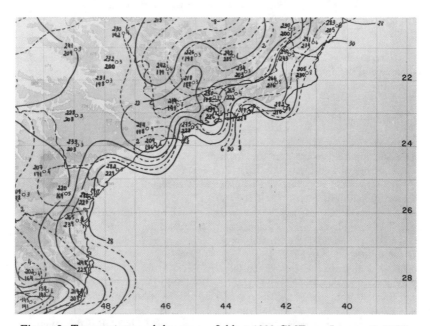

Figure 3: Temperature and depressure field at 1200 GMT, on January 2, 1987.

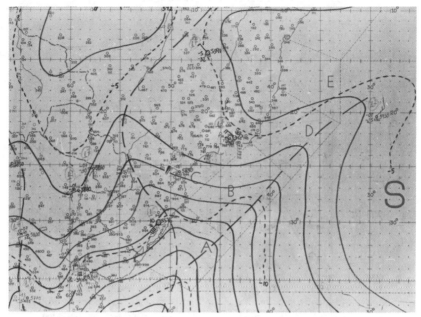

Figure 4: 500 hPa topography field at 1200 GMT, on January 2, 1987.

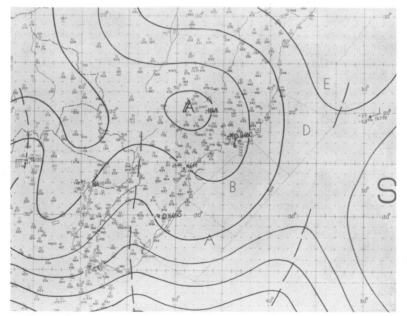

Figure 5: 100 hPa topography field at 1200 GMT, on January 2, 1987.

1. Absence of jet stream over Rio de Janeiro area since 12/30/86;

2. Discrete increasing of the temperature from the 1000 hPa until about 200 hPa; NW wind in all levels with dry and warm air flowing.

The Skew-T, Log P diagram shows, subsidence on January 1–2, on 590 e 580 hPa levels, respectively; Showalter Index values 5.0 e 3.5.

The mesoscale analysis shows the following dominant conditions in the Rio de Janeiro area:

1. 01/01/12:00 GMT - Cold front trough, expansion of the macrocyclone with temperature field 26°C, RH < 60%, pressure 1014.6 hPa (Figs. 7 e 8).

2. 01/02/00:00 GMT - Deepening persistent cold frontal through, T = 27°C, RH < 60%, pressure 1011.4 hPa (Figs 9 e 10).

3. 01/02/12:00 GMT - Significant expansion and deepening of the macrocyclone. Quasi-stationary synoptic features, T = 31.7°C, RH < 60%, pressure 1013 hPa (Figs. 11 e 3).

4. 01/02/18:00 GMT - Frontal trough about 100 km westward of Rio de Janeiro, T = 36°C, RH < 50%, pressure 1010 mb (Figs. 12 and 13).

5. Displacement of the frontal trough (item 5) localized in Mangaratiba area, reaching the Guanabara Bay at about 21:00 GMT, where basic conditions were dry (depressure 18°C) and warm (39°C), the interaction between the thermodynamic conditions of the trough and the basic conditions of the sea surface caused the severity of the storm.

The lack of radar observations and deficient satellite images due to the GOES W position in the period of the event, prevented a better view of the development stages of the storm. Coupling of radar observations and satellite image could allow better decision on the class of the synoptic entity involved in the disturbance. Therefore we used the misoscale analysis for the remarks mentioned in item 2.

The objective analysis of the vorticity field in the macrocyclone shows maximum value at 12:00 GMT - 01/01/87 and the 24 hours vorticity advection with its core at about 1,500 km eastward of the area. Moreover at 12:00 GMT - 01/02/87 the vorticity field maintains itself quasi-stationary with strong intensification (Figs. 14 and 15).

4 CONCLUSION

From the observational analytic study we have achieved strong evidence of the participation of a synoptic entity of the class of microcyclones, Fugita (1981), imbedded in the trough generated by the dominant macrocyclone conditions.

The scalar amplitude of the misocyclone was in accordance with the pattern of such microsystems. Its extension was about 40 km, and its area of critical activity inferior to 10 km, or 3,000 m in the Guanabara Bay where its severity was the highest.

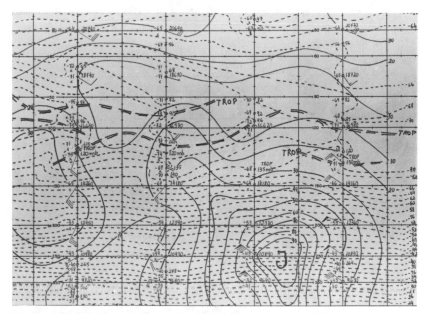

Figure 6: Vertical time cross section from Galeão (International Airport of Rio de Janeiro) from December 31, 1986 to January 3, 1987.

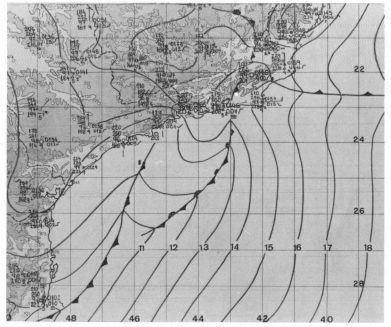

Figure 7: Mesoscale surface chart at 1200 GMT, on January 1, 1987.

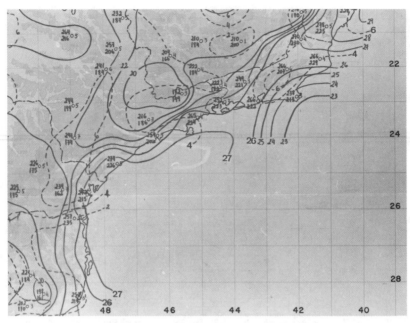

Figure 8: Temperature and depressure field at 1200 GMT, on January 1, 1987.

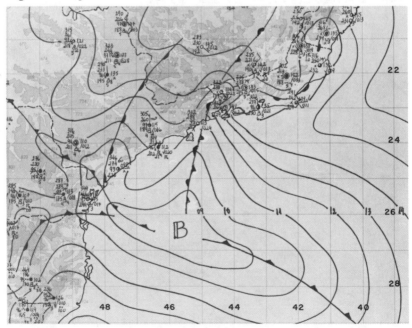

Figure 9: Mesoscale surface chart at 00 GMT, on January 2, 1987.

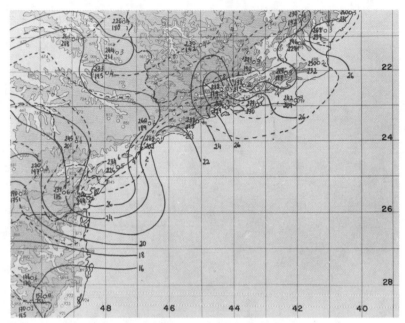

Figure 10: Temperature and depressure field at 00 GMT, on January 2, 1987.

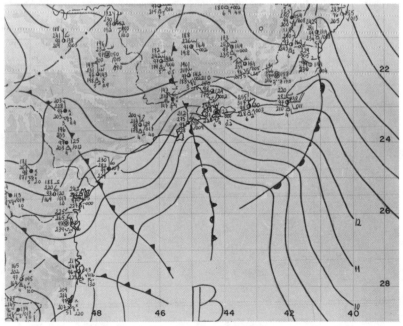

Figure 11: Mesoscale surface chart at 1200 GMT, on January 2, 1987.

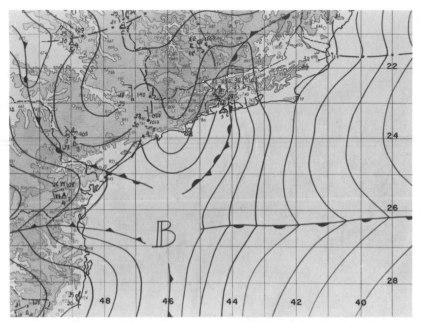

Figure 12: Mesoscale surface chart at 1800 GMT, on January 2, 1987.

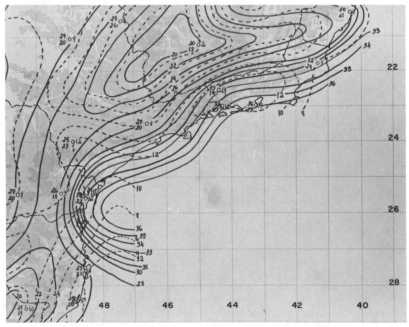

Figure 13: Temperature and depressure field at 1800 GMT, on January 2, 1987.

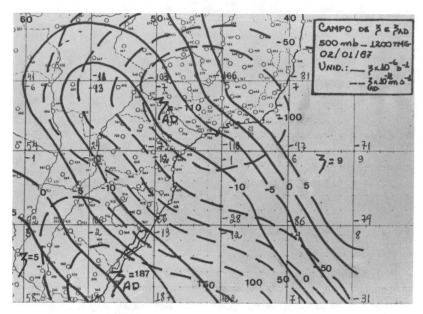

Figure 14: 500 hP vorticity field at 1200 GMT, on January 1, 1987

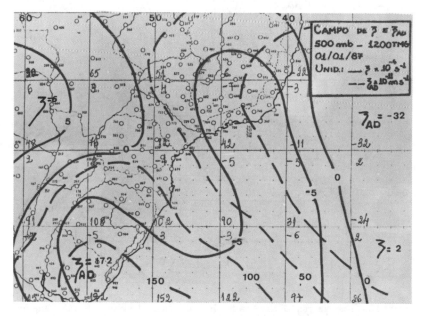

Figure 15: 500 hP vorticity field at 1200 GMT, on January 2, 1987

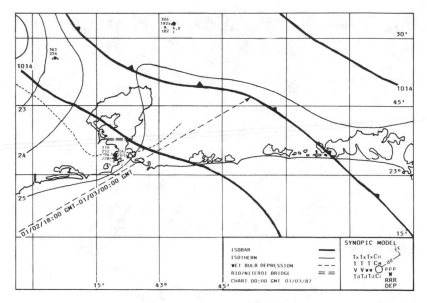

Figure 16: Misoscale surface chart at 00 GMT, on January 3, 1987.

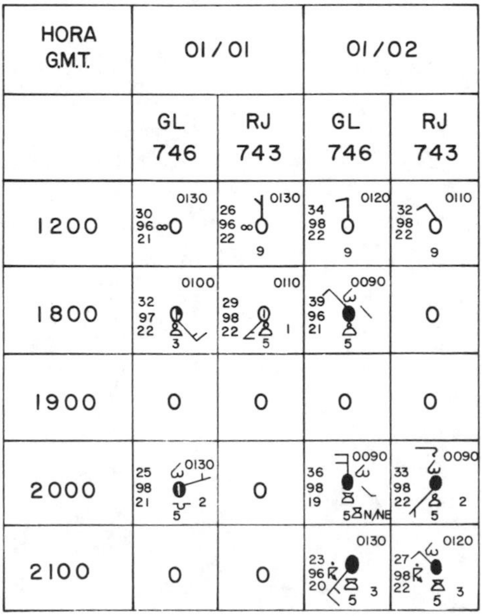

HORA G.M.T.	01 / 01		01 / 02	
	GL 746	RJ 743	GL 746	RJ 743
1200	0130 30 96 ∞O 21	0130 26 96 ∞O 22 9	0120 34 98 O 22 9	0110 32 98 O 22 9
1800	0100 32 97 22 3	0110 29 98 22 5 1	0090 39 96 21 5	O
1900	O	O	O	O
2000	0130 25 98 21 5 2	O	0090 36 98 19 5 N/NE	0090 33 98 22 5 2
2100	O	O	0130 23 96 20 5 3	0120 27 98 22 5 3

Figure 17: Time diagram of the weather in the area of the city of Rio de Janeiro.

The objective analysis was a re-enforcing information of the blocking action of the tropical anticyclonic cellula of South Atlantic over the acting synoptic system over the area of Rio de Janeiro.

No jet stream systems was detected in association with the storm during the period of the event.

The atmosphere-ocean and the atmosphere-surface interactions, and especially the dynamic effects of the eastward Guanabara Bay orographic systems were important forcing factors of the severe intensity of the storm.

The economical importance of several coastal installations in the State of Rio de Janeiro — such as offshore oil platforms, nuclear power plants, the Port of Rio de Janeiro, several marinas — justify the installation of the Meteorological Radar in order to give conditions for an effective Coastal Management Program, as well as to prevent oceanic accidents, to preserve lives and to protect property.

We have no doubt in saying that such microsystems have caused some of the severe meteorological disturbances that have occurred in Brazil.

Some synoptic analysis concerning the southern section of the coastal region of Brazil, have showed patterns of dynamic macrocyclones, similar to the one showed in this study. This system shows a series of trough disturbances, in fan model distribution generated by perturbation in the basic flow of the macrocyclone, caused by the interaction atmosphere versus surface conditions, such as topography, source or loss of humidity and/or warming. Frequently such trough-lines deepen, leading to the analyst to consider them as a frontal or quasi-stationary instability discontinuities. Such disturbances cause strong intensity weather conditions with notable persistance and large spatial scale; in the class of Grosswatter, Baur (1963).

The analysis of the misoscale chart of 00:00 GMT de 01/03/87 (Fig. 16) and the time diagram of the weather in the area (Fig. 17), shows the mature development stage of the storm over Guanabara Bay between 08:00 and 21:00 GMT de 01/01/87.

REFERENCES

[1] Alcântara, F., A.B. de Camargo (1969). "Manual de Análise do Diagrama Skew-T, LOG P", Rio de Janeiro, Brasil, Ministério da Aeronáutica, Diretoria de Rotas Aéreas, 111 pp.

[2] Barry, R.G. and A.H. Perry (1970). Synoptic Climatology Mathuen & Co. Ltd., London.

[3] Doswell, C.A., III (1982). "The Operational Meteorology of Convective Weather". Volume I: Operational Mesoanalysis. NOAA, Technical Memorandum, N.W.S. NSSFC, 5, 131 pp.

[4] Fernandez, P.J.J. (1973). Subsynoptic Convergence. Rainfall Relationships Based Upon 1971 South Florida Data. U.S. Department of Commerce – National Oceanic and Atmospheric Administration, 76 pp.

[5] Fujita, T.T. (1981). Mesoscale Aspects of Convective Storms. Proc. IAMAP Symposium. Hamburg, 25–28 August.

[6] House, D.C. (1960). "A basis for the Prediction of Severe Local Thunderstorms". Paper presented at the IAS 28th Annual Meeting. New York, 25–27 January, 12 pp.

[l] Lage, R. and M.A.F. Silva Dias (1984). Estudo de Tempestades Severas Associadas com o Jato Tropical na América do Sul. Paper presented at the 3rd Brazilian Congress on Meteorology, Belo Horizonte: 289–293.

[8] Maddox, R.A. (1983). Large-Scale Meteorological Conditions Associated with Mid-Latitude, Mesoscale Convectives Complexes. *Mon. Wea. Rev.* **11**: 1475–1493.

[9] Petterssen, S. (1956). "Weather Analysis and Forecsting", vol.I, McGraw-Hill, 428 pp.

[10] Purdom, J.F.W.; R.N. Green; J.F. Weaver; R.M. Zehr; and D.A. Lubich (1985). Satellite Data Support to the Pre-Storm Operations Center, May-June 1985. CIRA Paper no. 3, Cooperation Institute for Research in the Atmosphere, Colorado State University, Ft. Collins, CO, 75 pp.

[11] Rodgers, D.M.; D.L. Bartels; R.D. Menard; and J.H. Arns (1984). Experiments in Forecasting Mesoscale Convective Weather Systems Preprints 10th Conf. on Weather Forecasting Analysis, Clear Water, Fl., AMS, Boston, MA: 486–491.

[12] Rosman, P.C.C. and Valentini, E. (1989). Recent Erosion in the "Stable" Ipanema-Leblon Beach in Rio de Janeiro, Proc. VI Symp. Coastal and Ocean Management, 11-14 July, Charleston, Paper Ref. 366.

[13] USP. Departamento de Meteorologia (1986). Introdução ao uso de Modelos Diagnósticos Para a Precisão do Tempo. São Paulo, IAG-USP, 62 pp.

[14] Zehr, R.M. (1986). Analysis of Mesoscale Air Masses with VAS Retrievals. Reprinted from preprint volume, Second Conference on Satellite Meteorology/Remote Sensing and Applications, May 13–16, AMS, Boston, Mass, 347–352.

"IN SITU" DETERMINATIONS OF DISPERSION AND TRANSPORT PARAMETERS AT PIRAQUARA DE FORA (RJ) – BRAZIL, WITH HELP OF A FLUORESCENT DYE TRACER

João S. F. Roldão [1]

1 INTRODUCTION

This work deals with "in situ" determinations of the transport and dispersion parameters at Piraquara de Fora cove, near the site where the first Brazilian nuclear power plant has been installed.

Figure 1 shows the experiment site at the coast of Rio de Janeiro State. In order to avoid public concerns and problems of radiological protection, a fluorescent dye tracer was used to label the cooling water pumped from Itaorna cove and returned to the sea at Piraquara de Fora.

The field method used to measure the local transport and dispersion characteristics can be understood as a generalization of the so-called "Danish Method" introduced by Harremoes (1966).

This methodology, which was originally developed for the use of a short-lived radioactive tracer (in general ^{82}Br), is based on the monitoring of an artificial "cloud" which is formed by the dispersion of the radioactive tracer (instantaneously injected) during its entrainment by the local currents. The obtained results can be generalized to simulate the ones expected if a continuous injection had been performed. The main advantages of the method are an important reduction in the amount of injected tracer, which is directly related to cost and safety aspects (in the case of radioactive tracer), as well as simplification of the injection procedures.

The use of tracers has increased around the world specially where costly coastal works (like ocean disposal projects and monitoring programs) need accurate information on the local transport and dispersion mechanisms, as pointed out by Gunnersom (1987). Previous results obtained at the coast of Rio de Janeiro are reported by Marri (1973).

2 FIELD EXPERIMENT

Rhodamine B (color index 45100) was selected to be used as fluorescent dye tracer. In spite of its relatively high adsorption tendency by sediments, it works quite well

[1] Programa de Engenharia Civil, COPPE, Universidade Federal do Rio de Janeiro, Caixa Postal 68504, Rio de Janeiro, RJ 21945, Brazil.

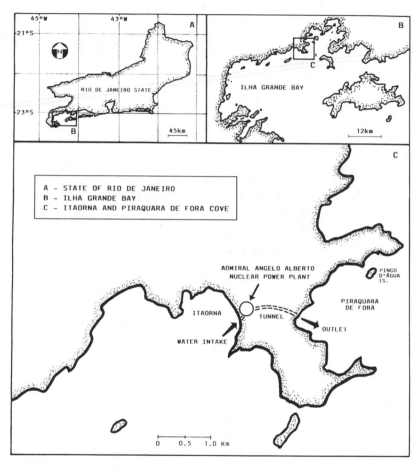

Figure 1: Map showing experiment site.

in clear water, which is the case of the Piraquara de Fora cove. This dye is relatively stable as concerns photochemical decay, cheap and easily available in Brazil.

1 Kg of Rhodamine B was diluted in 20 l of local sea water and methanol to avoid density differences between the tracer and the receiving water. Instantaneous injection was performed by pouring the whole volume in a place situated in the zone of influence of the effluent outlet. At the same time, four weighted cross-shaped drogues were launched in order to compare their displacements with the movement of the tracer cloud. Each drogue had an underwater sail 1.5 m wide, 3 m long, and placed 1 m from the water surface.

The injection was made on June 8, 1982, at 09:30 AM at the beginning of the flooding cycle of a spring tide (local amplitude is around 1.5 m). The field activities were carried out during the pre-operational stage of the power plant, when no temperature changes had been observed in the pumped water.

A Turner filter fluorometer, model 111, with a through-flow cell fed by a 1/2 HP centrifugal pump was installed on a small boat to detect the dye tracer. A strip-chart recorder was connected to the fluorometer in order to record the variation of fluorescence in time, as recommended by Turner (1984). As the boat was crossing the dye cloud, water samples were collected at the outflow tube of the fluorometer at 15 second intervals. These samples were protected from sunlight to be later analyzed at the laboratory. Their concentration was measured with a spectrofluorometer by the continuous scanning technique introduced by Behrens (1973). The time each water sample was collected, was noted on a chart paper by an event marker activated by a specially developed device ("bip-biper"). This device was able to send audio signals via a transceiver (walkie-talkie), to the three bases situated on the shore, where theodolites measured the position of the moving boat at 15 second intervals.

The boat, which was kept at constant speed (1.3 m/s), was oriented to intercept the tracer cloud in few transversal lines (around 5 lines) and a longitudinal one along which the fluorescence concentration distribution was measured. These concentrations were later plotted on the local geographical map using pairs of angles measured at each individual time.

The set of transversal and longitudinal concentration distribution lines are the basis for a computer program (DISPE) to interpolate spatially the "in-situ" results obtained, in order to prepare the final presentation of each tracer cloud.

The computer program also includes routines which convert measured angles to coordinate distances, and introduces corrections for the time delay between the instant of observation of the boat position and the measurement of fluorescence. This delay is a function of the boat speed, the length of intake tube, and the pumping flow rate. Figure 2 shows the cloud No.2 detected at Piraquara de Fora.

The symbols correspond to concentration intervals: the "small cross" (+) represents the chosen background (0 to 0.1 ppb), B for concentrations from 0.1 to 1.0 ppb, C from 1.0 to 2.0 ppb, E from 2.0 to 3.0 ppb, ... Q from 10.0 to 12.0 ppb and T from 12.0 to 16.0 ppb. The dimensions of the symbols, in this particular cloud, correspond to a square of 9.5m × 9.5m in the field.

Figure 3 presents a general view of the displacement of the tracer and the final position of the drogues at Piraquara de Fora cove.

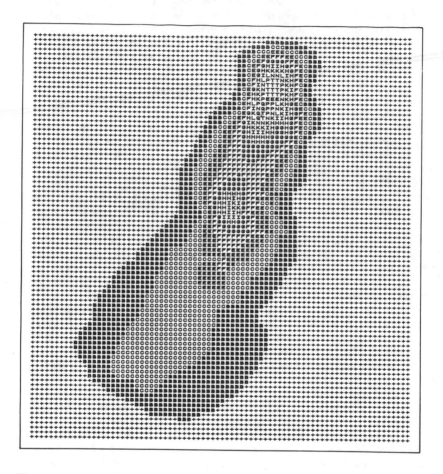

Figure 2: Longitudinal and transversal distribution of dye concentrations of Rhodamine B. Cloud 2 at Piraquara de Fora.

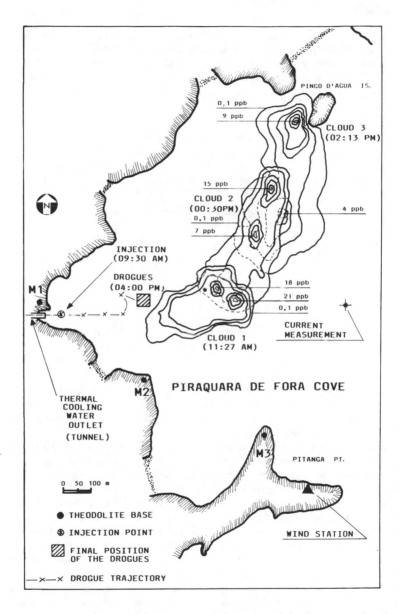

Figure 3: General view of displacement and dispersion of the fluorescent dye cloud at Piraquara de Fora.

3   OBTAINED RESULTS

The bulk movement of the tracer cloud, as usual, is summarized by the displacement of its center of gravity. The calculation of the coordinates and the time (t) associated to the center of gravity of each cloud is also carried out by a routine of the DISPE program. Table I summarizes the path of labelled sea water at Piraquara de Fora, during the tracer experiment.

Table I: Displacement of the center of gravity of the dye cloud.

Cloud	Time after Injection (h)	Coordinates of the Center of Gravity (m) X	Y	Mean Velocity (m/s)	Direction of Displacement [1] (°)
0	0	556,810	7,454,995	–	–
1	1.95	557,640	7,455,149	0.12	79
2	3.00	557,900	7,455,507	0.12	36
3	3.93	558,063	7,455,737	0.08	36
4	4.71 [2]	558,222	7,455,870	0.07	50

NOTE: [1] clockwise angle in degrees from North.
         [2] estimated by the peak concentration.

Interference caused on the theodolites sight when the boat was sailing behind the Pingo d'Água island prevented the complete detection of cloud No.4. Fortunately its peak (maximum concentration) could be detected and was used to replace the center of gravity as shown in Table I.

Figure 3 gives an idea of the differences between the movement of the tracer cloud and the drogues. The final position and the path of the drogues are marked in the same figure, where they arrived after a rather fast movement along the straight line and slow movement along the curved line. It is believed that the drogues were pushed out of the artificial main stream created by the cooling water outlet and were kept in a nearly stagnant region were only weak eddies existed.

Measurements of surface wind (about 4 m/s and oriented towards NE) showed accordance with the general displacement of the tracer cloud. Currents were measured at a fixed station, with a local depth of 8 m. Values of 8 cm/s were observed with strong fluctuations, preventing any correlation to the tracer movement.

Local dispersion characteristics were determined by a log-log graph plotting the variances calculated along the longitudinal and transversal axis and the average time of the selected crossing ($\bar{t}$) as shown in Figures 4(a) and 4(b).

These data allow to calculate the empirical coefficients a and m of the general equation:

$$\sigma_i^2 = a\,\bar{t}^{\,m} \tag{1}$$

where,

σ_i^2 = variance of concentration distribution along the i axis (cm^2);
i = coordinate axis, $i = 1$ (longitudinal), $i = 2$ (transversal);
$\bar{t}$ = average time associated to the line which
      crosses the center of gravity along the axis i;
a, m = regression coefficients.

The local dispersion characteristics, here presented by the longitudinal (K_x) and transversal (K_y) dispersion coefficients, can be calculated by the general definition of these coefficients as :

$$K_i = \frac{1}{2}\frac{\partial \sigma_i^2}{\partial \bar{t}} \qquad (2)$$

where,

K_i = dispersion coefficient related to the axis i (cm^2/s).

The regression equations for the data presented in Figures 4(a) and 4(b) are:

$$\sigma_x^2 = 2.2 \times 10^{-2}\,\bar{t}^{\,2.5} \qquad (3)$$

and

$$\sigma_y^2 = 3.0 \times 10^{-5}\,\bar{t}^{\,2.9} \qquad (4)$$

Figures 5(a) and 5(b) show the conventional plot of K_i versus L_i. The "length scale of diffusion" (L_i) is here arbitrarily set as 3 times the values of σ_i. The regression equations of the these plots are:

$$K_x = 7.5 \times 10^{-2}\,L_x^{\,1.20} \qquad (5)$$

and

$$K_y = 9.3 \times 10^{-3}\,L_y^{\,1.31} \qquad (6)$$

4 CONCLUSIONS

The attempt to use conventional drogues to measure the direction and velocity of local currents at Piraquara de Fora cove has failed completely. It seems that the performance of drogues at Piraquara de Fora is strongly dependent on the selection of the launching point, as a consequence of the important distortion in the natural current field caused by the cooling water discharged by the Admiral Angelo Alberto Nuclear Power Plant.

The general path of the tracer in the receiving water could be easily detected, and from that the direction and velocity of labeled water was measured. These results helped in the final decision of selecting proper sites for the continuous monitoring of the effluent of the power plant.

The transversal dispersion coefficient of Piraquara de Fora cove showed to be rather close to the previously obtained at Itaorna cove, but the longitudinal dispersion coefficient was quite different from those obtained at Itaorna. The main reason is that the current field at Piraquara de Fora is strongly influenced by the effluent discharge. The obtained results were later used as a first step for the calibration of a mathematical model to forecast the transport and dispersion of radioactive pollutant at Piraquara de Fora cove.

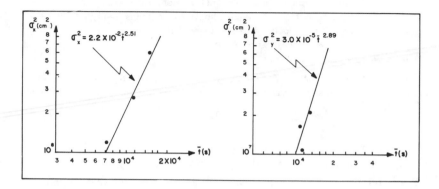

Figure 4: Longitudinal (a) and transversal (b) variance versus mean transit time of the dye cloud.

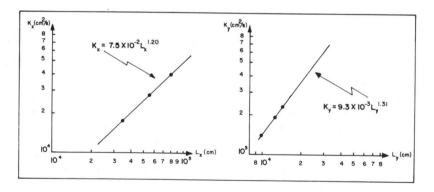

Figure 5: Longitudinal (a) and transversal (b) dispersion coefficient versus length scale of diffusion.

Acknowledgements: The author thanks the "Comissão Nacional de Energia Nuclear" (CNEN), and FURNAS Centrais Elétricas S.A. which made this work possible.

REFERENCES

[1] Behrens, H. (1973). Eine Verbesserte Nachweismethode fuer Fluorozenzindikatoren und ihre Anwendung zur Feststellung von Fliesswegen im Grundwasser. *Z. Deutsch. Geol. Ges.* Band **124**: 535–544.

[2] Gunnerson, C.G. (1987). "Wastewater Management for Coastal Cities. The Ocean Disposal Option". World Bank Technical Paper no.77, Washington DC, 366 pp.

[3] Harremoes, P. (1966). Prediction of Pollution from Planned Waste Water Outfalls. *J. Wat. Pollut. Control Fed.* **38** (8): 1323–1333.

[4] Marri, A. (1973). "Traçadores Radioativos no Controle da Poluição Costeira", M.Sc. Thesis, Universidade Federal de Minas Gerais, Belo Horizonte, 130 pp.

[5] Murphy, C.R. and K.C. Miners (1978). "Turbulent Diffusion Processes in the Great Lakes". Inland Waters Directorate, Scientific Series no. 83, Ontario.

[6] Roldão, J. and G. Goretkin (1984). Calibração de Modelos Matemáticos Aplicáveis à Simulação do Transporte e Dispersão em Águas Costeiras: Uso de Traçadores Fluorescentes. 1. Sem. de Modelagem Numérica do Mar, INPE, São José dos Campos, 13 pp.

[7] Turner. (1984) "Circulation, Dispersion and Plume Studies" – Fluorometric Facts – Turner Designs. Mountain View, CA.

TOURISM VERSUS CONSERVATION
IN FERNANDO DE NORONHA ISLAND, BRAZIL

Dieter Muehe [1]   Denise Rivera Tenenbaum [2]   Maria Teresa M. de Szechy [3]

1 INTRODUCTION

Since its discovery, in 1503, the Island of Fernando de Noronha has had several uses, such as: military base, station for the quarantine of animals, penal colony, and recently as a tourist resort. Disorderly occupation and predatory use of its natural assets systematically caused ecological imbalance.

Several initiatives of an isolated nature have been developed in the last years so as to define the best way of using the Archipelago rationally (Fundação S.O.S. Mata Atlântica, 1988). Tourism has been the interesting basic activity for its development (HIDROSERVICE, 1986), but it causes problems and incompatibility in its uses (Comissão Coordenadora do Plano de Desenvolvimento de Fernando de Noronha, 1986).

Conscious of the problems created by tourism expansion and searching for a definition of the uses compatible to the restoration and the maintenance of ecological equilibrium, the previous administration of the Archipelago, represented by the Estado Maior das Forças Armadas (EMFA), organized a multidisciplinary group to gather data for the elaboration of the Master Plan for the development of the Archipelago in 1986.

To achieve this objective, in a preliminary analysis, our work proposes to identify *conservation areas* i.e., liable to be used for tourism without degrading the environment, and *preservation areas* where human interference would be virtually non-existent. In view of time restrictions for field work, and insufficient past data, we adopted the techniques of integrated evaluation, partially based on perception, having in mind the orientation of future studies as well as the identification of areas for emergency action.

[1]Departamento de Geografia, Instituto de Geociências, Universidade Federal do Rio de Janeiro, Rio de Janeiro, RJ 21945, Brazil.

[2]Departamento de Biologia Marinha, Instituto de Biologia, Universidade Federal do Rio de Janeiro, Rio de Janeiro, RJ 21941, Brazil.

[3]Departamento de Botânica, Instituto de Biologia, Universidade Federal do Rio de Janeiro, Rio de Janeiro RJ 21941, Brazil.

2 STUDY AREA

Fernando de Noronha Archipelago is situated 546 Km from the city of Recife on the north-east coast of Brazil, 3°52'S and 32°24'W. It comprises 20 islands and islets, the main one having a surface of 17 km² (Fig. 1). The climate is semi-arid tropical, the dry season being from August to January. Average yearly precipitation is approximately 1,000 mm and the average monthly temperature varies from 26°C to 28°C. Because of high evaporation rate as well as related to the oceanic location, sea water salinity is relatively high (> 35 ppt). The thermal amplitude of the superficial waters is low, usually inferior to 4°C a year, thus inhibiting thermal convection and the renewal of nutrients. The sea water average temperature is 24 °C.

Under the influence of trade winds that blow towards the Equator (Dietrich *et al.*, 1975), the Archipelago is inserted in an oceanographic region of westward marine currents and dominating wave direction ranging from SSE to E. Consequently, Fernando de Noronha's SE coastline is strongly affected by local hydrodynamics, the explanation for its irregularity. The deep water wave height varies usually from 0.5 m to 2.0 m, but 5.5 m to 7.0 m high waves occur exceptionally when they come from SSW and WSW.

The Archipelago is the eroded remains of the top of a volcanic formation which has a base of 60 km diameter and is 4,000 m high. It is situated in the fractured zone that is transversal to the meso-atlantic dorsal area. Its morphology relates directly to the erosional processes associated to climatic and oceanographic conditions and rock hardiness. These conditions explain the alternation of bays, eroded out of clastic rocks of reduced resistance, such as volcanic tufts and cinders, and high cliffs carved in the lava flows.

As Fernando de Noronha is an oceanic island, some outstanding ecological aspects regarding biota should be mentioned. The already harmed vegetal cover and the presence of endemic and migratory species are contrasting particularities of this system as environmental quality is concerned.

The terrestrial ecosystem was altered by anthropic influence, its vegetal cover reduced, deforested and burned or replaced by exotic species. Of the original insular Atlantic forest, only 5% remains at sites of difficult access. Endemic birds (*Vireo gracilirostris* and *Elaenia ridleyana*) and migratory ones (*Pluvialis squatarola* and *Arenaria interpres*, from the Neartic region; *Ardea purpurea* and *Hirundo rustica*, from the Paleartic region) are threatened by the modification of their natural habitat and by particularly predatory attacks from lizards and rats carried to the island (Comissão Coordenadora do Plano de Desenvolvimento de Fernando de Noronha, 1986).

In contrast, the marine ecosystem has not been much affected by man's interference and thus became a haven for the sole existing community of 'rotating dolphins' (*Stenella longirostris*) of the South Atlantic. Sea turtles (*Chelonia mydas* and *Eretmochelys imbricata*) lay their eggs yearly on its beaches. The island is remarkable for its coral richness: 10 of the 18 species found along the Brazilian littoral can be found there (Comissão Coordenadora do Plano de Desenvolvimento de Fernando de Noronha, 1986).

Up to 1938, Fernando de Noronha was part of the state of Pernambuco, when, due to national security reasons, the Archipelago's administration passed to the

Figure 1: Localization of the Fernando de Noronha Archipelago.

Army. It became a Federal Territory in 1942. During the sixties it was once again under the administration of the Armed Forces. The first civilian governor was appointed in 1987 and in 1988 the Archipelago was annexed to the state of Pernambuco again, according to the new Constitution.

The local population, nowadays concentrated in the main island, comprises about 1,500 inhabitants, most of them being government personnel (civilian or military), or people dealing with fishing and tourist activities. Farming and cattle raising, extractive and industrial activities are limited by the topographical and climatic conditions of the island. The income thus created is insufficient for its population, which thus becomes economically dependent on the Government.

Fernando de Noronha stands out as a national historical heritage, concentrated in the Vila dos Remédios, built during the Portuguese occupation on the XVIII century after successive French and Dutch invasions.

3 METHODOLOGY

Information used in the ongoing process of environment evaluation was gathered from July 13 to July 19, 1986, from bibliographic survey, interviews with specialists and from the observation and gathering of biological and geological material.

The adopted methodology is based on Mader and Remson (1978), consisting basically in the attribution of certain values to the environmental factors ensemble so as to adequately characterize an area for a stated use. Two basic procedures characterize the applied methodology: division of the region into sub-areas, and the calculation of capability ratings for each of the sub-areas according to their type of use. The region was divided into 500 m sided squares; surveys were limited to 12 sub-areas selected on the northwest littoral of the Archipelago (Fig. 2).

The capability ratings were obtained step by step as follows:

1. Survey and selection of environmental factors taken as a diagnosis for a preliminary evaluation:

   • Landscape aesthetics
   • Coastal geomorphology
   • Water quality
   • Hydrodynamics
   • Biological aspects
   • Accessibility

2. A priori statement of weight coefficients which express the relative importance of environmental factors suitable to the proposal. Weight coefficients were classified according to Mader and Remson's scale (1978):

   0 - no importance
   1 - very low importance
   2 - low importance
   3 - moderately important
   4 - highly important
   5 - very high importance

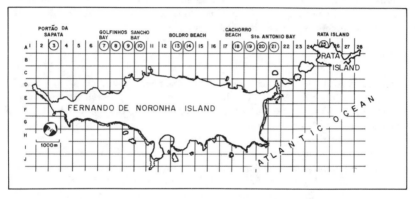

Figure 2: Division of the region and studied sub-areas.

Table I shows weight coefficients obtained by arithmetic mean of the values attributed by each member of the working team which comprised: 4 biologists, 1 geographer, 1 professional deep-water diver, and 1 local fisherman.

Table I: Weight coefficients.

	USE OPTION	
ENVIRONMENTAL FACTORS	TOURISM	PRESERVATION
Landscape aesthetics	5	1
Coastal geomorphology	3	4
Water quality	4	4
Hydrodynamics	3	0
Biological aspects	4	5
Accessibility	3	2

3. Capability values were attributed to each environmental factor for each sub-area of the study, comparatively and according to the proposed type of use. Capability values were obtained by the arithmetic mean of the values given by each member of the working team. Table II shows the aspects considered for the evaluation of each environmental factor.

Table III shows classification scales used for capability values. Evaluation of the landscape aesthetics was made by the use of Fine's Method (1968) employing a geometric scale, which is more extensive to minimize subjectivity caused by personal differences, such as sensitivity, psychological state of mind, past experiences and socio-cultural level of the working team.

4. Calculation of the weighted capability values, which result from the multiplication of the environmental weight coefficient by the capability value of each studied sub-area.

5. Calculation of capability ratings of each studied sub-area corresponding to the sum of the weighted capability values of each type of use.

Tourist and preservation maps were made where each studied sub-area is represented by relative capability ratings which are expressed as a percentage of the maximum possible rating. This rating is determined by the sum of the product of weight coefficients by the highest capability value (i.e., 5).

4 RESULTS

From Table IV we obtain the relative capability ratings of the studied sub-areas. Figs. 3 and 4 represent, respectively, areas fitted to conservation minded tourist use and preservation, that is, undisturbed by anthropic action.

Table II: Environmental factors: aspects considered.

1. Landscape aesthetics	4. Hydrodynamics
• visual perception	• waves
− coastal	− wave climate
− submarine	− wave breaking type
	− period
2. Coastal geomorphology	• currents
• texture	− direction
− rocky outcrops	− velocity
− blocks	
− gravels	5. Biological aspects
− sand	• community evaluation
− silt + clay	− species association
• composition	− abundance/dominance
− biodetritic	− species richness
− not biodetritic	• species evaluation
• topography	− ecologically limited species
− length of beach arc	(e.g. threatened, rare, endemic species)
− height of beach berm	− ecologically important species
− width of beach berm	• ethological aspects
− beach and shore face gradient	− feeding areas
− seasonal variation of beach profile	− breeding areas
	− migration areas
3. Water quality	
• temperature	6. Accessibility
− seasonal variation	• access type
• pollution	− by sea
− chemical	− by land
− physical	• time and distance
− biological	
• turbidity	

Table III: Scale of capability values.

FINE'S SCALE (for landscape aesthetics)		CONVERSION TO OTHER ENVIRONMENTAL FACTORS	
VALUES	MEANING	VALUES	MEANING
0–1	Unsightly	0 – 1	Low
1–2	Undistinguished		
2–4	Pleasant	2 – 3	Medium
4–8	Distinguished		
8–16	Superb	4 – 5	High
16–32	Spectacular		

Sancho Bay and Cachorro Beach are the most adequate for tourist use, followed by Santo Antonio Bay and Boldró Beach which also rate well for this type of use. Golfinhos Bay and Portão da Sapata have good ratings for preservation followed by Sancho Bay, the latter having high relative capability ratings for both types of use. No sub-area shows low adequateness rates either for tourism or preservation.

If the two maps shown on Fig. 3 and Fig. 4 are compared, one verifies that there is no superposition between areas with high tourist potential and those needing preservation, with the exception of the area near Sancho Bay. Thus, if Sancho Bay and all of the northern extreme of the island up to Portão da Sapata and also all of the smaller islands of the Archipelago are included in the preservation area, and considering preservation as the priority, one arrives at the zoning presented in Fig. 5.

Table IV: Relative capability ratings.

SITE	TOURISM	PRESERVATION
Portão da Sapata	50%	81%
Golfinhos Bay	68%	89%
Sancho Bay	84%	75%
Boldró Beach	71%	46%
Cachorro Beach	82%	60%
Santo Antonio Bay	73%	61%
Rata Island	65%	61%

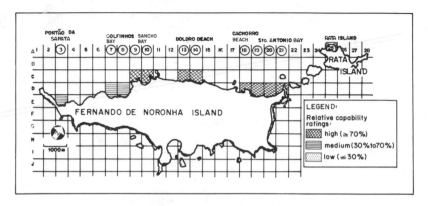

Figure 3: Potential use for tourism.

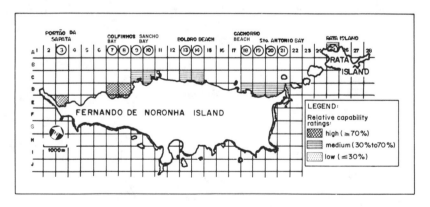

Figure 4: Potential use for preservation.

Figure 5: Coastal zone planning for tourism and preservation.

5 FINAL CONSIDERATIONS

The applied methodology has proved itself to be advantageous, an excellent tool for integrated environmental evaluation. It is especially adequate for integrating multiple sources of knowledge. This methodology allows us to arrive at satisfactory results in a short time and with low costs, providing satisfactory resolution potential, in a certain way redeeming the worthiness of human perception, which is often left out in favor of multivaried quantitative techniques. One must emphasize that such methodologies are not mutually exclusive. They should be added up to provide the best diagnosis.

Despite the powerful intuitive component used to arrive at the results, they coincided with the ones later obtained when using traditional methods such as thematic map interpretation. The maps prepared by the Federal Government in order to create the National Marine Park of Fernando de Noronha, based on agro-ecological zoning (Decree no. 95922, April 14, 1979) show the same limits we defined for preservation and conservation areas.

Aspects of the studied area, relative to the quality of natural resources, their importance to species maintenance and to regional ecology, the similarity to other areas and their contribution as concerns the national park and reserve system, should be considered when dealing with conservation (NOAA, 1982). The quality of the historical and cultural heritage, of natural resources, the scenic beauty, the adequacy to recreational and educational activities and to the establishment of basic infra-structure should be evaluated before tourism implantation.

Due to its tropical oceanic situation and natural scenery, the island is suited to tourism and also scientific work. Some studies which have already been developed permit us to identify a threatened ecosystem. In spite of the need and desire to preserve the whole area, a kind of ecological tourism is certainly possible in areas that might be delimited and controlled inside the sector between Porcos Bay and Santo Antonio Bay, on the northwest coast of the Archipelago.

Among the studied sub-areas, Santo Antonio Bay, Cachorro Beach, Boldró Beach and Golfinhos Bay should be carefully analyzed when tourism is developed in the Archipelago. Urgent action should be taken to stop or to minimize the effects of existing anthropic interference. The construction of a port at Santo Antonio Bay, domestic waste disposal in Cachorro and Boldró beaches, as well as frequent and numerous bathers and boat visitors to Golfinhos Bay, are some of the agents that compromise environmental quality maintenance in its biotic and abiotic aspects.

Maintenance of the preservation areas, in view of the particularities of the yet untouched ecosystem, is extremely important for studies in several areas of knowledge. On the other hand, environmental education programs associated to ecological tourism should be stimulated, as our country becomes aware that this natural and cultural heritage, with its unique scenery, must be protected as an ecological landmark of the Brazilian littoral.

Acknowledgements: We are grateful to the Comissão Coordenadora do Plano de Desenvolvimento do Território de Fernando de Noronha, especially to Commander Acylino M. de Lima for logistical support and to biologist Silvana Campello for her stimulus and help in our field work. We are also grateful to researchers Bárbara Fiori, Clovis Barreira e Castro, Dante Martins Teixeira, Débora de Oliveira Pires,

Flávia Cavalcanti Rabelo, Jorge Bruno Nacinovic, Liliane Lodi and Maria Júlia da Costa Belém whose valuable information helped the authors in the developing of this work.

REFERENCES

[1] Comissão Coordenadora do Plano de Desenvolvimento de Fernando de Noronha (1986). Considerações preliminares e diagnóstico sobre o meio ambiente de Fernando de Noronha. Engenharia de Sistemas de Controle e Automação S.A. Rio de Janeiro. 109 pp.

[2] Dietrich, G.; K. Kalle; W. Krauss; and G. Siedler (1975). "Allgemeine Meereskunde". Ed. Gebr. Borntraeger. Berlin, Stuttgart. 593 pp.

[3] Fines, K.D. (1968) Landscape evaluation: a research project in East Sussex. *Regional Studies*, 2: 41–55.

[4] Fundação S.O.S. Mata Atlântica (1988). Fernando de Noronha: desenvolvimento e preservação ambiental, subsídios ao debate. Frente Nacional de Ação Ecológica na Constituinte. Brasília. 63 pp.

[5] HIDROSERVICE Engenharia de Projetos Ltda. (1986). Plano Diretor de Desenvolvimento para o Território de Fernando de Noronha. Relatório final, v. 1-4. Estado Maior das Forças Armadas. Rio de Janeiro.

[6] Mader, G.G. and I. Remson (1978). Student group project on environmental land-use planning, *in:* "Geology in environmental planning". Ed. A.D. Howard and I. Remson, McGraw Hill, Inc. pp. 429–459.

[7] NOAA – National Marine Sanctuary Program (1982). Program Development Plan. U.S. Department of Commerce. Office of Coastal Zone Management. Washington. 95 pp.

ENVIRONMENT EXPLOITATION BY PREHISTORICAL POPULATION OF RIO DE JANEIRO

Oswaldo Heredia [1]   Cristina Tenório [1]   Maria Dulce Gaspar [1]

Angela Buarque [1]

1 INTRODUCTION

Little attention has been given to the study of the prehistoric populations who inhabited the central southern coast of Brazil until recently, as regards their ways of life and adaptations to the different coastal microenvironments. The indigenous population built "Sambaquis" (mounds made up of the debris left over from the consumption of fish and shellfish), and this was considered as the sole and sufficient description of the coastal way of life, so different from others developed in what is now, the Brazilian territory. At the same time there were no serious attempts to determine the antiquity of human occupation along the coast. The earliest stage of human occupation of the coastal area would have taken place between 10,000 and 6,000 B.P. in areas today flooded by the rise in sea level in the post Pleistocene, although there is no archeological evidence to support this hypothesis. The first established absolute dates place the earliest settlements at ca. 5,000 B.P., but there have been no serious attempts to correlate different cultural phases with the existing chronology.

Our first contacts with the area allowed us to determine that, in spite of the great cultural homogeneity derived from the almost exclusive dependence on marine resources, it was possible to notice differences in the types of resources exploited and in the technological equipment used. In order to determine these particularities, the authors have been working at the Museu Nacional, since 1981, on the research project called "Environmental utilization by the Prehistoric population of the State of Rio de Janeiro". The specific purpose of this project was to establish the cultural contexts in the area being studied as well as to define the mechanisms of environmental manipulation that were employed by the prehistoric population in the different stages of the occupation of the coast.

During the project development we undertook several fieldwork expeditions, devoting special attention to a survey which covered the greater part of the state, including not only marine coastal environments but also some island areas. At the same time we conducted excavations in 12 prehistoric settlement sites, with

---

[1]Departamento de Antropologia, Museu Nacional, Universidade Federal do Rio de Janeiro, Quinta da Boa Vista, Rio de Janeiro, RJ 21942, Brazil.

various occupation layers, permitting a diachronic analysis of the cultural remains, mainly artifacts made from stone, bone, shell and teeth. In one exceptional case it was possible to recover a wood artifact. Most of these artifacts were used to obtain or to process foods, although the same raw materials were also used to make ornaments. These remains are always found among the refuse of mollusk shells, fish and mammal bones, on the whole, these are the main source of information on the way of life of prehistoric coastal inhabitants.

The coast of Rio de Janeiro State is 800 km long and the geomorphology of the shoreline is quite varied. Long beaches facing out the high seas can be found, while others are closed off by bays and barrier beaches; there are also islands which are exposed to the high seas on their western sides having beaches with still waters on the opposite sides.

The researched sites were found in these different environments thus permitting the following classification. Figure 1 indicates the location and the names of these sites.

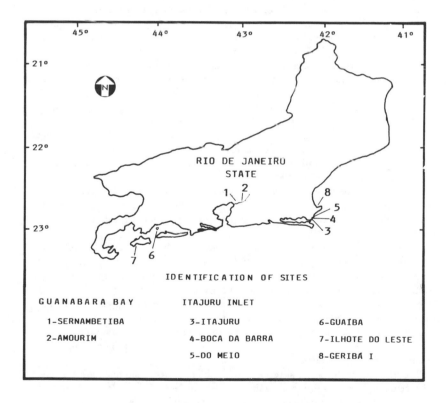

Figure 1: Location of studied sites.

2 HUMAN SETTLEMENTS AND THEIR ENVIRONMENTAL LOCATION

The most utilized location for prehistoric human settlements along the coast seems to have been at the end of bays, close to mangrove swamps. In such sites, were found the richest cultural deposits and the strongest evidences of prolonged occupation, namely the food remains left by the inhabitants. The examples we have, consist of large mounds resulting from daily subsistence activities during relatively long time periods. The mangrove swamps offered an unsurpassable potential as food-source as it combines marine, riverine, and terrestrial environments. Generally the inhabitants occupied the higher areas, well protected from the surrounding watery environment, at relatively short distances from marine resources (fish and bivalve mollusks), easily found on and or near muddy beaches. The majority of the shellfish recovered was bivalves which lived in the muddy waters and generally did not need rocky terrain for fixation and proliferation. There is a strikingly smaller frequency in the consumption for gastropods, indicating smaller quantities of these species available in this environment. The fish remains in the archeological register suggest a preference in the exploitation of the species that swim up rivers to spawn. The mangrove swamps have a specific vegetation which has numerous aerial roots, such as those of the *Rhisophora mangle* specially adapted to watery environments. These roots were used as support by dense colonies of *Ostrea rhizophorae*, which was an important source of food. This environment was also suitable for the proliferation of many species of crabs. Dear, capybaras (*Hydrochoeros hydrochoeris*), alligator (aligatorideos), various rodents and monkeys from the Atlantic forest complete the sources of food and/or raw materials for the making of artifacts.

In the southeastern region of Brazil, the areas near to the large bays consist of vast "lowlands" with mild slopes towards the sea. Due to this geomorphological situation, the various changes in sea level during the last 10,000 years caused large land areas to appear or disappear, depending on the sea level variation. A rise of only 2 m on the sea level could trap the land population against the "Serra do Mar" mountain range. In those occasions, elevations that were between the mountains and the sea became small islands where man could live and utilize the natural resources well known to him. This explains the existence of numerous archeological sites with abundant marine fauna deposits at 4 or 5 km distance from present day beaches.

The basic tool kit recovered at the sites does not show any great complexity. The artifacts are generally made out of fish bones shaped into projectile points which would be attached to the ends of spears used to capture fish in the shallow waters mentioned above. Some of these projectile points were shaped to allow them to be tied to the spear so that a barb stuck out in the opposite direction of the spearhead. Thus, a fish caught with the spear would be stuck on the barb making it difficult for it to be lost. The presence of these projectile points along with the seasonal formation of shallow lakes and pools suggest the environmental exploitation described above.

The size and depth of the sites located on the mangrove swamps indicate that their occupants returned time and again to the same place. This is also suggested by numerous layers of superposed campfires, each layer indicating a single occupation. There were probably no permanent settlements on any of these sites, as they would require a different kind of utilization of the space, and an internal organization with differentiated places for specific activities. The burial of the dead in the dwelling areas possibly shows that different groups occupied the site at different times. The great "Sambaqui de Sernambetiba" (Beltrão et al., 1979) in Magé has the following present day dimensions: 100 m long, 80 m wide, and 5.50 m deep, which signifies approximately 50,000 m³ of sediments accumulated by human activities. In an area of more than 8,000 m², relatively small human groups occupied sectors which were later abandoned, then occupied again by the same or another groups along the following seasons. Thus, the "sambaqui" was not formed by a successive accumulation corresponding to the permanence of one group, but by numberless accumulations distributed throughout the surface area. This is indicated by the limited extension of the series of superposed campfires and by the existence of many of these series spread out on the whole surface of the site, making it impossible to determine the spaces corresponding to any single group.

Examples:

a) Sambaqui de Sernambetiba
   Despite being partially destroyed by a road which cut part of its north side, and also by levelling which removed at least 50 cm of its total height, it measures today 100 m in length E/W, 80 m in width N/S, and 5.50 m in depth down to the level flooded by the water table.

b) Sambaqui de Amourins, Magé (Heredia and Beltrão, 1980)
   Partially destroyed (40%) in the west sector by the erosive action of a nearby river which changed its course, thus destroying the sediments.

2.1 Settlements located on the banks of inlets

They can be characterized by their sheltered position in relation to the natural agents which affect unsheltered beaches, particularly wind. These canals are influenced by tides, although some parts have a depth which permits navigation, there are also relatively shallow inlets. The banks of these canals were occupied by human groups who did not form great mounds such as the sambaquis. These discoveries apparently correspond to short occupations since they do not show dense sediments. There is a dominance of bivalves in the deposits, even though there is a higher amount of gastropods than in the sambaquis, the latter undoubtly an important source of food. These species (gastropods) proliferated in the shallow inlets favored also by the warmer and less turbulent waters of the canals.

The sambaquis found at the end of bays were evidently occupied annually or seasonally, but the sites on the banks of lakes or canals were real camp sites, not necessarily occupied every season or every year. The groups that came to these settlements, probably visited other campsites scattered around the area, including some further inland.

There seems to have been intense movements, never occupying the same spot for a long time. In Itajuru site, can be found exceptionally, layers rich in cultural remains until a depth of 2 meters, although there is a hiatus between one layer and another which shows little or no occupation. Only in the last level it is possible to verify a longer permanence on the site by a larger group of people.

No special instruments or weapons were needed to capture the animal species, the gastropods could be caught by hand and their shells broken with a stone to

Figure 2: Profile of excavation at Itajuru site.

extract the mollusk, as well as for the capture of crabs and bivalves. In these sites, specifically in Boca da Barra, there is a significant incidence of lithic instruments used to grind materials. There are rudimentary pestles and one mortar, stone hammer and supports, which show that some materials were ground by the inhabitants of the site. We were unable to recover plant foods, but their consumption was probably very important. Habits such as the painting of the bodies of the dead demanded the use of these grinding instruments to extract the dye from mineral or vegetable raw materials.

Fishing in the Itajuru canal was apparently of secondary importance, as there is no dominance of fish remains. Only in the Itajuru site, a significant quantity of unretouched quartz flakes was found, which the authors consider as having been used as knives to scale fish, although there was no attempt to make a blade. In deeper levels of the site corresponding to the more ancient inhabitants, crystalline quartz with sharp cleavage planes was found taken from carefully chosen veins not necessarily near to the site. This could be considered as an indication that the changes in sea level increased the mollusk colonies and their importance as a source of food, so that fish became less important.

Examples:

a) Itajuru site: depth 2.00 m, formed space layers indicating a lack of periodicity in the occupation of the site.

b) Boca da Barra site: small campsite, depth 1.20 m, some deeper points due to burials.

c) Meio site: superficial campsite with a depth of 0.60 m.

2.2 Sites on sheltered beaches on islands facing the continent

These sites have many of the characteristics of the ones mentioned above, they are protected from ocean waves, and have still and shallow waters. The inhabitants of these sites had close at hand a variety of gastropods and fish which were clearly the basic sources of food. The environment was very rich in sources of food so that seasonal movements in search of food were unnecessary, causing these island dwellers to be relatively sedentary. As island dwellers and having more than enough food, must have demanded some kind of demographic central (not necessarily undertaken in the case being studied) since a great increase of individuals would have created an imbalance in relation to the available resources.

The site on Guaíba Island (Heredia, 1984) seems to have had a permanent population for a longtime, which lived in the same small beach, as can be verified from the great quantity of sediments with cultural remains.

The Guaíba site has sediments 2.00 m deep. There is a great quantity of food remains In these sediments, especially shells of the bivalve *Pinctada imbricata* and numberless species of gastropods which proliferated in the still shallow waters between the island and the continent. This small island had very few terrestrial food resources in spite of its dense tropical vegetation. Being so close to the continent permitted the group to exploit some resources, especially raw material such as the bones of land vertebrates used to make weapons and ornaments.

The numerous burials found indicate a prolonged and continuous occupation by many generations of the same ethnic group. On Guaíba Island, the burials are not found among the food remains as in the Sambaquis but on the edges of the mound, as if throughout the occupation a specific place of burial was maintained, while the food remains were accumulated at a short distance, also in a specific spot. On Guaíba Island we can discern a certain spatial organization different from the other sites being studied.

2.3 Settlements on open beaches affording some natural protection

These were researched on beaches in Búzios (Fig. 3) and Ilha Grande (Fig. 4). In general, there were no settlement sites placed on the middle of long, straight beaches exposed to the waves and sea winds, although it is possible to find traces of campsites probably used for a short time. It was better to settle at the ends of these beaches, where a hill or some other elevation could protect from the constant winds. The prehistoric groups preferred the back of the hills, opposite to the sea but at a short distance from the beach where it was possible to obtain food. The most common resources were fish and bivalve mollusks. The open beaches were not suitable for the reproduction of gastropods. The constant beating of the waves on certain beaches permitted the proliferation of a food resource unknown in a calmer environment: the sea urchin. As concerns its quantity, the sea urchin cannot be considered an important food source, but apparently, its consumption is linked to culinary preferences, probably conditioned by the high quantities of potassium available. Geribá I site with many burials, seems to have been a site to catch sea urchins, as there are plenty of them on the rocks around the site.

At Ilhote do Leste site, on the Ilha Grande, human groups occupied the hill side opposite the sea of the hill which divides the long exposed south beach in two.

Figure 3: Geribá I site in Búzios.

Figure 4: Ilhote do Leste site on Ilha Grande.

There, they came into contact with the resources form the open beach. At the same time, resources from a mangrove swamp, like crabs and oysters were found in a canal that links two island lakes and forms a closed food resources system. The lakes, the canal and the sea offer resources practically all year round. In spite of the abundance of food, the enormous area of the Ilha Grande offered conditions for an isolated way of life such as the one on Guaíba Island described above. The studied settlement indicates by its relatively small size that it was not intensely occupied in prehistoric times. This seasonal occupation was probably complemented by others of the same kind.

2.4 Settlements on the banks of open sea beaches without shelter

These are common where long open beaches expose the continent to unfavorable factors from the sea (high winds and rough seas) and lack of natural protection. Surveys conducted along these shorelines, particularly in the extreme north of Rio de Janeiro State allowed us to determine the absence of settlements on the beaches. Recent ethnohistorical information shows that the hinter land was occupied, until historic times, by different groups which exploited resources other than marine. It was established that the older settlements were on the inner part, at the line of beaches separated and protected by high dunes. These dunes prevented the rivers to reach the sea forming lakes or swamp areas with varied resources, not necessarily of marine origin.

Thus, the settlement area was located on slightly higher grounds in the swamps, visited by aquatic fowl, capybaras, deer and alligators, all of these still abundant. The human population exploited mainly bivalves, which are able to develop in an environment with very low salinity resulting from the large amount of freshwater from the rivers. Fishing was also practiced by these groups, but it was not so important as the lake mollusks to the diet. These environments produced a large volume of food, due to the proximity to the sea although without the natural inconveniences of an open beach. The coast of Farol da Barra, São João da Barra County, Rio de Janeiro, can be mentioned as a good example.

2.5 Settlements located on mild slope terrains affected by tides

These were benefited by the animal resource which developed as a result of the tides, which determined that there were great amounts of bivalve mollusks in the muddy areas, some gastropods in cleaner rocky sections or on the sandy beaches, and crabs in the mire. When the tide went out vast areas were free to be used by human groups who built genuine islands from food remains. There are almost no land animals for they would have stranded or drowned in the flood tide, and fish seems to have been secondarily exploited. The search for food took place probably during low tide, which allowed easy circulation in the areas around the settlement.

This seems to have been the case in the lowlands around Guaratiba (5) which has numerous settlements sites. The food resources seem to have been rich, and a high population density is attested by the great quantity of sites, but it also seems that there was no great technological innovations, as the greatest part of the food was easily gathered by hand.

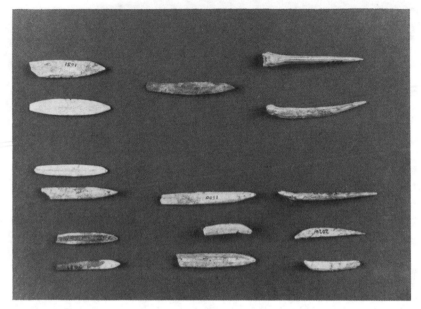

Figure 5: Bone artifacts found at Telégrafo site in Guaratiba.

3   CONCLUSION

The search for places rich in resources seems to have oriented the occupation of the littoral in pre-historic times. The study of the remains show that some sites were directed towards marine exploitation and others towards swamp exploitation. On the other hand, these studies can be useful for the understanding of shoreline evolution and sea level variations.

In view of the difficulty to have carbon dating in Brazil, we cannot affirm whether the choice of those places was related to the presence of different cultural groups or to an adaptation of the same culture along time.

These questions may be answered in the near future taking into account the technological development, either in our country or abroad. Therefore, these archeological sites should be preserved, as has been considered by the present methodology of coastal zoning and management. However, for such preservation to be effective, the population as a whole (including municipal and State agencies) must be aware of how important those sites are for the understanding, not only of our own heritage, but also for the changes in the littoral zone.

Acknowledgements: This project is being developed with financial support from "Museu Nacional da Universidade Federal do Rio de Janeiro" and "Financiadora de Estudos e Projetos" (FINEP).

REFERENCES

[1] Beltrão, M.C; O.R. Heredia; M.D.B. Gaspar; and S.M. Neme (1979). Coletores de Moluscos Litorâneos e sua Adaptação Ambiental — O Sambaqui de Sernambetiba. Arquivos do Museu de História Natural, vol.III, UFMG.

[2] Heredia, O.R. and M.C. Beltrão (1980). Mariscadores e Pescadores Pré-Históricos do Litoral Centro-Sul Brasileiro. Sep. Pesq. Antropologia no. 31., S.Leopoldo.

[3] Heredia, O.R.; M. Gatti; M.D. Gaspar; and A.M.G. Buarque (1984). Assentamentos Pré-Históricos nas Ilhas do Litoral Centro-Sul Brasileiro: o Sítio Guaíba. Rev. Arqueologia, Museu E.Goeldi/CNPq. Belém.

IMPACT ON A PRIMITIVE FISHING COMMUNITY IN MARICÁ COUNTY, CAUSED BY URBANIZATION

Edna Maia Machado Guimarães [1]

1 INTRODUCTION

Human space results from a combination of variables which act in diversified scales and times, where each place has its own particularities according to its history and its social formation.

The fishing communities we study in this paper, although influenced by the more important urban growth movement of the metropolis of Rio de Janeiro, have reacted in a different manner to the urbanization process, maintaining "old" ways of life and spatial forms while the "new" ones are being established.

It is precisely this co-existence of the "old" and the "new", this "rugosity" as suggests Milton Santos (1978), that marks the particular character of this portion of the space of Maricá.

Thus, this study intended to investigate the organization of a portion of the space of Maricá, trying to understand the transformation process in its spatial projection and its relation to environmental conditions.

2 THE STUDIED AREA AND THE FISHING COMMUNITIES

Maricá County is situated east of Guanabara Bay, in the metropolitan area of Rio de Janeiro (Fig. 1).

Two types of space opposed by form and use are found: to the north of the lagoons, irregular areas of low hills used as poor pasturage and ill kept farmland; on the other side starting from the lagoons up to the shoreline, plains, which formerly were mangroves, now drained and urbanized or divided into plots.

The littoral of Rio de Janeiro State is part of the "quaternary coastal plain which results from the realignment of the littoral by marine deposits and alluvial debris of old submerged "rias" (Lamego, 1945). This realignment process created numerous bays, coves and lagoons which have "permanent" or "intermittent" bars separated from the sea by barrier beaches.

[1]Departamento de Ecologia, Instituto de Biologia, Universidade Federal do Rio de Janeiro, Rio de Janeiro, RJ 21941, Brazil.

The realignment of the shoreline is more advanced in Maricá than in other parts of the littoral of the state: a long barrier beach almost a straight line links two rocky points: the false Sugar Loaf to the west and Ponta Negra to the east. Thus the lagoons of the Maricá system were formed, where, little by little, salt water became brackish because of the numerous rivers that flow into them.

In the narrowest part of the barrier, temporary inlets opened from time to time permitting the drainage of the water accumulated by rain which flooded the low boggy borders of the lagoons when they filled up. Sea water also entered the lagoon before the inlets were closed again by waves and tidal currents. In this way the water level was kept, and the salinity and the biota were renewed.

Such geoenvironmental conditions formed an excellent habitat for specially rich and varied fauna and flora.

Archeological studies affirm that during millenniums, natural resources offered by those environments along the Brazilian littoral were used by men for fishing and catching mollusks and crustacea (Kneipp, 1984).

According to historians, the first europeans who settled in the XVI century on the littoral of Rio de Janeiro lived from fishing either in the lagoons or in the sea (Bernardes and Bernardes, 1950).

Nowadays, the municipality has a 362 km² surface of water stretching, from west to east, by Maricá, Barra, do Padre and Guarapina lagoons. The Maricá Lagoon System is connected to the sea by Ponta Negra Canal built by Diretoria de Saneamento da Baixada Fluminense in the thirties.

Such characteristics cause Maricá to become a recent target for tourism and vacations. Other resort regions such as Araruama and Cabo Frio are farther from Rio de Janeiro and are already saturated. On the other hand, real-estate speculation, which is always associated with tourism, has found in Maricá a favorable region for high cost enterprises, guaranteed by its attractiveness and beautiful scenery. Moreover, due to its proximity to the Great Rio area — approximately 45 km — and good transportation, the number of real estate developments and condominiums has multiplied, which represents an alternative to permanent residences for people of the middle class income who work in Rio de Janeiro and Niterói.

The fishing communities studied here, are located in the area of the Municipality of Maricá, on the southern border of Maricá and Barra lagoons. In this spot of the barrier beach there are conflicting interests: on the one hand the fishery nucleus, wishing to preserve the lagoons and their intermittent inlet, on the other hand real estate speculation under the pretense of needing sanitation drained border land and even invaded the lagoon. We studied Barra de Maricá, Zacarias and Vila dos Pescadores nucleuses. (Fig. 2).

In the last 30 years transportation policy adopted by the state and federal government directed spatial organization through the opening and paving of roadways.

Amaral Peixoto road has a great influence on the metropolitan expansion of Rio de Janeiro towards Maricá and also the Rio-Niterói bridge which made transportation easier. Urban expansion has been stimulated by land parcelling.

As concerns traditional fishing community, plotting becomes the main function of environmental transformation agent. As a mechanism of land expropriation and appropriation, parcel development disrupts fishing activity, breaking the existing equilibrium between nature and that activity.

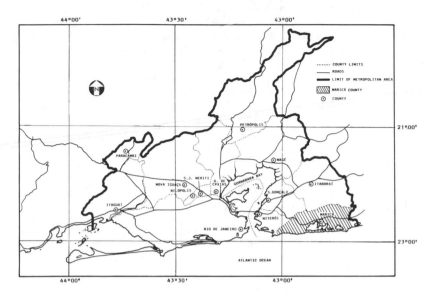

Figure 1: Metropolitan area of Rio de Janeiro and Maricá County.

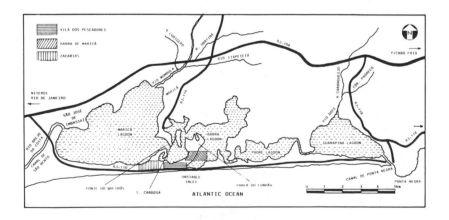

Figure 2: Location of studied communities: Barra de Maricá, Zacarias, and Vila dos Pescadores.

This occurs by expulsion and/or removal of communities from their original bases, new land developments taking their place.

Land fills, removal of vegetal cover, land displacement for road paving are starting points for environmental transformation. Lack of water renewal in the lagoons, reduction of water depth by draining, land fills and embankments, water pollution by waste disposal, complete the picture of impoverishment.

Urbanization impact is not only restricted to physical environmental transformations, though.

New life styles, new social values, new cultural standards begin to coexist and compete in the daily life of traditional communities.

This homogenization occurs by means of what Milton Santos calls "perverse universalization", because it does not reach people in the same way, being in fact the main discriminatory agent of the total space, increasing the wealth and the power of a few and enlarging poverty and fragility of the great majority.

Coupled with the decadence of the fishing activity, new opportunities are offered, which create new ways of insertion in urban economy for the remaining communities.

This insertion does not occur satisfactorily as it causes the rupture of traditional patterns of the social group, thus affecting its organization and altering the life quality of the communities.

3 METHODOLOGY

Through description and analysis of the ways of life of the three communities we tried to record their particular forms of insertion in the present spatial organization and the effects of this change when considering their socio-economical and cultural level and the man-environmental relation.

Data were obtained by direct observation, from private and public interviews, and from questionnaires.

The communities were described according to their present size and to their present population structure, which permitted us to infer on their suffering from the impact of these transformations and their potential of reaction to those changes. They way that the communities interact with environment was evaluated by their production activities (Burdge and Johnson, 1977).

Parameters such as family income, their diet and infrastructural aspects of their dwellings were used to measure the survival strategy of each of those communities and to make evident their spatial differentiations and their internal contradictions.

4 RESULTS

Data obtained permitted us to describe the communities and to characterize them as to:

• population size and structure (Fig. 3);

• social-economic aspects (Fig. 4 and 5);

• environment interaction.

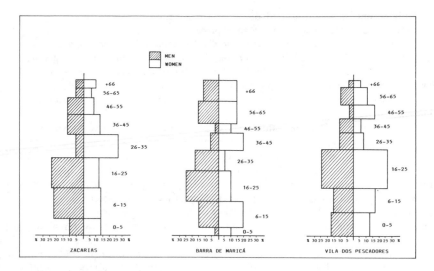

Figure 3: Populational structure of the communities.

Interaction Man-Environment happens especially in the sphere of productive activities, either to satisfy their basic needs or the desire to create economical surplus.

We understand as *productive activity* all activity which results in "conditions" for the individual survival and the reproduction of the social group. These "conditions" include resources such as income, food, housing, clothing, health, education and social well-being, safety, etc.

In the communities of the study, productive activities are mainly "linked" to the primary and tertiary sectors: fishing in the lagoons, trading and services in the nucleuses neighborhood and in the town of Maricá.

As concerns occupational structure of the communities the production situation was defined as follows: (Fig. 4)

1. *Active Population* (AP) — all individuals who have generating resources activities.

2. *Non Generating Income Population* (NGIP) — all who do not have any income generating activity, thus depending from someone else.

3. *Pensioners* (P) — those who receive sums from any official source: pension or retirement pay.

From the analysis of these data it was verified that the age group form 16 to 66 years old is the productive one. Moreover, as it is the biggest percentage of the class "Active Population", the male population was considered as defining the occupational categories as follows: (Fig. 5)

- *Fisherman* — Fishing activity in general, in all modalities found and also in those related or derived from manufacture, repair and handling of the fishing apparatus, maintenance and the commerce of fish.

- *Employed Workers* — Activity with explicit work.

- *Part-time Workers* — Contracts with previously established wages and people who, although not belonging to the fisherman class, work without a written contract and receive variable wages.

- *Fisherman and Others* — Fishermen who, besides having fishing as the main activity, have eventual jobs as odd job men.

In order to measure survival strategies found in the communities, we tried to evaluate results from these activities by analyzing the following aspects:

- family income,

- diet,

- infra-structural situation of dwellings.

These aspects clearly show the heterogeneity of the social class shaped in each community by the historical process of changes of use of space. Considering the three communities it was possible to notice the spatial differentiations and internal contradictions of each of them.

5 DISCUSSION

5.1 Barra de Maricá

In Barra de Maricá, the mingling of the fishing community in the summer people community is very high. Some forms-appearances persist in unmodernized old huts in the old professional tools, which are rarely used now. "Forms-contents" change with the new life styles, and new social problems to be faced.

Moving from a simpler productive form, peculiar to the non skilled fishing community, to urban forms of services, the community loses its professional characteristics. When proletarization begins, labor is not supplied, the community loses its habits and traditions, the people become outcasts in the city as needy and unqualified population.

Community integration in the urban system of production will redefine all roles played in the productive area, influencing family relations, weakening the role of the "paterfamilias" and also redefining the role of woman in the economics of the group and emptying the community as young people emigrate to the city.

5.2 Zacarias

Meanwhile, the Zacarias community took advantage of their special conditions. Being somewhat isolated in the rustic strip of the remaining barrier beach, it interacts intimately with natural resources, coupled with inaccessibility to urban equipment such as supermarkets. Another particularity is a possible interbreeding which,

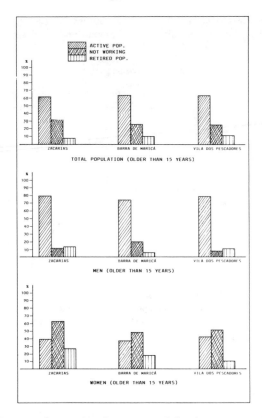

Figure 4: Occupational structure of the three communities.

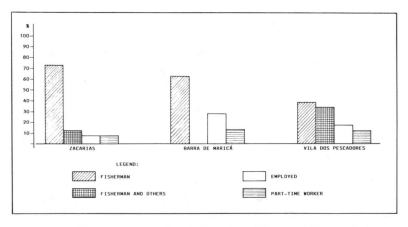

Figure 5: Occupational categories of the population.

favoring family closeness, permits maintenance of traditional production and of survival.

To this community, fishing means space-activity, which besides giving fundamental means of group survival, it also symbolically expresses freedom and autonomy on which the fisherman's social identity is based. Though he has difficulties in his life, his speech proclaims an idealized situation where his autonomy is reinforced. In the opposition and complementarity of the colony versus canoe, the Zacarias fisherman builds his social identity. Through this relationship, relations between sexes are defined as well as hierarchies within the group. "Fishery" is a socially masculine space. What is done there is considered as "work" and gives social status as a fisherman. Woman's space is in the hut, where she "helps" but she does not "work".

As concerns the survival strategies used, Zacarias maintains a way of life where the relationship with the natural environment is emphasized. This can be understood by analyzing the diet of the community, full of native food items, which costs them no more than the effort to pick them up in the barrier beach or in the lagoon.

Huts, as form-appearance, seem to crystallize a dynamic process to transformation of the "old" into the "new". But, as a space in use, they clearly show the older form-contents, where domestic activities are held in the open air, on the porches and in the improvised kitchens, and the recently created new space plays the secondary role of store room.

In Zacarias, more than in Barra or in Vila dos Pescadores, the "old" and the "new" intermingle to build the space of the community. Old forms show up: in the old huts which have not yet been remodeled; in the old way of using newer dwellings; in the centenary canoes; in the natural diet which does not dismiss the small fish from the lagoon or the vegetation from the barrier beach; in the esteem the fisherman has within the community; in the silent and discreet help from the women which gather wood in the beach barrier, prepare dyes for the hammocks, entertain themselves with fish but "do not work"... The "new" forms are in dwellings reconstruction; in the questioning, even if only among a minority of young people, of the fisherman's future as regards environmental changes; in how young girls invest in their future when they study and get prepared for the jobs the big city offers; in the recently acquired electric lighting, which brought with it refrigerators to keep fresh fishes and to cool drinks sold to tourists on week-ends and holidays... and also color TV, of course.

5.3 Vila dos Pescadores

It is a recently-built, poor, second-rate space of new forms which is inhabited by a social group with no affinity to it, partly because the group did not make it. Yet forms are new because of what they contain in their appearance, as new kitchens, new bathrooms with running water, masonry houses in walled lots, with tiny backyards in each house unit. In this nucleus, there are mixed contents from various origins and times. Not only the traditional fishermen from Maricá were taken to this area, but also migrants from several parts of the country, construction and urban workers who have stayed there in the last 20 years. The fishermen are the more numerous ones, but because they are inserted in such a different context they are slowly losing their identity, and also their old way of keeping themselves by fishing from the lagoon and the balanced interaction with the barrier beach environment.

6 CONCLUSIONS

We pointed out several contradictions and we are aware that they also exist in society and in space. In the studied communities, these contradictions form a resistance point, either because of their forms-appearances or their forms-contents. With the passing of time, these contradictions accumulated in each community, as the expressions of the transformations and changes in society, thus creating attrition between the "old" and the "new", a spatial "rugosity" where they survive as communities.

Acknowledgements: This work was supported by FINEP (Financiadora de Estudos e Projetos).

REFERENCES

[1] Bernardes, L.M.C. and N. Bernardes (1950). A pesca no litoral do Rio de Janeiro. *Rev. Bras. Geogr.* **XII** (1): 17–53.

[2] Burdge, R.J. and S. Johnson (1977). Sociocultural aspects of the effects of resource development. *in:* "Handbook for Environmental Planning: The Social Consequences of Environmental Change", J. McEvoy III and T. Dietz (ed.). John Wiley & Son, USA.

[3] Kneipp, L.P. (1977). Pescadores e coletores pré-históricos do litoral de Cabo Frio, Rio de Janeiro. *Col. Mus. Paul. Ser. Arqueol.* **5**: 1–169.

[4] Lamego, A.R. (1945). Ciclo evolutivo das lagunas fluminenses. *Bol. Dept. Prod. Min.* **118**: 1–48.

[5] Santos, Milton (1978). "Por Uma Geografia Nova". HUCITEC/EDUSP, São Paulo.

HEAVY METALS POLLUTION MONITORING THROUGH
THE CRITICAL PATHWAYS ANALYSIS: THE SEPETIBA BAY CASE

Olaf Malm [1]   Wolfgang Christian Pfeiffer[1]   Luiz Drude de Lacerda [2]

Marlene Fiszman[1]   Neusa R. W. Lima[1]

1 INTRODUCTION

The methodology of the critical pathway analysis has been widely employed to monitor the environmental impact of nuclear power plants in the aquatic environment.

According to this approach, among the nuclides released by the plant, some, due to their physico-chemical behavior, biological accumulation, and availability to humans, are critical ones; the pathways through which these nuclides are transferred to humans are the critical pathways, and the human group most exposed to the critical nuclides is the critical one. Thus, by monitoring the critical nuclides, a safety level of contamination for the whole situation can be achieved (Penna-Franca et al., 1984; Preston, 1975).

Our laboratory has applied this methodology to two different multimetal pollution situations (Lacerda, 1983; Malm, 1986).

The Sepetiba Bay is one of the most important fishery and recreational areas in the state of Rio de Janeiro, and presents typical environmental conditions of a very protected area along the Brazilian coast.

The main goals of this work are to assess the critical metal(s), the critical pathway(s), and the critical human group(s) inside the bay, in order to optimize monitoring programs for the situation with considerable economy of human and technical resources.

2 STUDY AREA

Sepetiba Bay (23°S, 44°W) is a 519 km² semi-enclosed bay, approximately 60 km from Rio de Janeiro city, Brazil.

Fluvial water inputs to the bay are concentrated along the NE coast, where the watersheds of five rivers are responsible for 95–99% of the total fluvial inputs to the bay. Among these, the Canal de São Francisco (CSF) and Rio Guandu (RG)

---

[1]Instituto de Biofísica Carlos Chagas Filho, Universidade Federal do Rio de Janeiro, Rio de Janeiro, RJ 21941, Brazil.

[2]Departamento de Geoquímica, Inst. Química, Universidade Federal Fluminense, Niterói, RJ 24210, Brazil.

constitute 75% of the watershed's total input, corresponding to an annual flow of 1.45×10^{11} l/s (Fonseca et al., 1978).

The industrial park (mainly metallurgical) located between two rivers (CSF and RG) discharges its effluents into them 3 km from the coast, thus providing a singlepoint effluent release (Lacerda, 1983). Moreover, the intensive utilization of the bay's biological resources enhances the possibilities of metal transfer to man through the marine seafood chain.

The principal geographical and hydrographical features of the Sepetiba Bay area are illustrated in Fig. 1.

Cu, Cr, Cd, Zn, Mn and Pb, the main metals released by the industrial park, were analyzed in the water and in suspended particles in the CSF and RG fluvial systems in order to evaluate flux into the bay.

Sediments are the dominant sink of metals in the marine system, in consequence it was included as one of the abiotic compartments to be monitored in the Sepetiba Bay project.

For the assessment of anthropogenic metal pollution, it is the non-lattice held fraction, instead of total metal concentration, which is of prime interest (Fiszman, 1984).

Therefore, a special extraction technique was developed to remove the available metals in the bottom sediments in a rapid, inexpensive way which at the same time was able to quantify the degree of anthropogenic discharges.

3 CHEMICAL ANALYSIS

Heavy metal concentration in all the samples was determined by flame atomic absorption spectrophotometry. River and estuarine waters were analyzed after filtration through 0.45 μm Millipore filters. Metals in suspended particles retained in filters (0.45 μm) and bottom sediments (63 μm), were extracted with HCl-0.1N and considered available fraction, and the residue with HNO_3:HCl:$HClO_4$ (3:3:1) considered as total content. All biological samples were chosen among the main seafoods normally consumed by the local population, and collected only from the bay area, where metals attained their highest concentrations. Samples were ashed at 450 °C for 24 h, dissolved in concentration HNO_3, and recovered in HCl-0.1 N, prior to analysis.

4 RESULTS AND DISCUSSION

Table I shows summarized results of the heavy metal concentrations in the estuarine area of the bay's main fluvial systems, CSF and RG rivers (Fig. 1).

The relative contribution of each metal to the total flux is: Mn > Zn > Cr > Pb > Cu > Cd. The particulate flux is greater than the dissolved one for all metals but Cd, and suspended particulate matter also showed the greatest metal levels, thus being an important compartment through which metal is transported in the bay.

Table II presents metal concentrations in suspended particles and bottom sediment from the most contaminated site, indicating the available fraction and total content respectively.

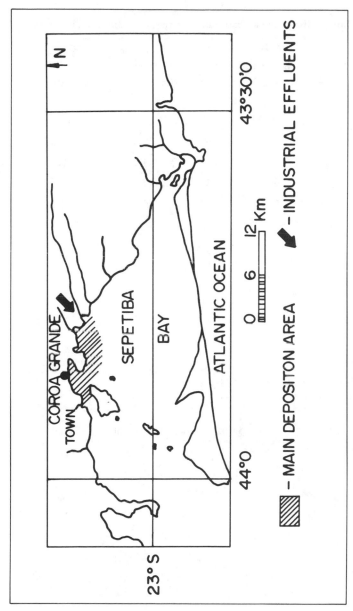

Figure 1: Localization of the studied area.

Table I: Heavy metal distribution in the bay's main estuarine area.

METALS	Total Dissolved Flux ton.y^{-1}	Total Particulate Flux ton.y^{-1}	Suspended Particulate Concentration μg.g^{-1} dw	Bottom Sediment Concentration μg.g^{-1} dw
Cu	0.89	1.80	57.3	19.3
Cr	5.30	5.60	109.9	52.7
Cd	0.80	0.10	4.4	2.5
Zn	2.00	9.50	476.1	282.5
Mn	3.90	16.50	468.3	195.3
Pb	1.80	2.70	131.2	50.4

Table II: Metal concentrations in suspended particles and bottom sediments from Coroa Grande. (Values in μg.g^{-1} dry weight.)

METALS	Suspended Particles Available	Suspended Particles Total	Bottom Sediments Available	Bottom Sediments Total
Cu	43.3	61.1	2.0	9.4
Cr	66.3	152	17.5	73.1
Cd	3.2	3.2	2.0	2.6
Zn	329	390	208	325
Mn	758	788	141	235
Pb	92.9	139	20.2	35.5

Table III: Heavy metal concentrations in seafood from Sepetiba Bay. (Values in $\mu g.g^{-1}$ wet weight.)

Metals	Cu	Cr	Cd	Zn	Mn	Pb
Mollusks						
Ostrea equestris	3.19	1.57	1.60	973	2.75	1.12
Cassostrea rizophorae	1.37	0.39	0.48	471	1.44	0.77
Mytella guyanensis	1.63	1.35	0.49	29.2	2.90	0.96
Tagelus plebeius	2.52	1.45	0.09	96.4	8.40	1.64
Anomalocardia brasiliana	0.76	0.38	0.40	19.5	4.15	0.92
Crustacea						
Peneus schimitii	3.47	0.76	0.08	37.80	0.50	2.38
Callinectes danae	32.80	1.51	0.34	39.50	4.12	1.96
Fish						
Mogil sp.	0.70	0.50	0.03	7.40	0.80	0.60
Cynoscium sp.	0.27	0.31	0.02	3.42	0.20	0.57
Micropogon sp.	0.54	0.77	0.04	27.30	0.97	1.08
Haemulon sp.	0.60	0.53	0.04	9.00	0.61	1.48
BSE	30	0.1	1.0	50	–	8

Table III presents metal concentration in the main seafood items consumed by the local population, in comparison with the Brazilian Standards for the Environment (BSE) for these metals in seafood.

Concentration in biological samples in general do not follow the same pattern as the abiotic compartments, although Zn has presented the highest concentration in both compartments. When comparing metal concentration of biological samples with those from BSE, Cd, although presenting the lowest concentration in abiotic compartments, overdose the BSE by a factor of 1.6 in one species of oyster, while Zn, by a factor of 10 to 20 in both oyster species. Cr, on the other hand, presented concentrations ranging from 3 to 15 times the BSE, in all the biological samples analyzed.

The population of a small town, Coroa Grande (Fig. 1), was identified as the critical human group, due to its location adjacent to the most contaminated area in the bay, its diet based on seafood, and its great consumption of the food items

254 COASTLINES OF BRAZIL,

With the highest metal concentration. A description of the analysis of population habits and fish production in the area is presented elsewhere (Lacerda, 1983). The critical parameters thus determined for the Sepetiba Bay situation are:

Critical metals :   Cr, Zn, Cd.
Critical pathways :   Suspended particles appeared as a
                             relevant transport compartment.
Critical food items :   Cr, all analyzed biological samples
                             Zn, oysters (both species)
                             Cd, oysters (only *C. rizophorae*.
Critical Human population: Inhabitants of Coroa Grande.
Biological monitor :   *Crassostrea brasiliana.*

Acknowledgements This work was supported by Financiadora de Estudos e Projetos (FINEP), Fundação de Amparo à Pesquisa do Rio de Janeiro (FAPERJ), Conselho Nacional de Desenvolvimento Científico e Tecnológico (CNPq), Comissão Nacional de Energia Nuclear (CNEN) and Universidade Federal do Rio de Janeiro (CEPG/UFRJ).

REFERENCES

[1] Fiszman, M; W.C. Pfeiffer; and L.D. Lacerda (1984). Comparison of methods used for extraction and geochemical distribution of heavy metals in bottom sediments from Sepetiba Bay, RJ. *Env. Techn. Lett.* **5** (12): 567–575.

[2] Fonseca, M.R.M.; M. Vieira; J.A. Chipe; and L.R. Ribeiro (1978). Qualidade de água da Baía de Sepetiba. *in:* Meio Ambiente Vários Estudos II. Fund. Est. Eng. Meio Ambiente, Rio de Janeiro, p. 316–334.

[3] Lacerda, L.D. (1983). Aplicação de metodologia de abordagem pelos parâmetros críticos no estudo da poluição por metais pesados na Baía de Sepetiba, Rio de Janeiro. PhD Thesis, Instituto de Biofísica, Univ. Fed. Rio de Janeiro, 182 pp.

[4] Malm, O. (1986). Estudo da poluição por metais pesados no sistema Rio Paraíba do Sul – Rio Guandu (RPS–RG) através da metodologia de abordagem pelos parâmetros críticos. M.Sc. Thesis, Instituto de Biofísica, Univ. Fed. Rio de Janeiro, 180 pp.

[5] Penna-Franca, E.; W.C. Pfeiffer; M. Fiszman; and L.D. Lacerda (1984). Aplicabilidade da análise pelos parâmetros críticos, usualmente empregada para instalações nucleares no controle da poluição do ambiente marinho por metais pesados. *Ciência e Cultura*, **36** (2): 251–219.

[6] Preston, A. (1975). The radiological consequence of releases from nuclear facilities to the aquatic environment. *in:* Impact of nuclear releases into the aquatic environment, IAEA, Viena, 3–21.

GEOCOSTA OPERATIONS – A PROGRAM OF OCEANOGRAPHIC EXPEDITIONS FOR THE BRAZILIAN INNER SHELF

Dieter Muehe [1]

The systematic research of the Brazilian continental margin, from geological and geophysical points of view, began in 1969 as a joint undertaking of different universities and governmental agencies, with strong support from "Diretoria de Hidrografia e Navegação" (DHN) of the Brazilian Navy, and financial support from the Brazilian research council (CNPq). This task was managed by representatives of all entities involved, as a Program for Marine Geology and Geophysics (PGGM). The oceanographic expeditions were called "GEOMAR Operations", and were performed mostly with Navy oceanographic vessels.

Researchers and institutions engaged in coastal geology, geomorphology and engineering very soon felt the need to conduct these studies on the inner shelf, according to appropriate methodologies — for instance: mapping in larger and more detailed scales, use of smaller vessels, and integration of studies in the submarine region with those on the coastal zone.

The first oceanographic expedition with this purpose inside the PGGM, GEOMAR X, was in May 1978, with the R V. *Almirante Câmara*, belonging to DHN. Current measurements were carried out and samples of bottom sediments were taken from the inner shelf, east of the city of Rio de Janeiro (Muehe, 1982). At that time, the need to implement a specific program for oceanographic operations on the inner shelf became clear.

In July 1979, a new expedition was conducted with the R.V. *Almirate Câmara*, in the same area as GEOMAR X, with the following purposes: surveying profiles with side scan sonar and conducting current measurements simultaneous to meteorological observations (Muehe and Sucharov, 1980; Muehe and Sucharov, 1981). In order to characterize these expeditions to the inner shelf, the identification "Operação GEOCOSTA" was adopted, followed by the name of the geographical region, in this case GEOCOSTA RIO I.

In 1983, the operation GEOCOSTA SUL I took place on the inner shelf in front of the mouth of Patos Lagoon, in the State of Rio Grande do Sul, also with the R.V. *Almirante Câmara*. The methodology followed the one adopted in GEOMAR X and GEOCOSTA RIO I, consisting of: sampling of bottom sediments by dredging and by coring, simultaneous observations of meteorological and oceanographical parameters — in order to evaluate the conditions of sediment transport — and

[1] Departamento de Geografia, Instituto de Geociências, Universidade Federal do Rio de Janeiro, Rio de Janeiro, RJ 21945, Brazil.

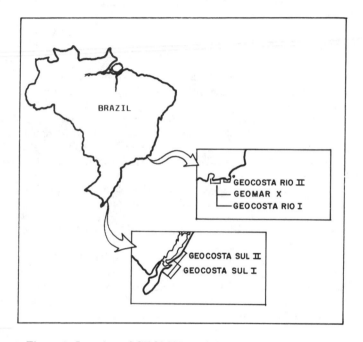

Figure 1: Location of GEOMAR and GEOCOSTA operations.

collecting material for the study of the significance of the fauna of ostracodes — used as a biological and ecological indicator and as a current tracer (DHN, 1983). In April 1984, the second operation took place, GEOCOSTA SUL II, covering part of the same region studied in the first expedition, especially the area in front of the Patos Lagoon, but extending further north towards Mostardas. It had similar goals to the first one, consisting of the study of present sedimentation by the use of sub-bottom profiles, side scan sonar, and sampling of bottom sediments for the mapping of sediment facies of the region (DHN, 1984).

Strategically, the second and third GEOCOSTA operations consolidated the idea of a specific program for inner shelf studies, which was finally approved on the XV PGGM Meeting, in November 1984. It was then decided that, besides the systematic work needed for elaborating the thematic maps — for instance, sedimentological, geomorphological, sediment transport, mineral resources charts — the GEOCOSTA operations should also be oriented towards generating information useful in coastal management projects. This view was reinforced during the XVII PGGM Meeting, in August 1986, when it was decided that the thematic mappings planned for those operations should include, whenever possible, the study of the adjacent coastal zone.

The GEOCOSTA RIO II, in March 1986, had already incorporated a good deal of those ideas. With the purpose of obtaining information so as to understand the evolution of the coastline in front of the Araruama Lagoon, this operation covered the inner shelf between Saquarema and Cabo Frio, an area east of the one studied during GEOMAR X and GEOCOSTA RIO I. This time, a smaller boat was used, the Av.Oc. *Suboficial Oliveira*, to map a region with depths varying from 30 m to 60 m, an inflatable boat and a fishing boat, to cover the region closer to the shore. The following investigations were carried out: sampling of bottom sediment, bathymetry, side scan sonar, measurement of physical and chemical parameters of the sea and intersticial water, and dredging of bottom sediments for benthonic analysis. Within the coastal zone, the emphasis of the studies was in the characterization of the geomorphology of the barrier beaches, the textural characteristics of the sediments, and the detection of paleochannels by means of sub-bottom profiling. The integration of the data obtained both at the inner shelf and within the coastal zone will hopefully allow for the reconstruction of the evolution of the area and estimate its future development based on sedimentological processes.

One problem that has not been successfully solved is related to the availability of oceanographical equipment, mainly currentmeters and wave gauges. Equipment for geological sampling, like dredges and core samplers, has been furnished by DHN as well as by the institutions participating in the PGGM. Acquisition of geophysical equipment for shallow seismic studies (3.5 and 7.5 kHz) or intermediate ones (sparker), besides an electronic positioning system, would represent important tools for the inner shelf studies.

In conclusion, four operations "GEOCOSTA" have been executed so far, concentrating only in two areas of the Brazilian inner shelf (see Fig. 1). This is not enough for a country which intends to develop a serious coastal management program in such a long coastline, which has several large cities along it. However, it does represent a starting point. Research groups in various stages of consolidation already exist, spread among several universities in Brazil. This allows one to foresee that, sooner or later, such studies will be carried out at other locations of the continental shelf. It is just a matter of time, as well as of funds being available. Also, it is worth noting that similar studies in the inner shelf have been made, although on a smaller scale and without being part of a global program. Among the institutions belonging to PGGM, three of them have vessels which are appropriate for oceanographic research, in the States of Bahia, São Paulo and Rio Grande do Sul. The use of these vessels far from their home base, although possible, is too expensive. This creates an obstacle for the integration of the efforts. At the moment, the lack of vessels controlled by PGGM represents the main obstacle for oceanographical research. Renting boats, besides its high cost, has the serious disadvantage of making it almost impossible to return to the spot of study when, for some reason such as bad weather or equipment malfunctioning, the expedition has to be suspended. In the State of Rio de Janeiro, an effort to solve this problem is being made: a first project has been developed for a research vessel, for multiple uses, able to navigate in shallow waters such as estuaries, lagoons, and the inner shelf. The decision for buiding a new vessel or buying one to be later adapted has yet to be made. At least three major universities in the State — Federal do Rio de Janeiro (UFRJ), Federal Fluminense (UFF), and do Estado do Rio de Janeiro (UERJ) — would benefit from such an acquisition.

Acknowledgements: With the purpose of implementing the creation of a specific program for the inner shelf, the author suggested the designation of "GEOCOSTA Operations" for these expeditions, with the joint agreement of DHN's officials, Cmte. Luiz Carlos Ferreira da Silva and Cmte. Hugo Bernardi Jr., at the time in charge of Division of Geophysical Prospection and head of the Department of Geophysics, respectively. They were responsible for the scientific activities then and for the schedule of DHN's oceanographycal and hydrographical ships, and their contribution towards the establishing of the program was significant.

REFERENCES

[1] Diretoria de Hidrografia e Navegação (1983). Operação GEOCOSTA SUL I. Relatório de Fim de Comissão. Ministério da Marinha.

[2] Diretoria de Hidrografia e Navegação (1984). Operação GEOCOSTA SUL II. Relatório de Fim de Comissão. Ministério da Marinha.

[3] Muehe, D. (1982). Relatório de bordo da Operação GEOMAR X. DG 32-XI, Diretoria de Hidrografia e Navegação, Ministério da Marinha.

[4] Muehe, D. and E. Sucharov (1980). Operação GEOCOSTA RIO I: Primeira Etapa. Relatório de Bordo e Resultados Preliminares. Anais Hidrográficos XXXVII: 65–112. Diretoria de Hidrografia e Navegação, Ministério da Marinha.

[5] Muehe, D. and E. Sucharov (1981). Considerações sobre o transporte de sedimentos na plataforma continental nas proximidades das Ilhas Maricás, RJ. Rev. Bras. Geoc. 11 (4): 238–246.

ENVIRONMENTAL EVALUATION OF THE COASTAL AREA OF MARICÁ DISTRICT: A METHODOLOGICAL ESSAY

Maria Fernanda S.Q. da Costa Nunes [1]   Edna Maia Machado Guimarães [1]

Maria Cristina Lemos Ramos [1]

1 INTRODUCTION

This paper is part of an integrated study of the coastal environment of the county of Maricá, Rio de Janeiro, where the environmental alterations of the urban expansion phenomenon were monitored.

The environmental conception of Silva e Souza (1987) was used in this work. For them "an environment is nothing but a parcel of the earth surface still under dominantly natural conditions or transformed in different levels by man". This conception, however, does not exclude the social factor, for, as Silva and Souza have noted, "nature and society ... consist of dimensions of environmental reality which cannot be dissociated".

2 AREA DESCRIPTION

The studied area is in the county of Maricá, east of the city of Rio de Janeiro, within the geographical coordinates 7,468,000 N, 7,458,000 S, 715,000 E and 736,000 W. It has an area of 210 km^2 which includes a lagoon system formed by Maricá, Barra, Padre and Guarapina lagoons up to Ponta Negra. It is limited by the Atlantic Ocean in the south and by Macaco, Camburi, Silvado and Padre hills in the north (Fig. 1).

The climate is classified as AW in Koppen System, with a hot and rainy summer and dry winter. The average yearly temperature varies from 22°C to 24°C, and the average yearly rainfall varies from 500 to 2,500 mm.

This area can be subdivided into two sub-areas limited by the Amaral Peixoto road:

1. To the south a coastal plain of marine formation is found, a Quaternary barrier beach ("restinga"), the lagoon system — in which the lagoons are in the process of being filled up by sediments — and cliffs. The sediments are marine-sandy and sand-clayish with or without hydromorphism. The soils are

---

[1] Departamento de Ecologia, Instituto de Biologia, Universidade Federal do Rio de Janeiro, Rio de Janeiro, RJ 21941, Brazil.

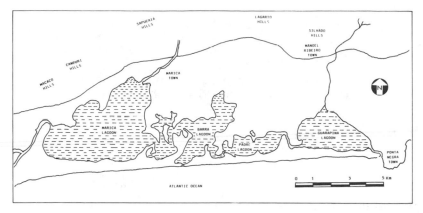

Figure 1: Maricá County: location of lagoons and hills.

of dystrophic humic-gley (RADAM, 1983), covered by primary herbaceous, shrubby and/or arboreous vegetation. The area dynamics is unstable.

2. The area from the north down to Ponta Negra, is not an accumulation area but a dissection one, varying from moderate to strong. This area presents structurally oriented dissection relief formed by asymmetrical ridges and cliffs which coalesce into colluvium slopes and convex hills and elongated steep hills with digited spurs with draining incisions varying from 158 m to 201 m and hillside inclines varying from 11° to 24°. These hills are part of the Paraíba do Sul Complex, of the archeozoic period, formed mainly by granite and gneiss (RADAM, 1983). The sediments are of clay and sandy-clay texture and soils yellow podsolic and red alic covered by pastures and secondary vegetation or the Atlantic Forest remains in steep areas.

The county of Maricá dates from the end of the XVI century, when "sesmarias" were donated, and Benecditine monks started the São José de Imbassaí settlement (Biase Simão, 1979) on the west border of the Maricá lagoon. Later on, at the end of the XVIII century, the hamlet was transferred to the higher northern border, not subject to inundations and thus a healthier place. This new settlement became a village in 1814, under the name of Santa Maria de Maricá. In December 27, 1889, at the beginning of the republican government, the village received the status of town in its present site.

Since the colonial times up to the end of the XIX century, the Maricá area was considered an "important agricultural center of the Lagoon Region" (Biase Simão, 1979). Paradoxically, at the same time it became a town, the village of Santa Maria de Maricá started its decadence, for its agricultural economy was compromised by the end of slavery in 1888.

After 1890, when the provinces became states, the new government, aware of the problem of sanitation in the Fluminense Lowlands, created several agencies aiming for the drainage and sanitation of the lowlands. One of them was the Departamento

Nacional de Obras e Saneamento (D.N.O.S.), which, from 1936 on expanded its role to encompass the whole country.

An important work of hydraulic engineering was made during that time which not only benefited sugar cane plantation and cattle raising in Maricá county, but made the use of big land parcels possible due to the reduction of the areas flooded by the lagoons.

From 1950 on, when the Amaral Peixoto road was paved, summer residents and tourists started coming to Maricá. The first real estate investment started in 1953 near the inlet of Maricá and Ponta Negra. From then on, pressure on the traditional fishing communities forced them out of the lagoon shores and out of the beaches. To the north, the semi-abandoned colonial farms were parceled into lots.

The accelerated growth of the city of Rio de Janeiro in the sixties also influenced its metropolitan area, including Maricá. The construction of the Rio-Niterói bridge shortened the distance between the Metropolis and Maricá, increasing the tourist flux and land values, which caused real estate speculation. This process and also land parceling into lots has been favoring urban expansion.

Relative to the traditional soil use in the county, "plotting" has taken the role of main environment transformation agent. Landfills, removal of natural vegetal cover, displacement of large amounts of gravel to pave new streets gave way to big environmental transformation.

However, the impact of urbanization is responsible for other transformations, beyond those of the physical environment. New life styles, new social values, new cultural patterns co-exist and compete in the day to day life of the local population, as discussed in the paper by Machado-Guimarães in this conference. Coupled with the decadence of the traditional activities, the new life possibilities which are offered create, little by little, new forms of insertion in the urban economy to the remaining population. This insertion, however, does not occur satisfactorily, as it creates a rupture with traditional patterns of the social group, affecting its internal organization and altering the life quality of the communities.

3 METHODOLOGY

The studies on environmental impact — as a type of environmental analysis — have been made at the same time as specific methodologies were being developed.

The main difficulties in finding a methodology that could deal with environmental complexity are centered in the double need of analysis and synthesis which would permit a holistic view encompassing environmental reality.

In Ecology, the concept of the Ecosystem as a functional unity of nature (Tansley, 1935), associated to the development of Bertalanffy's General Theory of Systems, originated in the seventies a series of works which applied a systemic approach to the study of biological systems. Those studies varied from extreme particularization and over detailing of the so called "nature unities" — which do not show the necessary comprehensive view — to a superficial global treatment — which does not present the information required for the understanding of the dynamics of the whole.

On the other hand, the urgency of environmental planning and management, in view of the growth of environment decay, which is directly related to the life quality of man, has recently brought out new "Environmental Evaluation Methods"

in developed countries such as the USA and Canada. The propositions of Leopold
et al. (1971), Sorensen (1974) and Bisset (1983) should be noted.

Nowadays, there are studies that propose a critical evaluation of existing methodologies such as the ones from Perazza *et al.* (1985) and Claudio (1987).

Basically, the different methods result in reports of items, matrices, maps and grids or diagrams, with different degrees of complexity. They also differ in other aspects, as for example:

- the range of application and use flexibility;

- the range of the environmental factors considered (physical-biological and social-economical);

- qualitative and/or quantitative base information;

- effectiveness of communication with the user such as lay authorities or community members;

- identification of the impacts on specific variables and, also, the ability to unite identified impacts;

- necessary resources;

- taking into account whether the impacts are: harmful and/or beneficial, temporary and/or permanent, short-term and/or long-term, direct and/or indirect, localized and/or spread;

- possibility of interdisciplinary evaluation;

- community participation, especially when attributing values to environmental factors and impacts; and

- evaluation of the magnitude of environmental effects and the importance of the impact, a difficult problem, owing to its subjectiveness.

The adopted methodology in this work is based on the interpretation of data obtained from aerophotographies and orbital images from LANDSAT-TM taken from 1964 through 1986. Thus it was possible to prepare maps of land use/land cover in the years of 1964, 1976 and 1986 ("source maps").

From these source maps, the geographical information system (S.A.G.A.) generated new maps showing the observed changes in land use/land cover, regarding their location, direction and extension. These new maps will be referred hereafter as "derived maps".

Thus, the urban expansion areas are detected and later on they are characterized through field work where data related to human aspects are gathered with the help of question forms and interviews. From them, the authors gather information on settlements, housing, population, production activities and life styles.

At the same time, other area data are delivered to S.A.G.A.: topographic maps, soil maps, geology, geomorphology and declivity data. Thus the work area is well defined in its geophysical aspects. These maps are superposed so that they can be analyzed in order to identify the critical areas.

Therefore, it is possible to indicate and to monitor the evolution of the use and of the dynamics of environment in time and in space.

4 PRELIMINARY DISCUSSION OF RESULTS

Table I presents the values in hectares (1 ha $= 10^4$ m^2) of the surface related to each of the use/land cover class in 1964 and 1976, as well as the percentage of change of that period considering 1964 as zero time. 1986 data obtained from LANDSAT-TM images is not yet available. However, field work made it possible to verify recent tendencies.

The *wetland* class was sub-divided into 11 sub-classes in level III. Consequently it is not included in the source maps. These results were dealt with separately in another study on wetlands.

Analysis of the source maps, show that there are marked changes in border areas of the lagoons and in those limiting Amaral Peixoto road and vicinal roads.

In the lagoon system, especially in the Padre, Barra and Maricá lagoons, the number of spits associated with internal circulation has increased.

New spits and wetland were observed in the Padre lagoon. Those areas are occupied by herbaceous vegetation used as extensive pasture for horses and cattle raising. The water surface and lagoon depth have decreased noticeably.

In the Maricá lagoon, deposition and sedimentation points are found in the mouth of the Ubatiba river and in the area which is parallel to the primary shoreline. The water surface has diminished 3.4%.

In general, new marshes (23%) and "tifetum" (20%) have appeared in border areas. The oldest ones have dried up and are now covered by grass and sedges, sometimes with shrubs too. Those areas which are now identified as *grassland* and *grassland with shrubs* are used for extensive pasture. They increased reasonably during the period of the study (12 years): 13.3% for *grassland* and 30.7% for *grassland with shrubs*.

Between the lagoons and the sea, the *barrier beach vegetation* is found, which is characterized by scattered bushes along the sandy land. Nowadays, considerable amount of this kind of vegetation is only found near the Maricá lagoon, as, from that area up to Ponta Negra, the land has been divided into recreational land developments (which are classified as *settlements*). Some of them are already occupied while others have not yet had constructions built on them.

Although the *barrier beach vegetation* has grown on former *sandy land*, growth of *degraded barrier beach vegetation* shows an increase of anthropic influence in the area which is caused by sand removal from the beaches for industrial purposes, domestic sewage disposal and the above mentioned land parcelling.

In the northern area of the lagoon system, *improved permanent pasture*, *grassland*, *grassland with shrubs* and *croplands* have also increased at the rate of, respectively, 41.4%, 13.3%, 30.7% and 117.0%. These data show intensification of man's presence in the area relative to agricultural and cattle raising activities. These prevailing activities cause the decreasing of areas formerly covered by native forests or secondary vegetation. The inappropriate management of deforested areas cause erosion and land slides, as can be observed in the Ponta Negra region.

The activity that showed the biggest increase (209%) among the identified use classes is mentioned in the sub-titles as *horticulture*, but in fact, it is a particular and recent use of the land, characterized by small land plots where simple dwelling were built. Part of it is sometimes used to grow basic crops for food and cattle raising. It was verified during the field work that these people do menial jobs, or

Table I: Change in land use in Maricá County.

CLASSES	AREA IN ha [1]		DIFFERENCE IN AREA (ha)	CHANGE %
	YEAR 1964	YEAR 1976		
lagoon	3397.25	3280.75	116.50 (−)	3.4
wetland	1596.50	1573.25	23.25 (−)	1.4
spits	121.00	126.50	5.50 (+)	4.3
beach	444.00	410.00	34.00 (−)	7.6
sandy land	239.25	191.75	47.50 (−)	19.9
bare land	91.50	83.25	8.25 (−)	9.0
land in ecological succession	1180.25	1216.00	35.75 (+)	3.0
grassland	896.75	1015.75	119.00 (+)	13.3
grassland with shrubs	2226.50	1542.50	684.00 (−)	30.7
improved permanent pasture	293.75	415.50	121.75 (+)	41.4
croplands	337.75	733.25	395.50 (+)	117.0
tree and other perennial crops	509.50	950.25	440.75 (+)	86.5
horticulture	32.75	101.25	68.50 (+)	209.0
settlements	1651.75	1626.50	25.25 (−)	1.5
barrier beach vegetation	354.25	238.50	115.75 (+)	32.6
degraded barrier beach vegetation	15.25	86.50	71.25 (+)	467.2
woodland	4274.25	3791.75	482.50 (−)	11.2
degraded woodland	773.50	901.75	128.25 (−)	16.6

[1] 1 ha = 10^4 m^2.

own a small trade which is always related to their housing unit. In most cases, the property is used as a consequence of cession, documented claim or even squatting. This sort of use clearly shows the expectation of future valuations of the real owners, which are real estate investors.

5 CONCLUSION

The methodology employed in this study is supported by the association of the techniques of remote sensing and geoprocessing with field work. Consequently, it was possible to monitor an urban expansion process and the resulting environmental impact.

The urban expansion phenomenon, as well as its effects, could be detected and measured in hectares, meaning the surface of the land use or cover which was lost or acquired. Examples of the effects of such expansion are: the use of hillside areas previously covered by forests for farming and cattle raising; and the reduction of the water surface of the lagoon system by increased sedimentation. Therefore, the environmental alterations were analyzed and estimated without ascribing any special set of values to the implied variables.

In the field work, the results given by the preliminary studies derived from geoprocessing were used. Thus, it was possible to detail, to single out and to qualify the effects of the urban expansion phenomenon on the local population, by employing their testimony.

The harmful, or beneficial, the short term, or long term effects, were included here according to the analysis of the data obtained from the remote sensors, and also, direct or indirect effects, those resulting from the interaction of several environmental elements, i.e., resulting from the environmental dynamics. As an example of the latter, the appearance of wetland, where formerly water of the lagoon system was found, can be mentioned. This process starts when sediments from degraded hills flow into the lagoons.

S.A.G.A. has permitted the union of data from several sources, as for instance in the map superposition method (Perazza et al., 1985), from which the "derived maps" were prepared (Silva e Souza, 1987). We could count on a reasonable flexibility as relates to the environmental variables used in our study. The works that have other purposes may unite primary sources with S.A.G.A. to obtain critical areas (as concerns physical-biological conditions and social-economic ones) to be monitored or avoided in certain projects.

The charts obtained from the S.A.G.A. analysis represent the situation found by codes or colors, and correspond to a synthesis of the present dynamics of the studied area. This may be clearly observed by anyone interested in those informations.

Thanks to the use of remote sensing and geoprocessing, all environmental variables of geographical mean were accompanied simultaneously in a specific period of time in all the study area. Thus, it was possible to make an interdisciplinary and integrated evaluation of the reality of the environment.

The analysis of the area in successive points of time, permitted the recording of the chronological evolution of the environment so that the modifications could be viewed.

The environment responds to the influences of the metropolis of Rio de Janeiro which cause modifications in the relationship between man and the environment and which could thus be detected, qualified and quantified. They were exposed in their spatial context keeping their geographical relations.

Silva e Souza (1987) emphasize the treatment by geoprocessing "as it considers directly the geographical dimension of the environmental impact, it surpasses the simple estimative analysis based on tabulations restricted to the discrimination of impacting actions and the answer estimative of the considered environmental elements".

From the analysis of the results, it may be concluded that this methodology is efficient and thus can contribute enormously to environmental planning and coastal management.

Acknowledgements: This work was financed by FINEP (Financiadora de Estudos e Projetos). The authors thank the Group of Research in Geoprocessing of the Geography Department (UFRJ).

REFERENCES

[1] Biase Simão, M.T. (1979). Pesquisa. INEPAC (mim.)

[2] Bisset, R. (1983). An overview of recent EIA methods. Symposium on EIA, Chania, Crete, UK. 25 pp.

[3] Claudio, F.B.R. (1987). Abordagens metodológicas na avaliação de impacto ambiental. Propostas de critérios de AIA em São Paulo. *Ciência e Cultura* **39** (5/6): 483–488.

[4] Leopold, L.B.; F.E. Clarke; B.B. Hanshaw; and J.R. Balsley (1971). A procedure for evaluating environmental impact. *Geol. Survey Circ.* 645, US Government Printing Office, Washington, DC, 13 pp.

[5] Machado-Guimarães, E.M. (1989). Impact on a primitive fishing community in Maricá County, caused by urbanization. Proc. VI Symp. Coastal and Ocean Management, Charleston, July 10–15, 1989, ASCE.

[6] Perazza, M.; M.J. Birraque; V.R. Link; and M.H.L. de Queiroz (1985). Estudo analítico de metodologias de avaliação de impacto ambiental. 13º Cong. Bras. Eng. Sanitária e Ambiental, Alagoas. CETESB, São Paulo, 63, 12 pp.

[7] RADAM (1983). Folhas SF-23/24. Rio de Janeiro – Vitória.

[8] Silva, J.X. da and M.J.L. de Souza (1987). "Análise Ambiental". Ed. UFRJ, Rio de Janeiro, 199 pp.

[9] Sorensen, J.C. (1974). A framework for identification and control of resource degradation and conflict in multiple use of the coastal zone. Dept. Landscape Architecture, UC. 50 pp.

[10] Tansley, A.G. (1935). Ecology 16, 296.

THE PARAÍBA DO SUL RETROGRADATION AND THE ATAFONA ENVIRONMENTAL IMPACT

Mauro Sérgio F. Argento [1]

1 INTRODUCTION

The mouth of a delta is an extremely dynamic environment; it represents an area of interaction between riverine and marine processes. Sediments, usually present in great quantity and varying considerably in size and grain composition, are transported by several river arms and are rapidly deposited at the mouths of the deltaic complex. The hydrodynamic processes which operate on such mouths have control over the water and sediment exit flowage, establishing the dissemination models and the material storage at the subaqueous part of the deltaic shelf. Other processes, including subaqueous mass-movements, begin to modify the model, bringing alterations into the depositional system. Such mass-movements have, at times, sufficient magnitude to affect the innermost deltaic sedimentary structures. Thus they explain the mechanisms responsible for the deformation of the sediment suites and for the formation of the sedimentary models of the offshore shelf.

The modification of sediments texture and the reaction of biochemical processes combined with subaqueous mass-movements, may cause retention and releasing of gases, especially of methane and carbon dioxide, thus showing a surface with a strong tendency to acoustical responses.

The deltaic area is extraordinarily dynamic due to the river-marine influence. On interdisciplinary terms it has lead to the writing of many works about its complexity. The following works concerning the subaqueous process are worth mentioning: Bea (1971), Bea and Arnold (1973), Coleman and Wright (1974), Fisch and Mc Clelland (1959), Garrison (1974), Coleman (1974), Hedberg (1974), Mead (1966), Moore (1961), Morgan et alii. (1963), Renz et alii. (1955), Richard (1967), Shepard (1955, 1973) and Singh (1974).

Coleman, Shuhayda, Whelan, and Wright (1974) presented a documentary on the different types of offshore mass-movements fronting the Mississippi delta.

Several types of deformation might occur on the river-marine interaction area, such as: peripheral slump planes, diapirism, radial tensions of eventual faults, mass-movements, bottom alterations caused by currents combined with nearshore waves and, finally, clay depositional flowage. Sediment deposition occurs mostly close

---

[1] Departamento de Geografia, Instituto de Geociências, Universidaade Federal do Rio de Janeiro, Rio de Janeiro, RJ 21945, Brazil

to the river mouths, gradually decreases seaward, fitting into successive rotational slump planes. The analysis of the existing deformations of this deltaic sedimentary environment must consider both the tectonic and atectonic processes.

This study is an attempt to explain the event which is presently occurring at the mouth of the Paraíba do Sul river and is causing a negative socio-economic impact on the Atafona population.

2 THE DELTAIC MOUTH PROGRADING PROCESSES

The meeting point of the marine and riverine environments at the mouth of the deltaic plain presents several subenvironments which are very different from each other: the main channel and its distributaries, the subaerial and the subaqueous natural levees, the bars of the distributaries, the distal bar, and the prodelta.

Material of sedimentary origin made up of sand, silt and clay arrives at the deltaic area. The hydrodynamic processes which take place here lead to a natural selection, concentrating the coarsest sand grains near the channel and dissipating the finest ones throughout a wider area seaward.

Figure 1, based on a LANDSAT Image by I-100, illustrates schematically the nearshore and offshore areas which are under the influence of the suspended material coming from the Paraíba do Sul river.

Figure 1 confines the study area in three distinct planes: the horizontal, the longitudinal and the vertical. For a better understanding of the actual processes, it is essential to combine the three information planes because together they furnish answers concerning the depositional environment boundaries, features and soil formations.

It is possible to understand the deltaic prograding process as well as its respective sedimentation through the model Coleman et alii. (1974) described for the South Pass Bar of the Mississippi. In this model, four regions with very specific characteristics are identified. Thus, region I is distinguished by turbulent diffusion and strong bottom friction, where the velocity of the fresh water decreases as it deepens seaward. It is on this area that the debouching bars begin to settle. In region II, the bars are already well developed and closer to the surface. It is a wave influence zone, having intense turbulence and rapid decelerations. The currents combined with the waves take various directions, subjecting, consequently, the deposited sediments, especially sand and clay, to more reworking. With the overbank splays and the deepening of the sea, a deep area is established in Region III, where there is an internal, hydraulic jump. Even though the velocity of the submerged currents is inferior to that of Region I, the currents are responsible for the sapping of the bars, thus explaining, by consecutive mass-movements, the progradation of such bars. Region IV corresponds to the expansion areas of weak buoyant (clay + silt), where there is great wind, wave and tide influence.

Consequently, as time goes by, different depositional planes are formed, confirming the prograding process previously described.

Continuous progradation combined with the successive currents which cap the sedimentation basis, make it possible to check the subaqueous mass from time to time.

Such processes usually act on the delta front bars, generating mass-movements such as slides (with intense mass-movement alteration) or slump (without internal

Figure 1: Interpretation of the material which arrives at the ocean through the Paraíba do Sul River.

mass-movement).

3 THE RETROGRADATION PHENOMENON AND THE ENVIRONMENTAL IMPACT IN ATAFONA

The small village of Atafona lies on the right margin of the Paraíba do Sul river mouth. Its population is of two different social classes: a group of low income people, basically of fishermen, who live there on a permanent basis settled on the riverside; and another one, of higher income, who only go there during summer vacations, holidays and week-ends.

For twenty years this area has been suffering from the effects of retrogradation and the population has been witnessing the destruction of their beaches and dwellings. Thus, the whole business life of the village has been affected, giving Atafona the appearance of a "Ghost City".

Figure 2 illustrates the geographical location of the Atafona village as well the destroyed area since 1968, time of the IBGE base card survey – 1:500,000 scale.

The search for an explanation of this retrogradation phenomenon has lead to several hypothesis. One of them is based on the decrease of sediment deposition at the river mouth, due especially to the great water volume retained by successive dams upstream, which would not only modify the riverine discharge at the river mouth, but also the texture of the transported grains. This area of strong dynamics of the river-marine agents would receive influences from a more intense, marine-erosive action, thus originating continuous alterations on the longitudinal Atafona beach.

Another hypothesis considers the combined dynamics of currents and waves at the Paraíba do Sul deltaic mouth. Continuous formation of bars on several arms of the Paraíba mouth and the stronger presence of the NE wind there result in big turbulent areas, contributing to modify not only the wave system on their basic parameters (direction, velocity, length, breakers, etc.), but also the spots of wave occurrence. Hence, such situation would reflect on the onshore forms, resulting in a strong erosive action with inevitable coastal progradation.

Nevertheless, the hypothesis presented in this work is that the Atafona area is sinking due to the occurrence of subaqueous mass-movements such as slumps, with subsurface, elongate retrogressive slides.

Argento (1979) shows the presence of a flooded drainage, previous to the quaternary deltaic plain and to the Paraíba do Sul deltaic progradation. The existence of successive bygone deltaic lobes confirms such hypothesis (Figure 3). The work of Xavier da Silva and Argento (1978) still shows a lead to the NE of the sedimentary suite of the present Paraíba do Sul river mouth.

The superposition of this information makes us infer that the present Atafona subsurficial area was a site of pleistocene silt and clay deposition. On the other hand, there is evidence that the sedimentary complex, made up of more recent bygone deltaic sheets (3rd. and 4th. Lobes), is sloping slightly towards Atafona, consolidating the possibility of a local incipient subsidence.

This hypothesis becomes stronger, if we apply to the Atafona present event the scheme of figure 4, where the occurrence and growth faults make the most recent prodelta clay deposits migrate along the existing sliding planes.

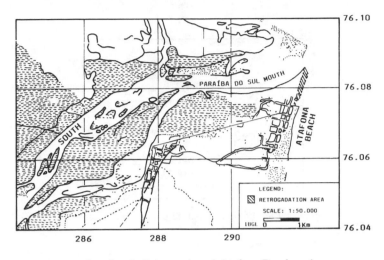

Figure 2: Paraíba do Sul mouth and Atafona Beach main area.

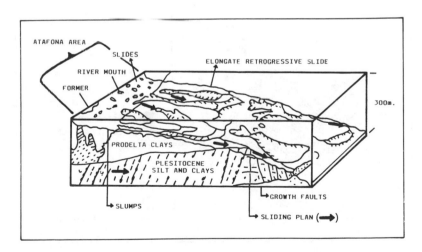

Figure 3: Spatial identification of the surficial deltaic sheets: Paraíba do Sul deltaic plain.

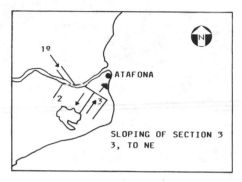

Figure 4: Paraíba do Sul deltaic plain: sloping sections.

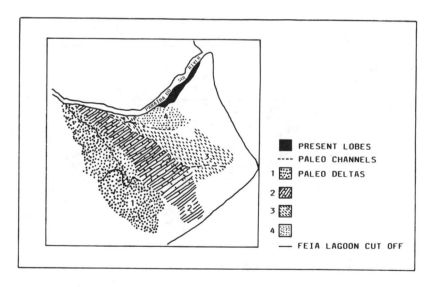

Figure 5: Diagram of Paraíba do Sul River mouth and prodelta.

The most recent sediments, deposited in successive upper layers, are influenced by subaqueous mass-movements, such as slumps and slides, which reflect as well on the layers that cap these depositional planes, such as the sandy Atafona deposits. Consequently, the Atafona village is located in an area, which suffers gradual sinking under the influence of this proccess whose effects are topographically visible. Figure 5 illustrates this hypothesis.

The retrogradation phenomenon observed at Atafona, on the Paraíba do Sul river mouth, is not an isolated one. Signs of a similar situation, which happened in the recent past, are evident for approximately three kilometers from the present Paraíba do Sul river mouth. The cutting off of the inner, ancient beach ridges reveal past Paraíba do Sul retrogradation phenomena.

Figure 6, made through the aerial photo-interpretation, documents what was stated here.

The occurrence of such phenomenon in the past, might not have caused environmental impact, due to the lack of population in the affected areas. Nevertheless, the present Atafona event is a significant example of negative environmental impact.

Even though this is a slow process phenomenon, without human losses, it brings incalculable socio-economic damages. Nearly the whole Atafona coastal zone was destroyed, including the historical Atafona lighthouse, which in 1976 was 200 meters from the shoreline. Three living quarters were completely destroyed by the invading sea. In less than seven years, at the river-marine confluence, a gasoline station, a fish warehouse and the main square of the village were destroyed. Most of the fishermen, that is, the lowest social stratum of the population, lost their houses and had to change their activities, altering, consequently, their "modus vivendi". The luxury houses of the higher classes, located at the seashore, were completely destroyed as well as the whole Atafona shoreline infrastructure. The attempt to reinforce the houses, nowadays, shows the population hopes to return to a past environmental equilibrium. However, the time of reaction is unknown: according to Figure 6, it is possible that the process may enter an accommodation phase due to the new situation of the dislocated layers. It is expected, due to the sort of repetitive chronological occurrences, that the regular, progradation phase of the river delta continues.

A visit to the site will confirm the negative environmental impact which presently occurs on the Paraíba do Sul delta mouth, more specifically on the Atafona village.

4 CONCLUSIONS

- This work offered a conceptual model of the Paraíba do Sul delta retrogradation.

- The deductive model was used on this investigation, using the model developed by the Coastal Studies Institute – LSU – for the Mississippi delta as reference basis.

- In our opinion, the present Atafona phenomenon results not only from the wave action combined with the currents, but, mainly from the effect of subaqueous mass-movements, offering enough magnitudes to affect the innermost parts of the deltaic sedimentary structures of the Paraíba do Sul.

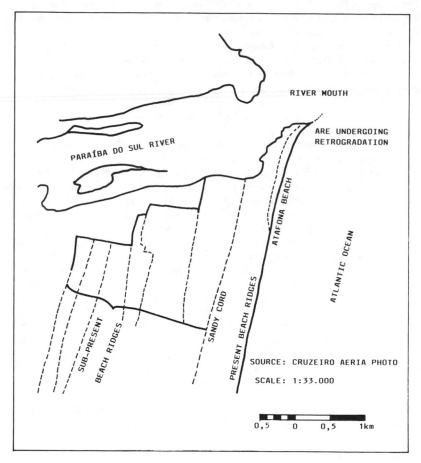

Figure 6: Aereal photo interpretation: Atafona Beach area undergoing retrogradation.

- Subsurficial documentation strengthens the hypothesis put forward concerning the Atafona area (Paraíba do Sul river mouth).

- This paper shows the dynamics of the deltaic progradations.

- The catastrophic events on Atafona beach are portrayed in this paper, with examples of environmental impacts.

Acknowledgements: Collaboration of Jorge Soares Marques and Maria Luiza F. Pereira is very much thanked.

REFERENCES

[1] Argento, M.S.F. (1979). The Paraíba do Sul Deltaic Plain — An Environmental System. M.Sc. Thesis, Inst. Geociências, Universidade Federal do Rio Janeiro.

[2] Bea, R.G. (1971). How sea floor slides affect offshore structures. *Oil and Gas Journal* **69** (48): 88–92.

[3] Bea, R.G. and P. Arnold (1973). Movements and forces developed by wave induced slides in soft clays. Preprints, Offshore Technology Conference, Houston, Texas, April 1973.

[4] Brooks, J.M. and W.M. Sackett (1973). Sources, sinks, and concentrations of light hydrocarbons in the Gulf of Mexico. *Journal of Geophys. Research* **78**: 5248–5255.

[5] Coleman, J.M.; J.C. Ferm; and R.S. Saxena (1972). Deltas: recent and ancient. New Orleans Geological Society, Continuing Education Seminar, Nov. 28–30, 169 p.

[6] Coleman, J.M. and I.D. Wight (1974). Formative mechanisms in a modern depocenter, in Stratigraphy and petroleum potential of northern Gulf of Mexico (part II). New Orleans Geological Society Seminar, Jan. 22–24, pp. 90–139.

[7] Coleman, J.M; J.N. Suhayda; T. Wheland; and L.T. Wright (1974). "Mass movement of Mississippi River delta sediments". Technical Report no. 174, Coastal Studies Institute, Louisiana State University; reprint from Proc. Gulf Coastal Assoc. of Geology Soc., 1974, pp. 49–68.

[8] Doyle, E.H. (1973). Soil-wave tank studies of marine soil instability. Preprints, Offshore Technology Conference, Houston, Texas, April 1973, pp. 743–766.

[9] Fisk, H.N. (1961). Bar-finger sands of the Mississippi Delta, in Geometry of sandstone bodies – a symposium. Am. Assoc. Petroleum Geologists, Tulsa, pp. 29–52.

[10] Fisk, H.N. and B. McClelland (1959). Geology of the continental shelf off Louisiana: its influence of offshore foundation design. *Geol. Soc. America Bull.* **70**: 1369–1394.

[11] Fisk, H.N. and E. McFarlan Jr. (1955). Late Quaternary deltaic deposits of the Mississippi River – local sedimentation and basin tectonics, *in:* A Poldevaart, ed., Crust of the earth – a symposium. Geol. Soc. America, Special Paper 62, pp. 279-302.

[12] Fisk, H.N.; C.R. Kolb; and L.G. Wilbert Jr. (1954). Sedimentary framework of the modern Mississippi Delta. *Journal of Sedimentary Petrology* 24: 76-99.

[13] Fleming, R.H. (1940). The composition of plankton and units for reporting population and production. Proceedings, Sixth Pacific Science Congress, San Francisco, Calif., 1939, pp. 535-540.

[14] Frank, D.S.; W.M. Sackett; R. Hall; and A.D. Fredericks (1970). Methane, ethane, and propane concentrations in the Gulf of Mexico. *Bull. Am. Assoc. Petroleum Geologists* 54: 1933.

[15] Gade, H.G. (1958). Effects of a non-rigid, impermeable bottom on plane surface waves in shallow water. *Journal of Marine Research* 16 (2): 61-82.

[16] Garrison, L.E. (1974). The instability of surface sediments on parts of the Mississippi Delta front. U.S. Geol. Survey Open File Report, Corpus Christi, Texas, 18 p., 3 maps.

[17] Hedberg, H.D. (1974). Relation of methane generation of under-compacted shales, shale diapirs, and mud volcanoes. *Bull. Am. Assoc. Petroleum Geologists* 58 (4): 661-673.

[18] Henkel, D.J. (1970). The role of waves in causing submarine landslides. Geotechnique, v.20, pp. 75-80.

[19] Martens, C.S. and R.A. Berner (1974). Dissolved gases in anoxic Long Island Sound interstitial waters (abstract). *Trans. Am. Gophys. Union* 55: 319.

[20] Meade, R.H. (1966). Factors influencing the early stages of the compaction of clays and sands — a review. *Journal of Sedimentary Petrology* 36 (4): 1085-1101.

[21] Mitchell, R.J.; K.K. Tsui; and D.A. Sangrey (1972). Failure of submarine slopes under wave action. Proceedings, 13th. Coastal Engineering Conference, Vancouver, B.C., pp. 1515-1541.

[22] Moore, B.J. and R.D. Shrewsbury (1966). Analysis of natural gases of the United States. U.S. Bureau of Mines, Pittsburgh, Pa., Information circular 8302.

[23] Moore, G.D. (1961). Submarine slides. *Journal of Sedimentary Petrology* 31: 343-357.

[24] Morgan, J.P. (1961). Mudlumps at the mouths of the Mississippi River, in Genesis and paleontology of the Mississippi River mudlumpls. Louisiana Department of Conservation, Geol. Bull. 35, pp. 1-116.

[25] Morgan, J.P.; J.M. Coleman; and S.M. Gagliano (1963). Mudlumps at the mouth of South Pass, Mississippi river: sedimentology, paleontology, structure, origin, and relation to deltaic processes. Louisiana State Univ., Baton Rouge, La., Coastal Studies Series 10, 190 p.

[26] Morgan, J.P. (1968). Mudlumps: Diapiric structures in Mississippi Delta sediments, in: Diapirism and Diapirs – Memoir 8, Am. Assoc. Petroleum Geologists, pp. 145–161.

[27] Nissenbaum, A.; B.J. Presley; and I.R. Kaplan (1972). Early diagenesis in a reducing fjord, Saanich Inlet, B.C.I. Chemical and isotopic changes in major components of interstitial water. *Chemica Et Cosmochimica Acta* 36: 1007–1027.

[28] Renz, O.; R. Lakeman; and E. van der Meulen (1955). Submarine sliding in western Venezuela. *Am. Assoc. Petroleum Geologists* 29: 2053–2067.

[29] Richard, A.F., ed. (1967). Marine geotechnique: proceedings, International Research Conference on Marine Geotechnique, May 1–4, 1967, University of Illinois Press, Urbana, Ill.

[30] Shepard, F.P. (1955). Delta-front valleys bordering the Mississippi distributaries. *Geol. Soc. America Bull.* 66: 1489–1498.

[31] Shepard, F.P. (1973). Sea floor off Magdalena Delta and Santa Marta area, Colombia, *Geol. Soc. America Bull.* 48: 1955–1972.

[32] Singh, H. (1974). The effects of waves on ocean sediments. Dames and Moore Engineering Bull. 44, pp. 11–21.

[33] Sterling, G.H. and E.E. Strohbeck (1973). The failure of the South Pass 70 "B" platform in Hurricane Camille. Preprints, Offshore Technology Conference, Houston, Texas, April 1973.

[34] Takai, Y. and T.K. Kamura (1966). The mechanism of reduction in water logged paddly soil. *Folia Microbiol.* Prague, v.11, pp. 304–313.

[35] Wright, L.D. (1970). Circulation, effluent diffusion, and sediment transport, mouth of South Pass, Mississippi River delta. Louisiana State University, Coastal Studies Institute Tech. Rept. 84, 56 p.

[36] Wright, L.D. and M. Coleman (1971). Effluent expasion and interfacial mixing in the presence of a salt wedge. Mississippi River delta. *Journal of Geophys. Research* 67: 8649–8661.

[37] Wright, L.D. (in press). Mississippi River mouth processes: effluent dynamics and morphologic development. *Journal of Geology.*

[38] Wright, L.D. and J.N. Suhayda (1973). Periodicities in interfacial mixing. Louisiana State University, Coastal Studies Institute Bul. 7, pp. 127–135.

[39] Xavier da Silva, J. and M.S.F. Argento (1978). Topographic Trend Analysis on the Paraíba do Sul Deltaic Plain. International Symposium on Coastal Evolution in the Quaternary.

RECENT EROSION IN THE "STABLE" IPANEMA-LEBLON BEACH IN RIO DE JANEIRO

Paulo C. C. Rosman [1]   Enise Valentini [1]

1 INTRODUCTION

This paper presents the findings of a diagnostic study contracted by the City Hall of Rio de Janeiro, concerning beach erosion problems.

The Ipanema-Leblon beach in the city of Rio de Janeiro is probably the most fashionable and well known beach in Brazil. Its importance to tourism and leisure is enormous, comparable only to the price of housing in the area. The beach, in the latitude 22°59' S and longitude 43°13' W, forms an arch 4.0 km long in an East-West alignment. It is a typical barrier beach and is divided in two segments, Ipanema and Leblon, by a very narrow canal connecting the Rodrigo de Freitas Lagoon to the sea (Fig. 1). At both extremities of the beach arch there are headlands, around which very little or no littoral transport is observed. Along the arch, the beach in Ipanema has always been wider than in Leblon. Nevertheless, until the mid seventies, Leblon was wide enough to have numerous volleyball, and soccer games played on the upper part of the beach.

In the late seventies the width of the beach in Leblon was diminishing considerably, and during a severe storm in 1978 the beach was completely eroded. Wave action reached the stepped-face seawall protecting and sustaining the littoral avenue following the beach arch. In front of this wall, under the previously three meter thick sand cover, a sewage pipeline with 1.2 m of diameter had been laid in the late sixties. Part of the pipeline was destroyed by wave action, and bathing in the Ipanema-Leblon sea waters was not recommended for nearly two months. For the local authorities the facts were quite puzzling as the beach had always been stable. In the past, even after strong winter storms the beach had always recovered its usual width. A diagnostic study, to be conducted with the available data, was contracted by the city hall.

As Ipanema-Leblon is most likely a pocket beach comprising a physiographic unit, no resultant longshore transport of sand could be expected. Consequently, only two sinks of sand are possible, the lagoon canal and the offshore bars. As could be expected, the very narrow lagoon canal, constructed in the late twenties, is always clogged with sand. From time to time the canal was dredged, and this

[1] Programa de Engenharia Oceânica, COPPE, Universidade Federal do Rio de Janeiro, Caixa Postal 68508, Rio de Janeiro, RJ 21945, Brazil.

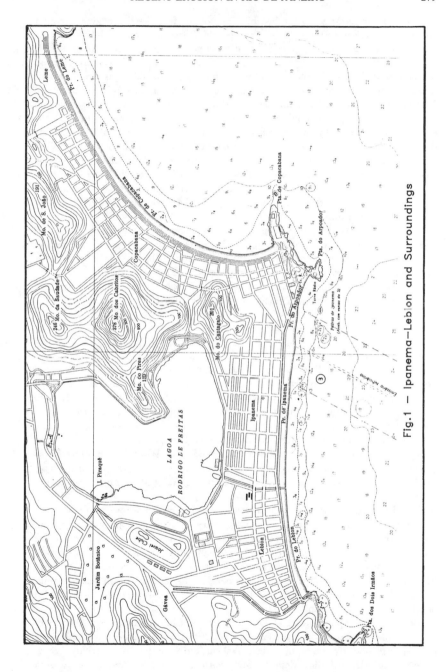

Fig.1 — Ipanema—Leblon and Surroundings

sand was never returned to the beach. The volume from each dredging is rather small in comparison to the volume of the beach. However, the cumulative effect of this eventual "sand mining" over the past forty years is quite significant.

Because there is a limiting seawall, the beach cannot respond freely, eroding and accruing according to the sequence of wave climates. Until the early seventies this limit was far enough and even major winter storms would not erode the beach up to the seawall. But the "sand mining" was slowly bringing the shoreline closer, and eventually a winter profile would meet the seawall. When this happened in 1978, the storm waves reflected by the seawall formed massive offshore bars at considerable distance from the shore line. Apparently part of this sand did not return to the beach during the following summer period, remaining in the offshore zone. And since then, a cycle of total erosion followed by partial restoration seems to have been established. That is, in the winter the beach is often completely eroded, and in the summer it is partially restored. Since 1978 the sewage pipeline has been destroyed several times.

In addition to the diagnostic study already done, a possible mean sea level rise in the region is under investigation. A recent and more far fetched discussion concerning an observed increase in mean wave energy in the eighties, is also under investigation. So far, the city has set policies concerning the destination of the dredged sand in the lagoon canal, and an artificial nourishment to the beach is under study which will probably occur in the near future.

2 EXISTING DATA

Two major studies were conducted in the region during the late sixties. One concerned the sewage outfall in Ipanema beach, and the other a rather large artificial nourishment project in Copacabana beach, both sites are shown on Figure 1. However, very few data from those projects were usable for the Leblon beach case. The Copacabana project presents thorough data concerning littoral processes in the Copacabana beach, such as a one year record of wave data collected by visual observation, beach profiles, sediment analysis, etc. The Ipanema outfall project has little if any data concerning conditions in the surf zone. Wave data employed, was based on the Sea and Swell Charts (1948), hindcasting, and on the visual observations used in the Copacabana project. No data regarding littoral processes in the Ipanema beach was presented.

For the diagnostic study, two basic data were necessary: wave climate and sediment characteristics. Given the inadequacies of the wave data available from the mentioned studies, the data presented for region 40 in the Ocean Wave Statistics (Hogben and Lumb, 1967), were considered sufficient and have been employed. Figure 2, based on the Ocean Wave Statistics data, summarizes the seasonal offshore wave climate pertinent to Ipanema-Leblon beach. The sand in Leblon beach is quite different from Copacabana, and therefore two small analyses had to be done. No beach profiles were available.

Bottom topography in a 1:20,000 scale Nautical Chart of 1988, and 20 years of tidal records in a nearby site, the entrance of Guanabara Bay, were available from the Department of Hydrography and Navigation (DHN) of the Brazilian Navy. Such scale was sufficient to allow detailed wave refraction analysis, and the tidal data easily transferable to Leblon Beach.

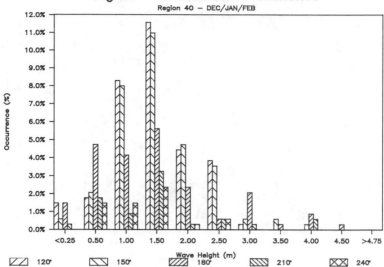

Fig.2a — Ocean Wave Statistics
Region 40 — DEC/JAN/FEB

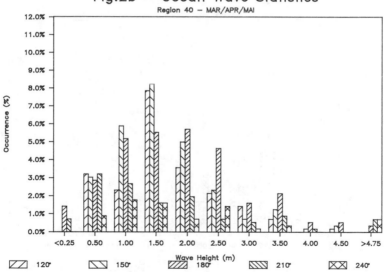

Fig.2b — Ocean Wave Statistics
Region 40 — MAR/APR/MAI

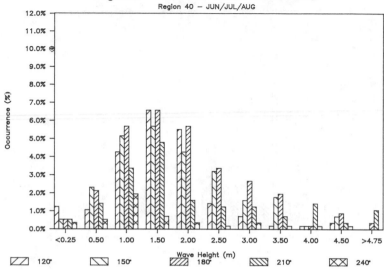

Fig.2c — Ocean Wave Statistics
Region 40 — JUN/JUL/AUG

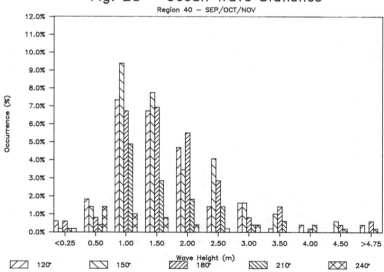

Fig. 2d — Ocean Wave Statistics
Region 40 — SEP/OCT/NOV

Tide regime in Rio the Janeiro is semidiurnal, with significant diurnal differences. Figure 3 shows the water level permanence curve, obtained from hourly records of water level during a two years period, 1977 and 1978. As indicated, the maximum spring tide level is 1.40 m above the hydrographic datum (MLLW). Figure 3 also shows the regions of water level variation due to meteorological effects.

As shown in Figure 3, storm surges in the region can be quite significant, as near 10% of the recorded water levels are above the maximum water level due solely to astronomical tide effects. Oceanographical studies conducted for the Angra Nuclear Power Station, indicate an average surge level of 0.28 m for the Guanabara Bay entrance, and of 0.55 m for the Angra site, about 80 km westward of Leblon beach. The maximum surge level recorded in Angra during 1972 and 1973 was 0.95 m. Figure 4 shows the difference between the recorded and the predicted water levels for May 17–18, 1978, at the entrance of Guanabara Bay. In those dates a severe storm occurred, and surge effects were over 0.80 m. Possibly this was the storm that caused the first erosion reaching the seawall at Leblon beach.

Since there are no long term wave records in the region, it was difficult to assess the occurrence of storms. A hindcasting technique could be used, but that would require an enormous amount of work, and was not strictly required for the purposes in view. As a way of circumventing this lack of data, we have used the press. Newspaper files, concerning sea storms in Leblon-Ipanema beach, from 1956 to 1987 have been collected and analyzed. For these 31 years, Figure 5 shows the monthly and seasonal frequency of occurrence of storms in the region.

3 BASIC HYPOTHESIS

The first fundamental hypothesis is whether the Ipanema-Leblon beach is a physiographic unit. There was little doubt that due to its prominence, there is no littoral transport around the Eastern headland, Arpoador point. However, the Western headland, Vidigal point, is much less salient, and some littoral transport probably occurs in exceptional conditions. In order to check this hypothesis, the net annual longshore transport was estimated, as described in the next item. A small net transport would reinforce the hypothesis, and that was verified.

As a physiographic unit in the form of a pocket beach, the littoral transport would be in alternating directions, and would be confined between the two limiting headlands. In some years a small residue could be verified in one direction, and in other years in the other direction, but in the long run the net transport would tend to zero.

In a pocket beach no significant lateral inflow or outflow of sediments is expected to occur in the time span of engineering projects. Therefore, in the case of Ipanema-Leblon beach, only two sinks of sediments are possible: the lagoon canal, and offshore bars. In the former the sand would be lost, because the dredged material of the canal was rarely returned to the beach. In the latter, the sand would be removed from the beach arch and deposited offshore by the strong onshore-offshore transport during storms. However this sand would eventually return to the beach arch, although that could take a few months. Sand could also be launched on the littoral avenue during storms and lost, but that is certainly in quite small amounts.

The existence of a seawall limiting the width of a beach, can modify the natural dynamics by which wave energy is dissipated. If storm waves hit the seawall the natural swash and backwash flow is altered, the waves are reflected, and much less energy is dissipated than when they swash freely over the beach. Hence, the reflected backwash flow can drag more sediments farther offshore, increasing the erosion rate. This is a feedback process, because as the beach is eroded it becomes easier for smaller waves to hit the seawall. And then the offshore bar will be formed further away from the beach. Consequently, when the wave climate returns to normal conditions, significant additional time will be required for the beach to be restored.

As far as it is known, the first erosion to reach the seawall at Leblon beach occurred during a storm in 1978. Considering the previous paragraph, the apparent increased erosion problem in Leblon since then, raises the hypothesis that the time span between storm seasons has been insufficient for the beach complete restoration. Therefore, a new cycle was set up; total erosion in the winter followed by partial restoration in the summer.

Finally, one has to conjecture why the seawall was not hit before. The hypothesis for that is an exceptional rise in the sea level due to the combination of storm surge, wave set up, and spring tide, occurring in a beach with a small sand deficit. Perhaps if sand had not been removed, via dredging of the lagoon canal since the forties, the beach would still be in fine shape.

4 SEDIMENT TRANSPORT IN IPAMENA-LEBLON BEACH

To investigate the littoral processes along a beach it is of paramount importance to know the wave characteristics in the surf zone. Parameters like breaking wave height, depth of break, and wave crest angle with the shoreline are fundamental. Measured values of such parameters are extremely scarce, and these data are usually obtained through refraction analysis.

Our deep water wave data base was the one summarized in Figure 2. For each of the five azimuths indicated, we have considered wave periods ranging from 4.5 to 12.5 seconds. The refraction analyses were done with a computer model developed at the Ocean Engineering Program of COPPE/UFRJ in the late seventies (Neves, 1979). Bathymetric data were obtained from nautical charts revised in 1988, in scales 1:71,000 and 1:20,000. Despite the computer model, it was a very laborious task due to the existence of a number of small islands. Computer models that perform simultaneously refraction and diffraction analysis for practical problems are still under development.

Parameters that characterize the beach sediment are also basic. No data concerning this were available for the Leblon segment of the beach. Some data were available for the nearby Copacabana beach and for part of Ipanema beach. A few samples were then collected at Leblon, in order to fulfill the minimum requirements for an acceptable analysis. Sediments in the region could be generally classified as well sorted medium sand, with D_{50} varying from 0.4 to 0.6 mm, having about 20% of fine sand and very little coarse sand.

The longshore transport in Ipanema-Leblon beach was estimated via four different methods; Caldwell (1956), Castanho (1966), Komar and Inman (1970), and SWANBY, developed by Swart (1976a, 1976b). A number of other methods like Bijker's (1971), could also be used, but the quality of the available wave data would not justify the effort. Further details on the merits of each method can de found in Valentini (1980) and Sayão and Kamphuis (1983). Figure 6 summarizes the estimates for the annual longshore sediment transport, resulting from deep water waves coming from each of the five azimuths indicated in Figure 2.

As could be expected, there are significant discrepancies among the estimates by the four methods, although the computed values of net annual transport were small in all cases. By the methods of Swart and Komar, estimates of about 100,000 m^3 in the Ipanema-Leblon direction was obtained. Caldwell method yielded a net annual transport of about 50,000 m^3 in the same direction, whereas Castanho method gave an estimate of about 30,000 m^3, but in the opposite direction. Given the wave data available, the confidence one can expect from such methods, and the small magnitude of the net annual transport, including reversed directions, we concluded that the Ipanema-Leblon beach could be considered as a physiographic unit.

The onshore-offshore transport was estimated by the equilibrium beach profile method described by Dean (1977). Two line methods, Swart (1974), require more refined data and were not employed. Figures 7a and 7b show the two extreme values obtained. In figure 7, S stands for the surge height, that is, the difference between the mean sea level (MSL) in storm conditions and the normal MSL; H_b stands for breaking wave height.

The most affected beach section in Leblon is about one kilometer long. Through Dean's equilibrium profile method we have obtained a total onshore-offshore transport ranging from 8 m^3 to 30 m^3 of sand per meter of beach length. This implies that in the stretch of Leblon beach most prone to erosion problems, up to about 30,000 m^3 of sand can be removed from the beach arch during a storm, and deposited in offshore bars.

The erosion due to onshore-offshore transport is most dangerous to Leblon beach in the winter months. Not only due to the more frequent storms, but also because in winter the beach is narrower due to the significant longshore transport towards Ipanema. Through Dean's method we have obtained estimates of reductions in the berm width ranging from five to twenty meters, see figure 7. Reductions due to the longshore transport are difficult to estimate precisely.

While the storm equilibrium beach profile can be formed during the few days a storm can last, a much longer period of time with proper wave conditions will be necessary for the full restoration of the normal beach profile. The amount of time will depend on the depth and distance at which the offshore bar is formed, and these are functions of the intensity of the storm. Besides, if the seawall reflects the storm waves, the offshore bar is bound to be formed further offshore.

Finally, the amount of sand lost via the lagoon canal had to be estimated. There were practically no records on the volumes of sand dredged from the canal over the past decades. The only reliable data covered only the years of 1983 to 1985, when about 30,000 m^3 have been removed. We estimate that a volume of up to 200,000 m^3 of sand may have been lost via the lagoon canal since the forties, because the dredged material was rarely returned to the beach.

5 DIAGNOSIS

The analysis of the available data has backed the basic hypothesis discussed in item 3. A thorough diagnosis would indeed demand a deeper analysis, and much more data than is available. Nevertheless, we think that a fair diagnosis has been

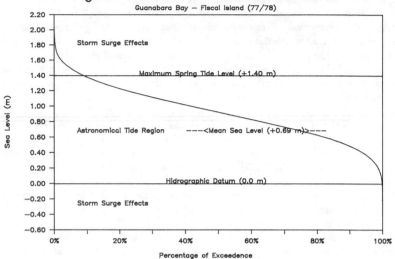

Fig.3 — Sea Level Permanence Curve
Guanabara Bay — Fiscal Island (77/78)

Storm Surge Effects

Maximum Spring Tide Level (+1.40 m)

Astronomical Tide Region   ————<Mean Sea Level (+0.69 m)>————

Hidrographic Datum (0.0 m)

Storm Surge Effects

Sea Level (m)

Percentage of Exceedence

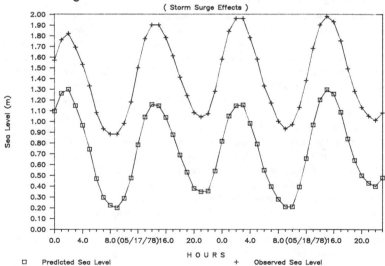

Fig.4 — Observed vs Predicted Sea Level
(Storm Surge Effects)

Sea Level (m)

(05/17/78)   (05/18/78)

HOURS

□   Predicted Sea Level   +   Observed Sea Level

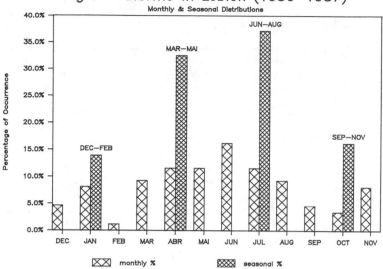

Fig.5 — Storms in Leblon (1956—1987)
Monthly & Seasonal Distributions

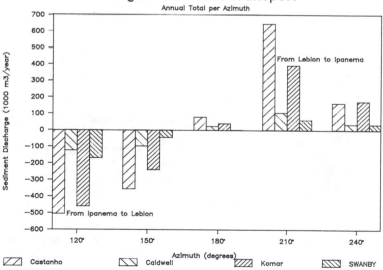

Fig.6 — Littoral Transport
Annual Total per Azimuth

Fig.7a — Equilibrium Beach Profile

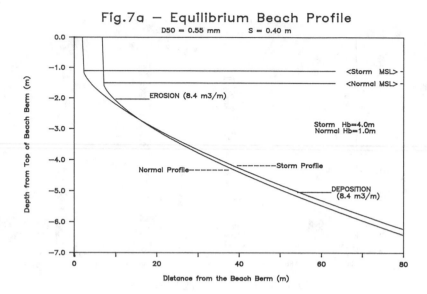

D50 = 0.55 mm   S = 0.40 m

Fig.7b — Equilibrium Beach Profile

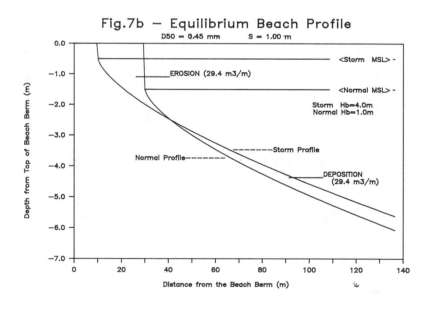

D50 = 0.45 mm   S = 1.00 m

attained.

We believe that the Leblon beach has been enduring serious erosion problems since 1978 due basically to two triggering factors. First, the fact that in 1978 the beach was for the first time eroded up to the seawall that sustains the littoral avenue. Second, that this has happened in 1978 because of sand deficit in the beach, caused by the numerous dredgings in the lagoon canal. And since then, a cyclic process of total erosion in the winter followed by partial restoration in the summer has been occurring.

When the seawall started to play a role in the littoral processes in Leblon beach, the sand deficit worsened, reaching a point that started the cycle. That is, during the 1978 erosion, a significant volume of sand was transported offshore, and after that the beach has never restored its original width. Therefore, part of the sand remained offshore, increasing the sand deficit. The sand deficit now is such that even mild winter storms can totally erode the beach. The problem is that the time span of good weather conditions between storms has not been enough to restore the beach to its pre-1978 conditions.

Evidently, the beach was totally eroded in 1978 because the available volume of sand was insufficient for the storms that occurred. And this volume was insufficient, at least in part, due to the loss of sand via the lagoon canal. The storm surge of 1978 shown in figure 4 did occur in conjunction with spring tide. Considering the wave set up, it is conceivable that on high water the sea level at Leblon might have reached 2.3 meters. In the case, only this elevation would mean a reduction in the berm width of at least 30 m.

6 RECOMMENDED SOLUTION

The recommended solution to the Leblon beach erosion problem is an artificial nourishment. In doing that the vicious cycle of total erosion and partial restoration would be broken, and the beach could resume its natural erosion-accretion cycle, without the seawall intervention.

The design of such artificial nourishment demands a lot of additional data, still unavailable, and much deeper studies. For that, a small primary nourishment of 50,000 to 100,000 m³ should be readily done, in order to prevent any immediate danger, and to allow proper time for the data collection and necessary studies. This primary nourishment is urgent since there is an actual risk for the stability of the seawall, and the littoral avenue it sustains, if the current situation persists. Further details concerning the recommended studies and necessary data acquisition can be found in (Rosman and Valentini, 1988).

7 CONCLUSIONS

The studies done with the available data, although enough for the purposes of a diagnosis, are entirely insufficient for the proper design of the recommended artificial nourishment. The disparity of results obtained with the longshore transport methods emphasize the need of, at least for the period of one year, comprehensive field measurements of wave data, sediment characteristics, beach profiles, etc... A detailed study will undoubtedly have to involve the lagoon canal, and physical as well as mathematical models will be necessary.

Although not exactly for the same reasons, the case of Leblon exemplifies the risks of unproperly constructing littoral avenues on the upper part of beaches. Littoral avenues are often constructed to enhance and develop the tourist attractions of a region. There is nothing wrong with littoral avenues if they are constructed out of the active zone of the beach. Otherwise they can trigger the extinction of the very reason for their construction. Unfortunately, this is too common a case in many cities along the littoral of Brazil. The ignorance concerning beach dynamics, together with the ambition to maximize the real state gains on the landward side of the avenue, are the major reasons for the current situation. Fortunately, Brazilians seem to be discovering the importance of proper coastal zone management, and hopefully in the near future many similar problems will be avoided.

REFERENCES

[1] Bijker, E.W. (1971). Longshore transport computation. *Journal of the Water- ways, Harbours and Coastal Engineering Division* **97**, WW4: 687–701.

[2] Caldwell, J.M. (1956). Wave action and sand movement near Anahein Bay, California. TM–68, U.S. Army Corps of Engineers, Beach Erosion Board, Washington, D.C.

[3] Castanho, J. (1966). Rebentacção das ondas e transporte litoral. Memória No. 275, LNEC, Lisbon, Portugal.

[4] Dean, R.G. (1977). Equilibrium beach profile. Report no. 12, University of Delaware, Newark, USA.

[5] Hogben, N. and F.E. Lumb (1967). "Ocean Wave Statistics", National Physical Laboratory, Ministry of Technology, London.

[6] Komar, P.D. and D.L. Inman (1970). Longshore sand transport on beaches. *Journal of Geophysical Research* **75** (30): 5514–5527.

[7] Neves, C.F. (1979). Um modelo numérico para refração de ondas monocromáticas. M.Sc Thesis, Ocean Engineering Program, COPPE, Universidade Federal do Rio de Janeiro, Brazil.

[8] Rosman, P.C.C. and E. Valentini (1988). Estudo sobre a erosão da praia do Leblon, COPPETEC Report-ET-17144, COPPE, Universidade Federal do Rio de Janeiro, Brazil.

[9] Sayão, O.F.S.J. and J.W. Kamphuis (1983). Littoral sand transport – Review of the state of the art (1982). Report No.78, Department of Civil Engineer- ing, Queen's University, Kingston, Ontario, Canada.

[10] Sea and Swell Charts (1948). U.S. Hydrographic Office, U.S. Navy.

[11] Swart, D.H. (1974). Offshore sediment transport and equilibrium beach profile. Delft Hydraulic Laboratory, Publication No. 131.

[12] Swart, D.H. (1976a). Predictive equations regarding coastal transport. Proc. 15th Coastal Engineering Conference, Honolulu, Hawaii, ASCE, pp. 1113– 1132.

[13] Swart, D.H. (1976b). Coastal sediment transport. Computation of longshore transport. Delft Hydraulic Laboratory, Report No. R968-I.

[14] Valentini, E. (1980). Os métodos de cálculo de transporte litorâneo e sua aplicação ao litoral de Natal–RN. PTS-08/81, COPPE, Universidade Federal do Rio de Janeiro, Brazil.

SUBJECT INDEX
Page number refers to first page of paper.

AUTHOR INDEX
Page number refers to first page of paper.